THE PROCESS OF THINKING

"
The descriptive act
the act of explaining'

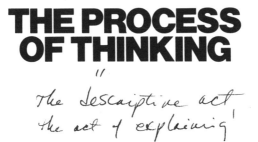

Educational Policy, Planning, and Theory
Series Editor: Don Adams, University of Pittsburgh

Marc Belth
The Process of Thinking

Martin Carnoy
Education as Cultural Imperialism
Schooling in a Corporate Society: The Political Economy of Education in America

Martin Carnoy and Henry M. Levin
The Limits of Educational Reform

Hector Correa
Analytical Models in Educational Planning and Administration

Seymour W. Itzkoff
A New Public Education

Donna H. Kerr
Educational Policy: Analysis, Structure, and Justification

Robert E. Mason
Contemporary Educational Theory

Henry J. Perkinson
The Possibilities of Error: An Approach to Education
Two Hundred Years of American Educational Thought

Richard Pratte
Ideology and Education
The Public School Movement: A Critical Study

Joan I. Roberts and Sherrie K. Akinsanya
Educational Patterns and Cultural Configurations: The Anthropology of Education
Schooling in the Cultural Context: Anthropological Studies of Education

Nobuo Kenneth Shimahara and Adam Scrupski
Social Forces and Schooling: An Anthropological and Sociological Perspective

Joel Spring
The Sorting Machine: National Educational Policy Since 1945

Norman C. Thomas
Education in National Politics

THE PROCESS OF THINKING

MARC BELTH

David McKay Company, Inc.
New York

The Process of Thinking

Developmental Editor: Nicole Benevento
Design: Pencils Portfolio
Manufacturing and Production Supervisor: Donald W. Strauss
Composition: Fuller Typesetting of Lancaster
Printing and Binding: The Colonial Press, Inc.

Library of Congress Cataloging in Publication Data

Belth, Marc.
    The process of thinking.

    (Educational policy, planning, and theory)
    Bibliography: p.
    Includes index.
    1. Thought and thinking.   I.   Title.
BF455.B345   153.4'2   77–23193
ISBN 0–679–30327–8

These three, each in his own time, have traveled long roads with me. To each of my good companions I offer this work:

Harold Bernstein
Stan Dropkin
Charles Ovans

CONTENTS

PREFACE

The primary assumption of this work is that a functional unity undergirds all the activities that produce the natural and social sciences, the historical inquiry, the aesthetic expression, and the common-sense investigations of the world we live in and celebrate. Not because all things in nature are made up of the same substance, but because a singular, determinable process operates in the way we think about the variety of things and operations that comprise our world.

In terms of their contents, the laws of nature are clearly different from the laws of society. The laws of poetic expression are substantively different from the laws of psychological explanation. Nevertheless, what is common to them is the process that produces them.

This is what the book is about. If inadequacies are found in the various chapters that explore the thinking activities of the several disciplines examined—and assuredly there are inadequacies—I hope that they are not so serious as to distract from the primary concern that this work intends to explore. That concern centers on the effort to answer several questions: How does thinking occur? What are the instruments of the thinking process? What, if anything, do we need to assume about human beings, nature, or society in order to understand the thinking act? What can be said about the thinking process so that it can be learned? What are the impediments to thinking, to learning how to think? Why do various manifestations of the thinking act appear so different from one another within the basic functional unity that is the cognitive process?

From this opening dogma (whose dogmatic character will, I hope, be dissolved as the book unfolds) let me indicate some things that the book is not about. Primarily, it is not an attempt to assert the frontiers of knowledge in any of the disciplines that we shall take up. Nor will it present a chronological development of a set of ideas in order to show how we have reached some present stage of thinking about thinking. Especially, it is not intended as a thoroughgoing study of the methodology of the various fields we shall be examining.

Neither does the book attempt to persuade anyone to believe that either human beings or nature are essentially rational. This latter I do not myself believe, though many do, and have argued this view exhaustively. I am not at all persuaded that people, or nature, left to their own devices, will in the end always come to rational decisions and harmonious solutions. The history of the human race hardly warrants such a conviction. I do believe, however, that human beings can xii

learn to think, and that the learning of this *forming* activity is our best, if not our only, hope in a world where the functions and powers of people and things are always flowing out beyond the already constructed bounds of the neat, institutional protection that other people have created. Even love, unformed by thought, has no protection against dissolving into slushy sentimentality or into a cruel oppression visited on those who fall out of the range of our standardized, "natural," love responses.

Neither the things in nature, nor the determinable, invented structures can, of themselves, properly serve us as substitutes for the thinking process. That process, being in essence creative, derives primarily from those human powers we call *imagination:* the capacity to analogize, to create imagery of worlds yet to be fashioned. It is to this that we must attend.

Let us agree, at the outset, that education, any kind of education that transcends mere training or indoctrination into already formed and established procedures, is designed to improve behavior by sensitizing it to ever greater levels of awareness. To this extent the work presents itself as a new form of behaviorism. Let us also agree that the most basic concern of education is with the deliberate nurturing of the thinking process in each of us. If we put the two together, then we may derive something like this: Education is a concern for the deliberate improvement of behavior by making it more and more cognitively determined. That cognitive determination is, in fact, the act or process of thinking, which is the subject matter of this book.

We are, so many of us I think, misled into the belief that we need learn only how to calculate, with great efficiency, what rules to obey within the systems that have organized our lives, and which to disobey for our greater advantage within those same systems, in order to find new dimensions of meaning and wonder. New worlds are inevitably made possible by uncalculated deviation from those rules. But how much more promising this would be if such deviations were calculated in the deliberate invention of new analogies in place of old docilities. New worlds become possible as thought becomes active in the creation of such new analogies.

In the preparation of this book a number of people have given their time and talents most generously. I should like to acknowledge my profound gratitude to each, while absolving them of any responsibility for what appears here. Indeed, their generosity is even more marked by their tolerant disagreements with some of my basic theses than by their approval of what I have written.

My thanks to: Professor Charles Tesconi, of the University of

111

PRE

Illinois, who read the book first and gave me much needed encouragement and kind advice. To Professor Don Adams, of the University of Pittsburgh, for his kindness in helping the book toward publication. To Professor Henry Perkinson of New York University for his special encouragement. To Professors Henry Wolz and George K. Herbert, both of the Philosophy Department at Queens College, CUNY, who read parts of the manuscript. And to John Walton, of Johns Hopkins University, who read the whole of it. All gave generously of their time in detailed notes that I valiantly tried to guide myself by. But none should be held to account for inadequacies, which are clearly only my own. To all those kind and patient students who worked with the book in manuscript form for a year before its publication, and who kept pointing out the innumerable places in which it was incomprehensible and to Nicole Benevento, who supervised the work through production, and Irene Glynn, who edited the pages. Especially to Elayne Bernstein, who worked over every page with me to improve its clarity. And, of course, to Zoé Belth, my tenderest and most enthusiastic critic.

MARC BELTH

Metaphor . . . is as ultimate as thought . . . a fundamental examination of metaphor . . . is . . . nothing less than an investigation of the genesis of thought itself . . . a dangerous enterprise.

—J. M. Murray

INTRODUCTION

Did the craftsman think, as he sat and worked at his bench, shaping shovels or violins, hammering iron link chains, or weaving baskets out of wood stripped down to thin and pliant reeds? Quite likely, if he followed out the form or the model, which he constantly kept alive in his consciousness of the act he was performing. Did he appear, however, obtuse and innocent of thought when he turned from this task to others, say, in the political arena, or in concern for the emotional well-being of his children? Quite possibly. But at his work he was full of thought, and active in it. This only demonstrates a fundamental thesis. We are not likely to be thoughtful about every domain of our experience in a world of ever widening experiences. We become thoughtful in specific problems, specific experiences, specific realms of act and judgment. The employment of models, which is the act of thinking, is always specific and limited. Even to generalize is a specific act, as Dewey once wrote, for generalizing is model building, or forming.

By *thinking*, as distinct from processes that appear to be thinking but are actually something else, I shall mean the "act of following out, and examining at the same time, a path, pattern, mapping, form, or formula until what has been called for in that map, path, pattern, form, or formula has been concluded and the whole of it has been considered for its inner and outer consistencies and its warrantable circumstances." It is, therefore, an *act* that includes a reflection upon itself.

What process do we follow in the "act" of thinking? And how? Mentally, we follow out all that is entailed in some model, analogy, or metaphor deliberately constructed so that we might entertain, in some systematic way, events of our experience. Thus, to "follow" at the conceptual level is to perform a mental act that would, indeed, be analogous to the physical act of following out something in observed nature.

But even so simple a statement is not without dilemmas. For, if it is "following out," we shall rightly expect of thinking that it issue forth in some form of behavior. That is, some overt act should follow the covert act of thought and be its manifestation, even if it is only the act of talking or writing. But because in common sense we always look for more than this, for more direct, overt behavior, and are eager to connect some form of external behavior with some act of thought that preceded it or coincided with it, we often take other kinds of acts as also being acts of thinking.

At any moment, it must be acknowledged, the act of thought could break out. But there is no assurance that it will. Sometimes it is simply not necessary, and sometimes it is not possible. It is not necessary when the forms that have been learned are satisfying to the situation, and resolve them. It is not possible when one has not learned what it is that one follows out in a situation, in a formulation, in a pattern or a path that is present. The ritualists, the actors out of myth, seem to be doing the same things that thinkers are doing, but in fact they are not. One builds and examines a road system through a forest of problems. The other gets onto the already prepared path and simply follows it until it reaches its end, and with it, whatever has been prepared at that end. One might even enjoy the "scenery," so to speak, on the path one is following, without being said to be thinking. For this specific act entails more than just the enjoyment of the "scenery," one's beliefs, rituals, behavior. Unless a person is in some way constructing, or reconstructing a path, directly or in imagination, he or she cannot be said to be thinking. Ernst Cassirer has said that we come to know only what we have ourselves had a "hand" in creating. In the same sense, we think only when we take a "hand" in what we are forming.

No one really believes it is an easy task to teach people how to think, to inculcate the habits of thinking. Psychologists, anthropologists, biologists, and physiologists have all probed deeply into the human condition, and have produced findings that are little short of dismaying to one who is concerned with the effort to plant and to nurture the conditions for the flowerings of cognition. So many impediments are held to exist as bars to its development: impediments of a social character, of the biological structure of human beings, of psychological needs that appear to be basic to people, that it would seem to be a miracle that thought ever manifests itself as human behavior. And yet it does, and in the face of the human condition, it remains always astonishing to observe it made manifest. In light of what is said of the human condition, thought must appear to be a dangerous inhibition to all our other impulses, needs, conditions, and desires. It is surely sought after, yet more often feared than celebrated. And yet it is celebrated, for it seems to be equally undeniable that thought alone marks the paths of civilizations' struggling up from the intuitive, "blood pulsing" responses to the primeval conditions of humanity.

It is a fundamental article of faith to believe that thinking can never be developed, even in a single human being, with any degree of completeness. Partly because all those other dimensions of human existence militate against it, and partly because we have no way of ever knowing what it means to say that a person is completely or totally thoughtful throughout a single day, or throughout life. And somehow there remains the notion that a person who is completely thoughtful, who is totally cognitive, is not simply a curiosity but truly a menacing creature who endangers the rest of us by cold, shall I say, heartless, contemplation of what he or she observes, or experiences, or says, or chooses.

To all these impediments there is also added the chilling way in which we usually approach the task of teaching, or learning, to think. I cannot resist the idea that all too many works devoted to the task of teaching how to think are plodding reductions of the whole process to logical and linguistic (but thoroughly) sterile games, in which thought is broken down into so many grammatic outlines, where the student is required to learn which pieces fit with which pieces, and which do not, however they may appear to do so to the untutored eye and mind. Small wonder that few ever learn what the act is really comprised of; even fewer, having discovered this much, ever come to employ this knowledge extensively or continuously.

It is not that these by now standard approaches are wrong or devoid of value for some, or even for a great many. On the contrary, it is the fact that they are right enough within their limits which makes thinking a really unappealing act or process to be undertaken. In so many cases we intuit, somehow, that we can reach the goals of cognition by other means, more immediate, more direct, more joyful, and more deeply satisfying than the coldly calculating approaches that are generally presented to us. If thinking is itself so spiritless, and the world so full of spirit, there seems to be a desperate paradox. Why not embark upon the spirited quality of life in the very quality that life reveals to us? Why the depressing torment of the syllogism, the linguistic calculus, the semantic and the syntactic analysis, where essential experience seems to require that this quality first be shaken out of sight before we can deal with it? Our very human drives and intentions must always resist it. Those who do not resist seem to be eager to avoid their essential humanity in order to achieve what only their humanity can impose. Thus the paradox: In order to be fully human, seek to become coldly logical first. It is the approach that creates this paradox.

It surely must be possible to examine and nurture the thinking process within the context of the existence to which it is applied. Thought, after all, is not external or alien to the human condition. It is as much a part of it as sexual needs, or spatial needs, or the needs of dignity, identity, and nourishment. It lies not outside the experienced world, but arises from within that world, from the transactions that bio-

logical-physical-historical-social-aesthetic impulses have with the physical environment that sustains and nurtures, or threatens and destroys
people. Language is not a mere appendage to a person, not an ancil-
lary trait that one could do without and still be human. It is as essential to one's humanity as eyesight, a digestive tract, and the soil on
which one lives. So thought is generated in this transaction of our
essential condition as humans and the essential environment that sustains and feeds us, and gives us our place to live. Thought is at work
in the perceptions we come to have of ourselves in that environment, in
the unique forms that we give to our language-making powers, into
which we embed our perceptions. Thought is present in the rules we
develop or imitate for handling ourselves and others and the things
that surround us immediately and at a distance.

Here, then, in this turbulence of living, we shall locate the characteristics of the act of thinking. And from this exploration we shall be
able to draw up some generalizations about what happens in that
process, if we are to bring it to a level of consciousness in order to
make it more capable of being learned in deliberation, and put to use
with greater economy and the promise of human fulfillment. In such
an examination we study not only the processes of thought, ab-
stractly, but also how the world moves to help in the shaping of those
processes, and how the individual affects and is affected by those
processes. Approaching thought in this way assures us at least of always being at the point of contact between humankind and world, for
it is thought, the individual's own or someone else's that he or she has
borrowed and continues to use, that makes possible the sustaining
relationships between the individual and world, between the individual and other selves. If the absence of thought satisfies a person,
promising that individual to reach fulfillment better than thought
could do, I can only say that it is because thought has been made insignificant or trivial, or ungainly, or inept in some presentation of it.
For nothing does for human beings what thought does. Impulse, intuition, divination—all serve human purposes, but they are not the
same purposes; they cannot be truly counted as better ways of reaching goals that thought has established. The conceptual goals of people
can be reached only by concept-using, and no human being is ever
without conceptual goals. I mean to show this at some length.

I know of no possible way of teaching how to think by the use of
formulas or by concise and abrupt shortcuts. I am convinced that anyone who pretends to make this possible is devoid of thought, and is
committed to a peculiar doctrine that makes thinking unnecessary.
The problems of the world do not come so well formulated, so consistently structured, that we can learn a tactic of unstructuring the

form of that problem, looking into it rapidly, and coming out with the proper conclusions. The dreadful fact about thinking is that it takes time, *and it demands action.* We can find no quick and ready solution to the profound dilemmas that confront us. The world is not a gigantic crossword puzzle, where the answers are already established in some private or secret dictionary that we need only to lay our hands on. Indeed, the world's problems are what we form them to be, and thus are as unique as the individual minds that create them. In nature itself there is no established dictionary that will provide us with the proper terms or definitions to fit the appointed spaces.[1]

1. Long after I had completed this book, J. M. Morse's *Prejudice and Literature* (see Bibliography) appeared. Had I read it earlier nothing would have been altered here, but I would have had the benefit of some brilliantly presented further illustrations of metaphors which sometimes prevent thinking and at other times are evidence of thinking at its most fruitful. Read it as a lovely corollary to Part 1 of the work that follows.

PART *1*

Some Problems in Identifying the Act of Thinking

In which it is shown that every explanation of the thinking act shows evidence that thinking is analogizing, whatever particular explanation of thinking is offered. Three such examples are shown.

The Problem of Defining Thinking and a Suggestion for a Resolution

THE DILEMMA OF APPARENT PRIVACY

What kind of an activity is thinking? How is it to be explained? Even more immediate, can we ever be sure that we are giving a valid or a testable description of the process? The problems arise, of course, from the obvious fact that thinking, much of the time, is a private affair, as William James has observed.

Consider the dilemmas that arise from these primitive questions. Is it best to construe thinking as a man talking to himself, as Socrates once held, in which he recalls and examines ideas in their self-existing purity? Is it wiser to construe thinking as the activity of the "mind" extracting the essences from things experienced? Is it better described as the "mind" developing the habit of contemplating images that have been impressed upon it? Is it the working of some innate power of an organism applying its own structure on formless events that we experience, thus preceding observations? Is it better to consider it as the activity of giving names and attributes to things, and then producing sentences describing them? Is it, perhaps, more fruitfully construed as some form of speech, overt or subvocal, which follows certain logical principles of deduction, inference, induction, and the like? Or is it better, as psychiatry suggests, considered as an activity in which memory creates a drive-tension that is brought to consciousness through the energy that produces an hallucination of an object desired but not present? Is there a suspicion arising that these may be evidence of different analogies being preferred?

At best, it would appear, thinking is widely accepted as occurring in some private domain, revealing some preferred analogy. Whatever the claims we make about the process, we can be persuasive only by making them psychologically and logically acceptable.

The problems are simply compounded when we attempt to make a common-sense approach. For even with the simplest statement that I think thus and so ("I think that Jones is right in saying it will rain tomorrow" or "I think I will be wasting time if I watch the football game today"), we are working on arguable assumptions about the characteristics of that thinking process. Generally, we assume the very process we are called upon to describe. What follows the phrase "I think" is an assertion, a conclusion, a question, the outcome of an activity of some kind. But just what that process is remains the problem. For, if—as common sense tells us—it is private, internal in some way, it cannot be actually, publicly, inspected. It can only be introspected. And introspection has a history of difficulties. But it is interesting to note that the term (introspection), as it is used, is a metaphor for "seeing." When challenged about what we think, the answer given does seem to imply that we "look into ourselves" in some way, for the purpose of checking the process and determining whether it was properly done, that we do indeed *think* what we have just asserted.

The trouble, more often than not, has been that although we metaphorize from the act of seeing, we come unguardedly to believe that it is more than a metaphor simply because it has been used so frequently. We believe it is a literal description of what, in fact, we do about the process whose outcome we have reported in some statement.

GETTING OUT OF THE BIND OF THE PRIVATE

The result of the recognition of the state of the problem has produced a whole series of recommendations of what it would be best to construe thinking as. That is, every view offered fixes on some overt event, somewhere, which it recommends as being most like what we ought to construe the thinking act to be. As John Murray has said, we need to give "to airy nothing a local habitation." The "is it like" questions with which this chapter began offer, each one of them, a different recommendation as to the best analogy to accept.

Is thinking like a man talking to himself? The analogy is to open conversation.

Is thinking like a man extracting the essence of an experience? The analogy here is perhaps to an explorer whose activity is to collect things and to look for all the common qualities of the things he has collected, so that he can talk about them under some generalized or universal form; or somewhat differently, it may be to someone who squeezes flower petals to draw out their "essences."

Is thinking like a woman inspecting images that have been impressed upon her mind? The analogy is to a photographer examining a series of pictures under a special light in a darkroom, and seeing a sequence and a relationship of similarities and differences between them.

And so on. But in each case, what has been done appears to be the only thing that could be done. We seek some external process that, for good reason, we feel will provide us with the formal procedures that we can accept as also being the procedures of the unseen and unseeable thinking process.

In this sense, then, the present work is somewhat different. Yet quite similar to others on this quest. I, too, will be looking for some existential process, and on grounds that I consider valid, persuasive, and defensible. I mean to argue that the process of thinking *is* the process of analogizing—itself a process that, I think, can be readily examined, tested, checked, modified, improved, and above all, learned —one that we not only can consciously learn, but also can consciously improve in use.

CONSTRUING THINKING AS ANALOGIZING

What does appear quite legitimate is the fact that, while each of the people represented above has chosen a different event to use as the basis of the analogy selected, I think it possible to capitalize on the larger process. That is, thinkers who have thought about thinking have all undertaken the same process—the process of analogizing. On this ground, then, it is reasonable to argue that the thinking process is the process of analogizing, of testing and analyzing whatever analogies are recommended or selected, and of reconstructing those analogies for more effective use in ongoing activities.

Let us begin with what appears to be common to all views, with the observable behavior of human beings that can be described as an effort to see more carefully what is in the world, and what is "in" what we say about the things in the world. What a person comes to see in the world derives not simply from the existential events, but also from the analogy an individual selects in order to explain and to account for what he or she cannot see, but which, one argues, must be present if the existential matters are what we claim they are. Thus, the thinking process is primarily the process either of employing some analogy as a model, or a frame for seeing what there is to see, or of creating an analogy, a model of some kind for seeing what there is to see and thereby propounding what cannot be seen as a condition for what can be seen. Such analogies (or models) become the "lenses" for "seeing" the world, and the activity of using, or constructing and *then* using, analogies is, in our terms, the "act" of thinking. One tangible event is used as material for analogizing another tangible event. But the *decision*, the judgment, though responsive to them, is not reducible to those tangibles. In other words, any given event can be explained in an infinite number of ways. This judgment is the *mental act* in its first stage.

TRUTH AND FALSITY IN ANALOGY

No analogy that has ever been developed and offered as an account of the thinking act is totally false. On the other hand, is any one analogy as good as any other? Isn't it, rather, that every specific analogy is an advocacy of a view of the world and needs to be treated as such? If it is then argued that this work is no less a matter of advocating a view, let me at least suggest that it is advocating at a different logical level: at the level of generality; that is, that although analogies are inevitable, this or that particular analogy is not. If I argue that all analogical efforts are evidence of the thinking act, it is quite different from saying that I prefer the Debater's model to the Chemist's model to explain thinking, or the Optical model to the Linguistic model, however good each of these may be. The employment and construction of each of these models *is* a manifestation of the thinking act, and must be treated as such. It is as valid to think of "thinking as debating" as it is to think of "thinking as mirroring." But no single analogy will solve all our problems, those problems which each specific analogue maker and user poses to another analogue maker and user. I show, in the second part of this book, how different models and analogies appear in different disciplines of inquiry into our lives and our worlds, and perform their tasks with remarkable success and penetration. And I show, too, how the ability to recognize the analogies in use and the deliberate borrowing of other analogies makes possible new thought; the recognition of existing inadequacies; and the construction of whole new worlds to be experienced.

A DISTINCTION AMONG *ANALOGY, MODEL,* AND *METAPHOR*

The fundamental aim of this book is to teach what thinking is. In our terms this requires teaching to recognize a *model*, an *analogy*, a *metaphor* in use; the imagery and concepts and perceptions that derive or are presented in the use of this or that particular model, analogy, metaphor; how to construct and use alternatives to these; and what cognitive consequences result from their construction and use. In order to do this I shall offer, at some length, detailed descriptions and illustrations of a process that will be a description, not of a private unseeable process, but of the act of thought become observable in some linguistic or other symbolic form.

Consider what is common to the three terms: analogy, model, and metaphor. All three refer to those constructs that are consciously chosen or deliberately created for purposes of reflecting upon some event under investigation. They are acts of employing symbolic representations of familiar, understood events as the means for dealing with unfamiliar matters in order to endow them with descriptions, explanations, and further exploratory conditions. From such constructs we are able to follow out, both logically and empirically, phases of the behaviors and the connectednesses of what is otherwise unfamiliar or unknown. By these means we give direction to our own further inquiries, as well as denoting or connoting the directions of behavior of those events. By these means we also make possible more critical descriptions of those events, offer explanations of their existence and their behavior, and make possible an understanding of them as events in a wider context of events. In such observations analogues, models, and metaphors are tested in empirical consequences, and the consequences themselves derive their meanings from the constructs employed.

Nevertheless, their differences must be borne in mind. A metaphor is only one kind of an analogy, and an analogy is but one kind of a model. Thus, MODEL is a *class name* (e.g., organic things), ANALOGY is a *genus* of model (e.g., trees), and METAPHOR is a *species* of analogy (e.g., an oak).

By means of a model we examine, in its totality, an event that is otherwise not examinable. By means of analogy we cross sorts of things with one another within the model, so that unfamiliar elements are treated in the terms of the more familiar or the more readily accessible. And by means of a metaphor we transfer the specific traits of one event to another so that the analogical relationship can be made clear and apparent (e.g., The camel is the ship of the desert).

A computer is constructed to carry out some functions normally performed by a human mind. If we accept this as valid, then an analysis of the behavior of that computer is construed as an analysis of human mental processes. To the degree that we establish and employ the computer as a model of thinking, we point to certain operations in the computer as analogues to the operations in the brain. When we address ourselves to that brain as the determinant of behavior (in humans or in the machine) we are treating *brain* as a metaphor for mind, which we construe as the judgment or the decision-making process of human beings. (This last, I show later, is a form of metaphor known as *metonymy*. But a more complete and detailed analysis of all three terms and how they function *as* the thinking process follows in ensuing chapters.) Let me give one further illustration of the interwoven relationship here. King Lear ends his life completely blind, railing against the storms, defiant against the fates that have destroyed him. But his physical blindness is but a metaphor for the blindness in which he had lived his life, blind to the love of the daughter who would never abandon him. The physical blindness, of course, is an analogy to the more "unseeing" ways of his thinking and behaving, of his demanding and his responding. And the whole model of the play is, indeed, a model in which "blind" power, because it is blind and uncontrolled, is a wildly destructive force in all humane relationships.

The metaphor, thus, is the most immediate manifestation of one kind of condition made to apply to another. The analogue is at the level of the conceptual transference. The model comes to serve as the basic context, or format, for the development and the telling, in this case, of the whole tale, the tale of "unseeing" destructiveness of moral, emotional force.

Analogical Bases in Some Prevailing Models of Thinking

I shall not go into any great detail in presenting or analyzing the content of any of the views of the thinking process that I am considering here. My purpose, rather, is to examine the models on which these various views are constructed, and to show how the analogies used produce the descriptions and explanations of that thinking process for each.

Nor do I present alternative views for the purpose of demonstrating which is defensible and which not, which is right and which wrong. Rather, I examine the grounds on which conclusions rest, what those grounds make logically obligatory, as descriptions and explanations of thinking, and what limitations must necessarily arise from this or that particular model and analogy. I am illustrating not conventional views of thinking, but how analogies undergird these views, in at least three examples.

THE ANALOGY WITH VISION

In classical and in modern times we find frequent evidence of treating thinking "as if" it were akin to the act of seeing. Not only Plato and Aristotle, but the Gestalt approaches of Koehler and Wundt, and many in between these, consider that to think is to be involved with the *seeing,* or *envisioning,* of ideas or relationships or forms; sometimes purely conceptual forms, sometimes the forms that appear to be implicit in the things of the world. The analogy, consciously or unconsciously held, obliges us to accept that the relationships that exist in the actual act of seeing also describe mental "seeing."

In actual experience our quest for knowledge is fulfilled when we learn to inspect things. The things we inspect have form as well as specifiable matter, as our actual seeing follows the laws of optics. In our inspection we note sequence, connections, relatedness. Therefore, our "seeing" into thought, that form of inspection called *introspection,* obliges us to seek out like characteristics in thinking. In this, however, there is no uniformity among the various representatives of the common analogy. In a Platonic world we inspect universal concepts that are antecedent to the things of the apparent world but are "reflected" in the things of that world. (Note how the term in quotes here has intimations of observation, of seeing.) In the Aristotelian universe we inspect things in the world for the universal qualities that lie embedded within them and that are "reflected" to us in our experiences of those things. In the Cartesian or Kantian world we are innately endowed with those forms or categories of perception that allow us to see the world in its physical traits. So, curiously enough, concepts, essences, and categories make vision of the world possible. Thinking gives us eyes.

To apply the act of seeing things in the world to mental events would somehow suggest that those events have characteristics that can be "seen." To give to "mental events" the analogical characteristics of mathematical forms is to construe the thinking act as having the logical structure of mathematics. The net result is that we find ourselves constantly in a tug between what the mind, as mind, perceives, and the ways in which the things of nature behave. When discrepancies between them occur, when the world seems less perfect than the universals of the mind, when they violate what the logic of mathematics allows us to see, the dilemma can become excruciating.

With John Locke, for example, the term "perception," a cognate of vision, is used with great frequency. In the briefest of terms, for Locke thinking is the act of perceiving what experience has written on the "clean paper" that is the mind. The mind "observes" because such impressions linger long enough to make possible comparisons of them with one another, to discern ideas to be the same or different. And this "envisioning" is what he calls thinking. He avoids any such doctrines as fixed essences or innate ideas that have absolute traits; but the basic analogy of vision is still present. The traits with which he endows nature, those events experienced that leave their impressions on the mind, are not of concern to us at the moment, so this comment on Locke is likely to be intemperately brief. Yet the point is not the whole construct of Locke's theory of thinking, but rather the primary analogy he has employed.

The strengths and the limits of the analogy are relevant to us. Its strength, briefly, lies in the attention that it gives to the relationship between whatever it is we now call Mind, and the experienced world to which attention must be paid. In this form of the analogy we humans are truly embedded in the world we need to sustain us, and to which we must continue to address ourselves. Whatever we do or say contains within it the evidence of this particular thought structure. But its inadequacy lies in the limitations that the eye itself has for seeing what is in the world. If we tend to see gross wholes and do not perceive what we now recognize to be part of the microscopic or submicroscopic world, then "insight," "introspection," will be equally limited in what it can think (or perceive). What we cannot have images of, we cannot think about. And that, it is clear, is a severe limitation in the analogy used.

Now one does not normally bring Locke and Plato together in consideration of the thinking process. And in terms of their conclusions, one can appreciate why this is so. Locke clearly resists the notion of innate ideas, as well as the notion of essences in reality. Yet the common use of the analogy of vision cannot be denied, and insofar as they are concerned with the *act* of thinking, the lingering vestiges of a kind of Platonism in John Locke can be understood. If they differ about what the mind "sees," they assuredly agree that it is best to construe the mind in terms of the power to "see" the world. And at that level, they share the strengths and the inadequacies of the analogy, primarily the problems attendant upon the idea of introspection. We do not get beyond them solely by considering the experienced world as something other than either of them did. We get beyond them, in this matter, only when we alter the visual analogue in terms of which the process of thinking is explained. Let us turn to one such alternative, not because it is better, but because it demonstrates that different traits and functions become identified as thinking.

THE ACTION ANALOGY

The most interesting aspect of using action as an analogy for thinking lies in the fact that it completely alters the character of the problem of observing the thinking process when defined as a strictly private affair. For, unless we divide things and their behaviors as Kant did, into phenomena and noumena—that is, into what can be seen on the one hand, and the power or force or spirit within, which moves the thing but cannot itself be seen, on the other—whatever act there is, is all there is and need be our only concern. Function, consequences, outcomes, and changes are all acts or activities. And if this is the analogue chosen to explain thinking, then the only thinking that occurs is that which shows some evidence in the changing external world. The unconscious, or the subconscious, whatever one may claim for these metaphysically, can have meaning for us only when they appear to us in some overt form. And then, of course, they are neither unconscious nor subconscious, but overt behaviors that had their origins in some interior yet active domain of existence that we come to know about only when they make their appearance. This, I suspect, is much like the hair on the face of a male, which comes into observable existence along about the thirteenth or fourteenth year of his life. We do not need to make a mystery of its sudden appearance. Having shown itself, we are led to a physiological explanation in order to discover that the substructure of the skin has always contained follicles that needed only time to appear. But this substructure, this subcutaneous condition, has an active state, and is as real in its earlier stages as it is in its later when it grows above the skin and makes the matter of shaving a choice now to be made. So thought, too, can be accounted for in terms of human biology, as Noam Chomsky says.[1]

Now, all behaviorist, positivist, and experimental psychologies, however else they may differ in their subanalogical preferences, share this analogue of action. Ryle commits himself to the act of speaking, or asserting, as being all there is to the act of thinking. Bruner commits himself to the act of classifying, of categorizing, as the act of thinking. Experimentalists more concerned with the behavior of human beings in the face of problems commit themselves to the idea that solving a problem that actually confronts them is all there is to thinking. Even the vision analogy can be treated in this action sense. This sounds, of course, rather stringent as I put it here, but it is rather more disciplined in the sense of establishing limits for inquiry than it is stringent or narrow.

The standard approach to the teaching of critical thinking derived from this analogy, from Aristotle through Dewey and beyond, has distilled this concept of thinking, of intelligence, into a series of steps that clearly reflect this particular analogy. Dewey's *How We Think* presents the classical formulation of it. Let me offer, however, a variation of this, which nevertheless is eminently faithful to that Deweyan tradition. W. E. Moore, in his *Creative and Critical Thinking*, begins his work with the following definition:

> Creative thinking may be defined as the formulation of possible solutions to a problem or explanation of a phenomenon. . . . Critical thinking [is] the testing and evaluation of these selections or explanations.[2]

The following, he writes, are the phases that must be pursued, the first three of which are the creative, the last two, the critical.

1. Recognition and defining of the problem.
2. The gathering of information.
3. Forming the tentative conclusions.
4. The testing of these tentative conclusions.
5. Evaluation and decision (or judgment) making.[3]

The difference between this approach and the vision analogy should be obvious. Every phase of Moore's five steps is an overt ac-

---

1. Noam Chomsky, *Reflections on Language* (New York: Pantheon Books, 1975), chap. 1.
2. W. E. Moore, *Creative and Critical Thinking* (New York: Houghton Mifflin, 1967), pp. 2–3.
3. Ibid., p. 6.

tivity of some kind; in the vision analogy, the process was that of a totally logical analysis of the terms involved in some purely conceptual formulation. There is none of the introspective quality in the second that there is in the first. The problems themselves are real, actual, apparent; and what is called for is an activity that measures the act of the things before us. Logical problems are not merely verbal, antecedent to, or apart from the world. They are the problems of the logic of an active inquiry into the actions of things. Experience alone stirs wonder and puzzlement; it provokes the guess, the trials undertaken, the hypotheses constructed. The activities called for in a world of action are entailed in the conditions of living itself; actions of economy, efficiency, accuracy of observation, attention to consequences in the world experienced, and so on.

Nowhere is this as clearly pressed as in Moore's inclusion of determinants, or codeterminants, of the processes of thinking. There are, he argues, social, psychological, and moral determinants in the individual inquiring, as well as in the problems he confronts. The total act of thinking, then, is the act of balancing these recognized determinants together against the objectives sought in the inquiry, of actively using all we have come to know of each, finding how they affect both the inquirer and the things inquired into, and reading out the consequences in this total context of activity. What we thus describe and explain is the how of things' behaviors, including the how of our responses and our ways of probing into them.

It is worth considering for a moment the strength of the action analogy, and against it, some of the claims made for it as more than just an analogy, which behaviorists such as B. F. Skinner argue for. Clearly, it is a persuasive approach to the problem of thinking, especially to the matter of teaching to think, whether we acknowledge the metaphor or not. Nevertheless, some claims that are made here need to be made clear.

To begin with, the concept "action" is a vague one. So vague, in fact, that although an explanation of thinking predicated on it will be very strong in many aspects, where it is weak, it is very weak. (At best, however, it may well be the most advisable analogy to choose, since—as I have been at pains to point out—there is no hard reality here to which we can address ourselves, which we shall use as the evidence for its truth or its falsity. And this, I repeat, underscores more fully than ever what I mean by saying that perhaps *the best way of considering the act of thinking is not in terms of this or that specific analogy, but rather as the act of analogizing itself.*)

As exact as our descriptions of substantive events in the world may be within the strictures of this analogy, when it is offered as a description of the thinking process itself, it can hardly be called literal. It has to be normative. That is, it becomes a recommendation for considering something that cannot actually be seen, or proven to be reducible to what can be seen. It could, very likely does, present a sound account of how people ought to behave and what they ought to do in this or that experience.

It is reasonable to assume that the events of the world do not come to us self-labeled. We give them labels, names, identities. We note and define problems. Nor do the discrete events, in any literal sense, even hint at or recommend those definitions. To be sure, they must be taken into account if they are to be the content of thought. But this does not mean that they "tell us what to do and what to say." Nor do the data we confront contain their own objectively determined solutions to *our* problems. Nature, as nature, in this conception, has no problems. If it did, it would really not matter much who looked, or what conceptual system was being employed in the observations being made. Is any observed data, when defined, explored, or explained, ever independent of some observer who brings some theoretical system to that observation and resolution? If not, as I think it is not, then can the thinking process (which Moore and others who are disposed to the use of the action analogy have defined) ever be "proven," demonstrably? For, what would then be implied is that the thinking act is simply a matter of pushing the data around this way and that, anticipating their later behavior, until we get them, the data, all right in their intrinsic forms, and then recording what in fact nature has revealed. What is more likely is that every such experiment or experience is a test of the meanings and assumptions of the model of thinking with which we had begun. Moreover, have we come, as yet, any closer to answering the basic question to which we have addressed ourselves: Just what is the act that we shall call thinking? Is it any less analogizing in Moore than in Plato? Evidently not.

With Moore we are in the midst of experience, of external events whose behavior puzzles us. We need to propound explanations and solutions in a context in which social, psychological, and ethical influences are at play. We acknowledge that in some way yet to be more fully identified these determinants of the problems have consequences, both positive and negative, in *what* we think; that is, they influence the recommendations we offer for their resolution. Nevertheless, it must be clear that it is not only the events themselves, as hard data, that have these consequences. There are also consequences from the way in which these data have been transformed into conceptual systems, into models for exploration and explanation.

The experiences of past researchers and the analyses of previous scholars serve us as a reservoir of models of thinking that we call upon as warranted guides for the inquiries to be made into all sorts of human experiences. When one such model has produced a sequence of successes in knowledge produced, it becomes, as Thomas Kuhn has shown, the "normal" way of making that type of inquiry in later, similar situations that need resolution and explanation. As such, success establishes it as the paradigm for future inquiry. It becomes the standardized model for the investigation of puzzles and problems that confront us.

In our terms, however, what we have done is to establish an analogy between the private act of thinking and the public act that is a disciplined investigation of the behavior of things and ideas in a context established by some conceptual system that includes not only a record of the past behavior of these kinds of things, but also the assumptions by means of which such past behaviors had been given names and meanings, sequences and continuity. The events themselves are not conceptual matters. But to call something a "social event" already has brought the conceptual into the picture. Human behavior is empirical to the extent that it is observable. But to say that behavior is "psychological" is to identify the conceptual system that has given it a particular significance, a terminology, a direction. That things occur is something that can be seen. But that there is "continuity and sequence" is what the mind ascribes to those observed events.

The whole, then, shows the inescapable characteristics of the invention of some analogy that connects what is seen with how we think about what is seen. There are, therefore, two symbol systems involved. What differentiates these two systems held now to be analogous to one another is the fact that the first is entirely limited to the realm of logic and a language that refers only to that logic, while the second attempts to provide a kind of a mapping system for some actual terrain of active, human, empirical experience through another language identified as a reference system. Each is presented as a description of the operations of the thinking act, when in fact the latter is indeed a description while the former is simply an invitation, or at best, a persuasive definition. But more of this later.

THE ORGAN ANALOGY

There is a third approach to the problem of thinking that we might consider. The first approach clearly addressed itself to a realm of pure ideas, a Platonist's realm, which may take any one of a number of variations. The second concerned itself with the effects that things and past beliefs and experiences, that social relationships and societal restraints and determinations, have on the characteristic activities of inquiry. The one can be charged by the other as being hopelessly divorced from the things that are of concern to us; the second can be charged by the first as being quite vague as to the determination and measurability of those empirical forces to which it addresses itself. So a third effort is mounted, whose intention is to attempt to identify, as positively (in a strictly empirical sense) as possible, just what organ or organism *does* the thinking, and how it does it. Hard research becomes impatient with vague and ambiguous names and notations and seeks to replace them with specific matters that can be carefully and critically observed. If we need to *see* what it is we are talking about, then such terms as "influence," "tendency," "mind," or "disposition" must either be given concrete referents or dismissed as hopelessly obscure.

If action is to be our quest, then let us be precise and look at how some specific organ functions, and observe the effects it produces in other organs and on the things around us. If we are to be certain that the descriptions we give are faithful to fact, then let us address ourselves to some determinate fact that can be described. A complete description of such a type makes it possible to check claims, to institute modifications and improvements, and to observe, quantitatively, the whole matter.

John Watson undertakes this approach, as does B. F. Skinner, among modern investigators of thinking. At the less technical level, the writings of Edward de Bono show the same intention. All are concerned with the role of the brain and the nervous system, both very tangible organs in the human body, both susceptible of experiment, observation, and measurement.

De Bono is not the most significant inquirer who might have commanded our attention. But his naiveté produces a simple enough example for our purpose, and he has achieved some popularity. He writes:

> The brain is a system in which things happen according to the nature of the system. What happens in the brain is information . . . and the way it happens is thinking. Since thinking in this broad sense determines what people do on any level from the most personal to the most international, it could be worth looking into some aspects of the brain system.[4]

4. E. de Bono, *Mechanism of the Mind* (London: Jonathan Cape, 1969), pp. 17–18.

For, he argues, if we can understand how any system works, we can improve its effectiveness; that is, we can institute methods for such improvements, for it would enable us to identify the indisputable physical source of errors and faults that are the consequences of malfunction in the system.

With fine consistency he observes that "language, notation and mathematics are useful *artificial* aids to thinking." Other artificial aids that might be invented depend upon our first understanding the facts; that is, the brain's operation itself. These artificial aids do not perform acts of thinking; they simply make possible a better operation of the brain, just as a pep pill that is swallowed cannot be described as the beating of the heart but rather as the stimulus to the beating of the heart. Thus is the mystery of thinking once again and for all time dissolved. The more complete the knowledge of the operation of the brain is, and the more precisely we distinguish this from artificial aids, the more positive is an understanding of what constitutes the act of thinking.

The similar approach that Skinner has made is too familiar to require more than the briefest note. We are less in danger of being misled, or of committing serious errors, he has continuously argued, if we avoid conjecturing over the unconjecturable, if we avoid theorizing where positive identifications and observations can be made. Now, if Skinner does not explicitly reduce thinking to the behavior only of the brain system, he does equate it with the entire neurological system. Observable stimulus-response states, which cannot remain private, can be measured, noted, and altered by altering stimuli. As we come to know more and more about the way in which electrochemical influences produce their effects in behavior, from the smallest and most subtle responses to the largest and most apparent ones, our knowledge of thinking becomes increasingly precise, and we are able to produce in individuals responses to problems that are immediate, exact, and errorless.

A much more direct (and delightful) work in this organ analogy is to be found in W. Grey Walter's *The Living Brain.*[5] For him, as for others using the same analogue, mind is simply (or rather, not very simply) the functioning of the brain, and to see it as anything else is nothing more than the carryover of old myths or old metaphysics that continue to give great psychological comfort, even though they are empty of explanations. The brain is an organ of electrical responses and the recorder of electrical impulses, which operates, has

5. W. Grey Walter, *The Living Brain* (New York: Norton, 1953).

operated, for all the centuries of our existence, in complete ignorance of itself as such an organ. With the work of Galvani in electricity, and of Pavlov in his studies on causes and conditions of behavior, the first steps were taken in the direction of the awareness of the function and the structure of the brain as the center and director of human electrical impulses. Now at last it became possible to develop a "physiology of the mind." "Mentality," Walter writes, is happier thought about "as a relation of dimensions in the same class as velocity." [6] But we should no more look for the specific mechanism of that velocity than a mechanic "would peer into his engine for the component of its velocity." (Interesting analogy, to say the least.) That velocity is simply a notation of measurement of the function of the engine itself, and not a unit within it. (Walter was one of the great contributors to the development and perfection of the electro-encephalograph, the instrument that magnifies and measures the minute electrical impulses inside the brain and is used so widely in the exploration and explanation, not only of the conditions of the body, but also of the "thought processes" in humans.)

But even here, we find Walter's acknowledgment of the function of models, and, although indirectly, of analogies. He writes:

> The model (constructed for purposes of examining in increasingly precise detail the operations of the brain) not only satisfied all the theoretical requirements predicted, but discovered phenomena for which no arrangement had been made, phenomena which nevertheless were found to correspond to those of the living brain under similar experimental conditions.[7]

Thus, within this literal or representative model, the functioning of the brain is, by definition, what we call mind, or mentality. Further, he writes, in a marvel of reductionism, "the brain is essentially the organ of personality." But this is precisely what we would be led to expect from the uses of some organ as the analogue for otherwise conceptual matters, especially when the analogical character is not recognized. And yet, curiously, he derides what he calls "intellectual materialists" who must always reify vague concepts, making them entities to be dealt with as tangibles. Nevertheless, he considers that his model allows him to deal with mind as a functioning of the brain, not as an event in itself. Yet that functioning, the model tells us, must be a functioning of some actual, tangible event. How far, then, has

6. Ibid., p. 260.
7. Ibid., p. 256.

he really freed himself from the dangers that he derides others for falling into? Has he not himself had to treat mind as a material event? Have not he and de Bono said the same things? From their analogies, aren't they both treating mind as tangible, organic operation?

Each of the advocates we have discussed emphasizes the literal statements he makes as being faithful to the facts to which he has addressed himself. They all, for example, share the dread of the kind of explanation of thinking that ends with an infinite regress; of getting into a situation where they would be talking about thinking about the thinking that has been done about the thinking that has been done—backward without end. For each, some firm and limited, yet complete, description is sought.

Curiously, they are all also concerned that the analysis offered shall not be treated *merely* as a metaphor (as a linguistic ornamentation), inevitably as an analogy that will ultimately be found wanting. And each develops richer analogies to prove his point. Let us consider this.

The Irreducibility of Analogies, Metaphors, and Models

RESISTANCE TO METAPHOR AND ANALOGY

In order to give warrant to the paradigm of thinking he has presented, Moore illustrates its literal force with a story of how General Eisenhower made the judgment to embark upon the assault of Europe in 1944. If the story is full of analogies, these are not to be considered as anything more than ornamentations upon a literally true description of the judgment-making process.

Skinner begins his book *The Technology of Teaching* with a discussion of "three great metaphors [which] have been devised to account for the behavior which distinguishes [the educated from the uneducated person]." What he intends to do, as he later shows, is to explode these metaphors, and to replace them with direct expository statements. Metaphors of "growth," "acquisition," and "construction" will be replaced, he says, because "any serious analysis of the interchange between organism and environment must . . . avoid metaphor." [8]

---

8. B. F. Skinner, *Technology of Teaching* (New York: Appleton-Century-Crofts, 1968), chap. 1.

What is revealed in all our illustrations, explicitly or implicitly, is the quest for a better model, even when it appears preferable to avoid the dangers of analogy. De Bono, throughout, is quite explicit in his uses of some model by means of which he plans to examine and describe, in empirical terms, the behavior of the brain as the thinking agent; but even for him, any model is at best an artificial means of coming to comprehend behavior that will finally better be understood by direct observation. And this, in the final analysis, will be the problem that we must consider.

It would appear that in certain arenas of inquiry the model and the metaphor are simply convenient but clearly temporary fictions. It would indeed seem that they are employed until the required powers and instruments have been developed by means of which we come directly at the data. In other inquiries it appears just as clearly that the metaphor and the model cannot be avoided since we are dealing, quite frankly, with matters that can never be seen. Poetry, for example, would be such a realm of thinking because what the poet expresses is his feelings, his visions of worlds that do not exist or might ever exist, or of worlds that do exist but that he perceives not as others do. Thus, poetry is the deliberate distortion of the familiar by means of a metaphor, until unexpected meanings and images suddenly recommend themselves.

Behaviorists, however, sometimes look into poetic expressions for direct evidence of the state of mind, or of the feelings of the poet, and attempt to expose those conditions that could be said to have "caused" the poetry. In this way poetry is transformed into the evidence for psychological investigations; a quest for exact descriptions of the states and the functions of the mind, apparent in this particular poem. Others, in order to avoid the psychologizing of poetry, are more likely to accept the metaphoric role as irreducible, acceptable not as a merely useful function but as the content of the poem. But in the fields of the natural and social sciences, if we take our earlier illustrations as evidence, the movement is always to get away from the metaphor and to use whatever models we require only for so long as we cannot get to the evidence directly.

THE PERVASIVENESS OF METAPHORS, ANALOGIES, AND MODELS

How shall we settle this argument, if indeed it can be settled? The intention, in at least two of the three approaches considered here, is to avoid a language that refers only to another language, and addresses itself, rather, to a language where each term refers to something in experience, something that can be observed. Because only in this way can we overcome the exasperating state in which words have no observable testing places, where words have no connection with the world and thus gradually drift off into what has been called mere vaporizing. But this, I have shown, assumes a condition of the existential world that the existential world does not appear to support. And if nature does not provide the evidence we demand, are we not also in danger, in the midst of our most diligent scientific inquiries, of "vaporizing"? Apples, water, air do not in nature come labeled "Eat me," "Drink me," "Breathe me." *We* label them. It is we who speak and classify, not nature.

Consider, for a moment, the language of that psychology that regularly employs terms such as "ego needs," "complexes," "drives," "repressions," "conditionings." Are these not segments of a metaphoric language? What words would we need to replace them in order to develop a true observation language? What, in human behavior, must we be clearer about in order to find those better terms? Are they not, after all, ascriptions we make to already observed behaviors, which still require an explanation beyond what has been observed?

Not even the most discriminating of scientific inquiries is free of this condition. The metaphoric language of science is so much a part of us that we do not always recognize that a "double helix" is a metaphoric phrase, that "fields of force," "kinaesthesia," "atomic structure," and "gravitational pull" are no less metaphoric than the metaphors of poetry. Nor can we long insist, without a rising embarrassment, that the laws of nature that are derived from continuous observation of the events in the natural world are as much "mind-dependent" as they are object-dependent. Models of unseen and unseeable worlds cannot be avoided if our quest is to give a fuller explanation of the world available to our senses. Science comes to rest only temporarily when we have found evidence of what we are looking for. It comes to rest when minds come to rest, when they no longer wonder, or doubt, or are curious. The history of science attests to this. It ceases, too, when we cease to consider our own involvements in explaining things, when we are no longer concerned to examine the classifying systems we have constructed or accepted, and becomes technology.

Another logical dimension must be considered here, which is much more complex and much more difficult to evaluate. It sometimes occurs, in scientific experimentation and theorizing, that the line between what is in fact observable and the concepts in use by means of which that observation is made becomes so obscured that we may well find ourselves entirely in the conceptual realm without concern for the fact that the referents to that concept could not possibly be empirical, that they could only be a fully developed conceptual system that comes to serve as the means for observing and commenting upon the empirical world. When the earlier parts of this system have been proven to be sufficiently faithful to the empirical world, later phases of the system take on the acceptability of that empirical evidence but develop a complete logical vindication in their own terms. If we remember the function that such theorizing performs, that it provides us with a structure for organizing and explaining the world of things, we can observe that, as it improves, it continues to do so with greater logical consistency, in greater and greater coherence with the known world. We finally seem to reach a point where it really does not matter whether the concept invented at some later time exists. It serves the function for which it was constructed, and that is all we can ask of it. It makes possible probings, explanations, sometimes predictions, and controls even though its physical existence may never be proven.

Nor is this the case only in physics and poetry. Every discipline that is evidence of the human being's continuing effort to offer more accurate descriptions and sounder explanations is a model-making and an analogy-and-metaphor-constructing activity. All of this can only lead to the conclusion that if we are to analyze thinking, we must address ourselves to the metaphors, the models, and the analogies that shape the paradigms whose traits and functions are what we can deal with as the thinking act.

Thinking as a Public Act

NO FINAL MODELS OR ANALOGIES

From our earliest days each of us unconsciously stores up "traces" of experiences that come to serve as the reservoir for the materials from which analogies can be constructed. Every memory becomes available matter for the construction of those analogies that permit us to inquire into inchoate nature. Every experience, every event observed, every social transaction undergone, every private feeling remembered, stands in that same office. Elements of them are available as data waiting to be transformed into materials for some model, analogy, or metaphor to be applied to some new event encountered or familiar event reconsidered. Every new model we construct, or new metaphor or analogy we employ, shows us the structure and function of the world in a new way, in the terms of that new model or that later analogy. No model that has ever been invented, or any analogy or metaphor, however familiar and widely used it has become, is the last possible model, analogy, or metaphor to be employed in our quest for fuller understanding, for better explanations, for more interesting and yet faithful descriptions of the world observed. The illustrations we have offered here are proof that we all grow in understanding as we invent, or someone presents to us, a clearer model, a better metaphor, a more insightful analogy to explain in a richer way what we have come to accept as standard.

USING MODELS OR BEING USED BY THEM

We need to distinguish between mere summoning up of memory out of our inherited social, moral, physical beliefs to resolve a dilemma, impulsive responses, and the "act" of thinking. If the limits imposed by this view of thinking appear to be narrow, at least it makes it possible for us to sort out those assertions in which we are *used* by models and metaphors of the past (as in mere memory) from those models and metaphors that are themselves evidence of our minds in action in a given situation.

From such a concept of thinking, all the observations and explanations, the reasoning procedures employed, are recognized as deriving from the very model with which we have begun and are becoming conscious of. They are no longer able to be offered as dicta, assertions of an objective reality that speaks for itself in its own, either precise or mysterious, language. The laws of nature we derive and pronounce derive as much from our models as they do from observed data. And with this, the dangers of pronouncing dogmas about the world observed and the world experienced diminish. For the context from which we speak, the "frame of reference," so to speak, of our observations, assumptions, descriptions, and explanations, are now discerned as the models by means of which that world is seen or evaluated. "Social determinants," "psychological sets," and "standards of behavior" are all part of the models we construct, or which have been handed to us. We can be used by these models, and manifest no thought at all, except the thought that someone else formed in the construction of that model. Or we can use those models "reflectively," that is, *use them* and remain aware of what the model makes it possible for us to see and understand in the world. Indeed, in this

sense, "to think" and not to be aware of the act would be a contra-
diction in terms.

There are some fundamental concomitants to this acceptance.
Metaphysically we assume, and on excellent grounds, that we cannot
always readily distinguish between statements about the realities of
nature and our fictions about that nature. Nor can we, in light of this,
commit ourselves only to material reality in our quest to make the
world comprehensible or more controllable. Our very comprehension
and control of nature is dependent upon mental constructs, not nature's own "ways."

Epistomologically, what we come to know are what our earlier
experiences, transformed into the materials of models, enable us to
understand of the newer experiences or investigations we undertake.
Biologically, it may well be the case, as Lewis Thomas has argued, that
the brain is the most public organ on the face of the earth, open to
everything; that the thinking that occurs results from the traces left
in that brain, not only from our own experiences, but also from the
experiences that others have passed around continuously. And it may
well be true that from this biological base we can more readily accept
the notion that we are all, always, borrowers from the nature that
sustains us and equips us for our continuing encounters.[9] But the
problem remains. We are either constantly being absorbed into some
prevailing model and following out its rules without further questioning or we become conscious of that model, explore it for its structural traits, its logical connectives, its inferential demands, and its
ultimate validity in the face of new experiences. The problem is always, then, one of either succumbing to some persuasive model and
being used by it, or turning to the model itself and grasping it to the
extent that we are the users of that model or some constructed alternative when it begins to show its inadequacies in our continuing
inquiry.

THE MANY WAYS THAT THOUGHTS ARE COMMUNICATED

Thought is communicated in the form of concepts systematically
organized and given material form; that is, made manifest to sensibilities. Unless concepts are in some way made sensible, clarity of
communication disappears. For we take what is manifest to be some-

---

9. L. Thomas, *Lives of a Cell* (New York: Doubleday, 1974).

thing other than what may have been intended by the communicator. Not every kind of communication, however, is evidence of, or is itself, the thinking act. All too often communication takes the form and the quality of exclamation, habits, feelings, desires, fears, uncertainties, and so on. They may well be clues to possible thought, but as expressions they are not thoughts. They simply represent themselves in their immediacy as sounds or shapes.

Communications of concepts manifest themselves to us, more often than not, as squiggles on a page or bursts of sound in our ears, whose code for translation we have already learned or must now learn. Less discriminate and precise, but no less communicative of thought, are drawings, paintings, sounds of music that we create or receive, movements in dance, gestures in acting, and even more ambiguous, flickers of expression on the human face in ordinary conversation. Without these, however subtle or however broad, whether definitive or ambiguous, how should we know that thinking goes on, or what thinking is going on? Stubborn convention continues to have it that thinking begins in passivity, or silence, which are forms of internal privacy. Yet, unless they are given form and manifest content, unless they appear in forms of public commentary or choices made, the "fact" of privacy leads only to the isolation that is incommunicability.[10]

Thinking, then, is advisedly spoken of here as the "act of following out" some conceptual plan made manifest in the "local habitation" of some symbolic, organized system. And this symbolic matter shows itself to us as a deliberately constructed analogue of the events we seek to inquire into, constructed into a model that represents all the data of our concern that we have chosen as relevant and important to our inquiry. From such a beginning it becomes possible to develop deliberate, critical procedures of thinking, which could not be nurtured as long as thinking remains a private affair. In this, too, we alter the meaning of "observation" of thinking. It is no longer a matter of trying to peer into some mind for some ephemeral process. It is, rather, observing the character of the model, the structure and function of the analogy in use, as it is communicated in some form. It is, in part, the examination of the logical structure of the sentences spoken or written, and the testing of the relationships between symbols and matters symbolized. It is the active analysis of the model as a model of events that goes beyond its linguistic form, into the total conceptual structure within which the symbols form a more com-

---

10. Gilbert Ryle, *The Concept of Mind* (London: Hutchinson, 1949), is by now the classic argument for this view.

plete picture of the world than the world itself presents. Assertions, sentences, appear as elements within that model, that map or form or formula, but it is the construct as a whole that gives meaning to the individual sentences used. Some models, or analogies, are too loose and uncertain in their inner relationships, ambiguous in their references, vague in their representations. These stand as awkward, confused, disjointed acts of thought. They are like clouded mirrors, within which an event can be seen only dimly, or which distort what they are created to reflect faithfully; or they are faced away so that they reflect other than what they ought to reflect. These last are readily recognizable, too, as metaphors for describing inadequacies of thinking. Sometimes the mirror itself is so framed and so gilded that we pay attention to the outer forms that contain it and never attend to the mirror in its functions. Thus the metaphors or the analogies, though they are still manifest acts of thinking, direct attention away from what is thought and toward the irrelevant framework. So, too, glittering metaphors sometimes distract from thought, from what is being said and intended.

If we accept this meaning of thinking as analogizing, we are no longer trapped in the helplessness into which we had been thrust when we were persuaded to believe either that thinking is, first and last, a private affair, or that it is simply a matter of faithfully reporting the world as it comes to us, in increasingly finer details. For as long as we remain conscious of the role of models, analogies, and metaphors, and become aware of how these are constructed, thinking can be seen as a process that is flexible, open, changeable, and moving because it is a conscious, conscientious effort to introduce better, more adequate, more significant representations of events in their features, their relationships, their functions. Thinking ceases, or cannot begin, when analogizing is either denied or lost sight of. When the process is identified only with the exact recording of what is there (literal description) or what is believed, and the analogy, or the model, is viewed either as an adornment to something fundamentally real or as a myth, it can no longer be analyzed and experimented with for alternative modes. We are being urged to look at the event "as if" it would appear to us directly. We must submit passively to the world in its intrinsic nurture. This is what Montaigne must have been arguing when he wrote that "he who follows another follows nothing." For discipleship stills the act of thinking in the disciple; his actions are directed by thoughts of others that have now been reified into dogmas, no longer open to the challenges of the curious and the reflective. As we give ourselves more and more unquestioningly to nature or to what other people tell us, there is less and less cause for thinking. The knowledge we have absorbed, which has become our private holding, is all we need. Therefore, thinking can be seen only as defiance or rebellion, which must surely be absurd.

We need now to look in greater detail at the logical structure of analogies, models, and metaphors, to see how they are constructed, how they are justified in use, and how they give direction to that process we call thinking.

Models and Analogies in Description and Explanation

In which it is shown that our models and analogies provide our several worlds with the qualities and quantities they come to have.

The Means for Thinking about the World

From the earliest days of our existence, of our absorption of the sights and sounds and motions of the world, what we see and hear are events that come to us in some connectedness. They are not comprehended as isolated entities. They are organized, limited, interrelated, and communicate a sense of direction. We learn as we learn what these relatednesses are, what the connections imply or portend, what follows from what, what is included with what. When the Greeks argued that learning, which is the gaining of knowledge and wisdom, calls for contemplation, and that the thinking life is the contemplative life, it is to this fact of implication that they were referring. We contemplate, carefully or clumsily, how words are entailed by words, how meanings are implied by meanings, how movements anticipate other movements, how faces suggest other faces, how beliefs are connected to other beliefs. For the world we experience comes to us in wholes, some immediate, some mediated, some close at hand, some more remote.

And yet, in our earliest experiences, none of the meanings of the world come to us directly through phenomenal experience. We hear sounds, creaks, breaks, voices, steps, clangs as distinct phenomena. And we see shapes, colors, and movements in the same way. But we neither see nor hear meanings. These come to us through symbols. Not single or isolated symbols. They come to us through whole systems of symbols organized into more or less discrete models to reflect or describe some aspect of the world outside those models. We spend our lives peeling the layers, so to speak, of the outer symbols in order to

28

understand the complexity of things, often without being conscious that we are doing so. We come slowly to learn what the "inner layers" of those systems (and the insides of things) are, what they mean, how they are connected to the outer levels. If we then learn to isolate some symbols, and apply them as isolated instruments to new situations, they nevertheless come to us originally in all their connectedness as models of worlds to be encountered and understood. We are never, as human beings, outside whole collections of models connected to other, wider models, by means of which the phenomenal and conceptual worlds are organized and symbolized. Indeed, they confuse the whole realm of our unconscious.

The model (or the analogy or the metaphor), then, gives us the language, symbols, and notational systems we use in making a description of something, an explanation of its existence and its behavior. The model, the analogy, and the metaphor make it possible for us to follow out some event in the world and provide us with the possibility of attaining knowledge and understanding. It is from some model that we derive the instruments for whatever explorations or observations we make, and the judgments with which we conclude. If, for example, we recognize that scientific descriptions differ from historical, literary, or sociological descriptions, it is because the models we use in the pursuit of knowledge in each differ from one another in traits and fundamental content. So also is it the case with explanations in the various types of inquiry we undertake. Nevertheless, it is worth considering these specific activities themselves: describing, explaining, interpreting, judgment making. At a general level we can recognize that, however different types of each of these phases of thinking are from one another, they nevertheless have common processive characteristics that make them all descriptions, explanations, and judgments in the unique, singular, ongoing, thinking act. Specific illustrations of these must await part 2. Here we consider their general traits.

Descriptions

Usually we accept that a description is a faithful report of some event that, as a result, can be recognized by someone else. That is, I describe a street by the features of the buildings on it, by signs that are there, by other such notations that will make the whole recognizable to someone. So the primary quality of a good description would appear to be the fact that it is a literal report of what is there. Unhappily, the matter is not quite so simple, for it presumes an objectivity that is belied in experience. Every description, inevitably, is also a description of my own perception of those events. Moreover, every description is cast into a language that has a syntax, a semantic structure, and a referential character that in part reports what is there, and in part what I, individually, have seen.

DESCRIPTIONS *OF* AND DESCRIPTIONS *AS*

Descriptions *of* and descriptions *as* cannot be separated from one another. Every description is both a description *of* something and a description *as* something. The description *of* something ought to be open to observation and to a check for its accuracy. But the description *as* something is inevitably an analogy. It is a description of this in terms of that, and to this extent it is private to begin with and public afterward, but in a way quite different from the public character of the event in isolation. The two descriptions inevitably flow into one another. The *as* form, the analogical description, derives from my history, my sensibilities, my command of language, my way of inferring the connectedness of things, and has as its referent some event in which I see the similarity. Thus, every description has one component that derives from the actual matters observed, and depends upon my powers of observation. The second component is sourced in thinking; it depends on the power to find or construct some analogy by means of which the observed event can be seen as a complex of connections, relationships, and inferences. The more complete a description of things becomes, the more it includes the analogical dimension, and thus the more understandable it becomes. In order to see what this would mean, try to imagine a physicist's description of a sunrise and compare it with a description of that same sunrise as offered by, say, a novelist (Lawrence Durrell's description of Alexandria, for example) or a poet. In the latter, the description includes not only the event, seen as a bit of phenomena in the universe, but also entails within itself both the phenomena and the perceptions that identify the viewer who is providing us with the description. From any description we could, when called upon, check the validity both of the description *of*, and the description *as*, some event.

The fact is that such descriptions are recognizable and understandable as more or less faithful reports of events perceived. The content of the description moves from the objectively accurate to the connotatively adequate report of events, physical and mental. In this way we are no longer in the dilemma created by the insistence that a description be limited only to that which is literally observable. The whole referent is made tangible, though not all of it is literal. Both aspects together show, as Geach insists, evidence of concepts that are employed in the judgments we make.[1]

THE REFERENTS OF DESCRIPTIONS

More formally, we may distinguish descriptions at two levels. We describe things in particular, and we describe classes of events. Nevertheless, in both there will be some referent for that description. (We will note later that in explanation referents have no such place.) There will be both a formal character and a functional character in the description. In some descriptions we will find that the event being described imposes obligations because of its phenomenal traits. Such traits, being intrinsic to the event, demand that we be as faithful as possible at a given time. But sometimes we are called upon to describe events for which such intrinsic traits are not available, even in the physical world. Here the role of analogy is greater than the literal, for it is the means of getting to the literal. We hypothesize a similarity between events in order to describe what cannot be seen, for we are analogizing it to something that we can see and that we claim is similar to it in important or pertinent respects.

Sometimes we are called upon to describe what, in and of itself, cannot be seen: connectedness, affective qualities, tendencies, inferred conditions. In this case, all we can do is address ourselves to what the symbols alone connote, since there are no literal events to which they refer that we can describe. Thus, some descriptions are actually intrinsically symbolic without specific reference to the intrinsic character of some particular thing in the world.

Yet, in every case, the description will have a referent, even though the nature of that referent changes with the different types of events we are attempting to describe. Even when the description is hypothetical or exclusively theoretical, a tangible referent of some kind exists to which the description refers. In some cases the referents are to the actual, literal features of something. In some, they are to the features of some matter analogized as being similar to what we would

1. Peter Geach, *Mental Acts* (London: Routledge & Kegan Paul, 1971).

see if we could see the thing. And in some, the description refers to some other symbol system.

Thus, even when we are concerned to describe actual features, emphasizing the literal or equivalent appearances of things in themselves, directly or in terms of other like things, analogy has entered.

PURE REPLICATION WITHOUT ANALOGY
IS IMPOSSIBLE IN DESCRIPTION

In the way that a single drop is as intrinsically water as a whole bucket, so the descriptive act shows all the traits of the process of thinking. But from our understanding of the character of description we come to recognize that no model that we construct, or that has ever been constructed, can be so exclusively literal to the world that it can eliminate the role of analogy. All too often literal descriptions are opposed to the analogical, to be preferred by those who insist on avoiding "fantasy." But even the simplest description, it has been shown, is couched in some language system that makes place for analogical perceptions or concepts. To look for nothing but exact "reprints" of the events of the world asks too much, both of the world and of our language. Neither can be reduced to replicatory precision. We must make choices. And however those choices may reflect observable events, they are nonetheless choices among alternatives. Such choices, inevitably, reflect more than the observable. They "reflect," too, what we "see" as a proper, or adequate, analogue for the observable and the unobservable within the observable.

What, then, would a totally literal description be like? (I could not even ask the sentence in that form. It would have to be: "What would a totally literal description *be*?" Not *be like*.) Even the most precise account would have to be some translation—onto paper, or clay, or metal; into a sentence, a gesture, a visual expression. And merely to repeat precisely what is there would further oblige us to do something more if there is to be any use in that so-called replication. It would have to be diminished in size or enlarged, have color added or deleted, have grid lines placed over it, have some points emphasized in some way and others deemphasized, be made of more handleable material, and such. Above all, there would have to be eliminations. Each of these choices derives from concepts organized into some conceptual model that directs these activities.

Nevertheless, we are concerned with the immediate events observed, or yet to be observed, in our description. Good analogies are, after all, tested against empirical data in some way, either directly or indirectly. But they fill out the description of an isolated event by contributing connections, directions, histories, futures. To use words such as "and," "not," "nor," "but," "neither," "right," "left," "anteced-ent," "generative," etc., within a given model-context, in order to offer a faithful description of the features of a street, obliges us to in-dicate some feature that would at least illustrate the meanings and uses of those terms. We may not see an "ego drive," as such. We might never be able to point ostensibly to the referents ("longing," "anonym-ity") in the sentence "I have a longing for anonymity." Yet, there are behaviors to which such phrases, terms, or sentences are conven-tionally applied, in an agreed upon semantic system. Even when we offer descriptions of gorgons, unicorns, or other mythical creatures, the referent is clear in the illustration, verbal or otherwise, of some fantastic collectivity of parts, if to no actual things.

We can only be led to the conclusion that in the matter of descrip-tion the decision to oppose literal to analogical is predicated on a questionable metaphysics of the structure of reality and of the human mind. For if every description requires the presence of referential terms, these referents will nevertheless still have analogical forms, features, or functions that give focus and meaning to that description.

The distinctions made between descriptions whose referents are (1) readily observable, (2) hypothetical, or (3) purely symbolic lead to a reinforcement of the ineliminability of analogies.

Sometimes we analogize what is present in order to apply it to something that is also present but unclear or unknown to us. Some-times we analogize in order to show what is similar among dissimilar things.

Sometimes, however, analogies of what is present are employed to propose descriptions of matters that are not now or will ever be pres-ent to us. This latter is what generally defines historical descriptions. What we have before us, as matters for inquiry, are not the events themselves, but a record of those events, some set of signs or symbols of those events; some artifacts that become the data we explore in order to develop a description of the event that can, in its actuality, never be encountered. What place we give the name for such evidence in a systematic statement that connects the event to other events de-rives in part from what is already known about that event, and in part from the model of explanation and interpretation into which we put the terms for that event. So, for example, a paragraph such as this from Herbert Muller's *The Loom of History* is surely an interesting mixture of the so-called literal and the analogical. He writes:

These Persians who finally led us to the Greeks, first wrote a glorious enough chapter of their own. They silenced the ghost of Ashurbanipal by creating not only the greatest but the most civilized empire yet known to history. Their early kings were remarkable rulers, with an eye to economics. . . .[2]

Are not the analogies as acceptably descriptive as the factual reports? If they are eliminated, would the description be the same, only more precise? Surely, it would be a very different kind of a description, evidence, Geach says, of a very different exercise of the mind. We could only prefer the *more nearly* literal to the more clearly analogical, but neither can be altogether dispensed with in any of our disciplines.

The Aristotelian definition of metaphor, that is, of giving something a name that conventionally belongs to something else, is basic to this analogical factor of the descriptive phase of the thinking act. In descriptions we transfer our knowledge of the features and functions of classes of things to those specifics that are our focus of inquiry. Or we transfer our knowledge of particular things in order to describe the whole class of events to which the thing belongs. We do this, he says, *on the grounds of an analogy that we discern or construct between those events.* On the grounds of that analogy, we use the terms legitimately applied to some event in order to describe another event. In this way, we are able to describe things that have occurred once and may never occur again, or events that clearly begin as private experiences. It is by analogy that we describe Caesar crossing the Rubicon, the fall of the city of Pompeii, Napoleon's obsessions, a headache, the behavior of molecules, frogs, and humans.

What we are led to is this critical observation. The describing phase of the act of thinking is that phase during which we construct, on analogical grounds, some model whose rules, definitions, and delimitations we will be following out in later phases of thinking, phases of explaining, categorizing (or classifying), interpreting, evaluating. *The description offered, in short, becomes itself the clarified model for the remainder of the thinking act,* and itself depends in part on observation, in part on control of the instruments (including, of course, linguistic) used in the description, and in part on the imaginative powers of developing analogies. To learn to describe, in short, is to learn to build a model, construct an analogy, fashion a metaphor, reflect some referent.

2. Herbert Muller, *The Loom of History* (New York: Harper & Bros., 1958), p. 102.

RULES FOR ACCEPTABLE ANALOGIES

The need for rules.   The most fundamental question now is that of establishing rules for the acceptability of descriptive analogies. How shall we test the warrant for the claim that the event I am now describing is enough like the event for which this description is being offered, and useful for the further phases of the thinking act? For inquiry not only into the unseen aspects of what is seen, but into the private mental acts? For it is safe to assume that mental events are as much a part of the furniture of our world as are physical events.

Purely theoretical or purely conceptual events are made manifest in some symbol system formed into a model by means of analogy. In many cases, even where we need to know how exact a replication the model or the analogy is to what is being modeled or analogized, we may never know. But the fact is, we may never need to know. It may be enough simply to turn to the consequences of the uses of the model or the analogue in order to determine its adequacy for our needs. (It may even reveal to us needs we could not otherwise have recognized.) But the model, at least, presents us with the symbols that are themselves firm data, and this prevents us from flying off into realms of mystery and miracle.

In any case, what we describe, in what language, and in what way, for what purpose, is determined by the relationship discerned in the model in the analogies constructed.

Five quick guides.   What, then, shall we look for in the construction of our analogies, or our analogical descriptions?

1.—A coherence and a consistency within the analogy. That is, the matters being analogized must "hang" together in the way that a picture (or a map) is made of parts that fit together logically and do not contradict one another.

2.—A correspondence between the elements of the analogy and the elements of the events to which the analogy is to be applied as a means for further inquiry. Selectivity is crucial. The analogy needs to contain within itself those aspects of the event being modeled that answer some specific concern or are projected as having primary meaning.

3.—There must be clarity in the analogue. That is, the analogy is being constructed for the express purpose of making apparent the traits, relationships, features, and functions that are obscure in the event for which this model is being constructed.

4.—The symbol system that is the analogy must have at least a stipulated or conventional validity, and where possible, enough empirical warrant to show that it is adequate to the task for which it is constructed.

5.—There must be rules for transforming the data of the world into the data that comprise the analogy. If lines are used for roads, if waves are used for light, if sound is used for feeling, there must be established a dictionary in which all the features of the events being explored are adequately noted in the symbol system of the analogy being created.

This is also a good set of recommendations for the development of an adequate description of anything, whether it be of a particular thing, a class of things, a concept, a feeling, a "state of mind." Its strength lies in this: If thinking is an act that requires referents, *it is some model, constructed analogically, that becomes that immediate referent.* The act of describing, it is clear, is the act of constructing that referent, by means of analogy, upon which all other phases of thinking focus. We explore the model, and through it, the world represented in the model. And the process of our thinking is the process that begins with the description that becomes the model and directs us by its rules.

Explanation

THE PURELY MENTAL ACT

Whether we are conscious of it or not, whatever we call an explanation, we derive from some explicit or implicit description that we have accepted or constructed. But even more than descriptions, explanations are purely mental acts. In the simplest common-sense terms we say *why* a thing is what it is only when we know *what* it is. In a more complex way we are able to offer an account of events only after we have developed models of those events by means of some valid, or warranted, analogy. *What* we are explaining is already present to us in that model, which is why we are called upon to account for it. Without a description of some kind, we have nothing to explain. Thus, the second fundamental phase of the thinking act is determined by what we have built into the model. When we say we have no explanation for something, we are acknowledging we have no adequate model for it.

We need to recognize what could be quite disconcerting. It may help us to overcome the great dilemmas we create for ourselves when we demand more from an explanation than explanation can afford. A world or a universe of vast distances and vast numbers of submicroscopic bits of energy can never be ultimately, absolutely, seen and recorded. All we can do is create for ourselves tangible immediacies to which we give wholeness and unity, knowing we will never be able to test the absoluteness of the identicality. If we expect more than this, if we expect absolute identification and don't get it, then everything becomes miraculous. It is for Jung, for example, a miracle that a broken bone heals. But this insistence that explanations be absolute, that detailed descriptions be of what is really there, demonstrates why humanity is fundamentally imperfect. What else could human models of humanity and nature allow?

Nothing comes so close to defining the heart of the act of thinking as does the act of explaining. There is one mode of thinking in which explanation does not serve this central role. This is the thinking whose outcome is some work of art, which is taken up fully in a later chapter. For now, however, I focus on those modes in which explanation is the "heart" of the "act." For, if to think is to follow out the rules, the inferences developed, the formal strictures of some model of inquiry of an event, mental or physical, then the conclusions we derive from that following-out are the explanations derived or constructed. To explain an event is to move from whatever is present before us in the model to what is not immediately present but can be inferred from it. It is, then, a statement about the condition, or the process, that is offered to account for what we have before us.

The question of what an explanation is, and why it is the heart of the thinking act, must be more completely analyzed. There are people who hold that having described something is to have given an account of it. But we are dealing with answers to two different questions here, not one. A description, the building of an analogical model of some kind, is an attempt to answer the question, *What* is it? This act, I have said, is the first phase of the thinking process. But explanation answers the very different question of "*Why* is it?" or "*Why* is it this?" or "*Why* is it this way?"

Sometimes, in order to extend the descriptive phase into the explanatory, the *why* question is transformed into the form, "*How* is it this?" or "*How* is it that it is this way?" which could, indeed, be answered by a description. Nevertheless, however complete the description offered of such a sequence, it does not fully respond to, or take account of, the inferential matters that are involved within the descriptions. Rather, it assumes that whatever is present before us *had* to be what it is because it is only a later phase of something we have described as immediately preceding it. Some "explain" a man by describing a boy's phases of growth into a man. But the need to explain the sequence remains. Even the most precise model we have constructed, the fact of phase following phase, of event following event, does not reveal, in the same observable way, the laws or causes that produced this sequence of phases. And thus the question of *why* remains unanswered. There is no logical basis for being satisfied with the statement of sequences as being all that is meant by the question of *why*, unless you have accepted a logical model in which this is entailed. It is clearly not enough to say that an explanation is nothing more than a series of increasingly complete, specific descriptions of any given event and all the interconnectednesses from which it arose, and toward which it is tending.

But what, other than an increasingly detailed description of events, do we seek in our inquiries into the world of things and the world of ideas? Quite simply, an *understanding* of whatever it is we are investigating within a context of events of which it seems to be a part or to which it belongs. What we want beyond the description is a comprehension of the career of "mechanisms," of powers at work that connect events to the event we now see and can describe. We want to understand not only what is but what might be, what might have happened, what might yet possibly happen. We want to understand connectedness, especially how events can be inferred from events in a context. We want to comprehend relationships between events that, on the face of it, seem to have no influence on one another. We want to grasp the mechanisms of transference, and transformation, how the "history," of an event affects the structure of that event. For these, we need generalizations, in the form of laws, from which explanations are derived. For such understandings, descriptions alone do not suffice. Indeed, the more precise and clear the description, the more the explanation becomes possible and appears needed. In the larger picture, then, descriptions are of particular events that we can discern the model as an *illustration of some generalization that the mind constructs as an explanatory system.*

WHAT MAKES AN EXPLANATION NECESSARY?

Clearly, the very character of events in the world makes explanation a necessary concern for us. Nothing in nature ever remains so static, is so complete and evident in and of itself, that by describing it we can give a complete account of it. In the changes that occur we need sometimes to understand origins we could never observe, or possibilities we must guard against or encourage so that they will or will not in fact occur. Then, too, we are always on the verge of being surprised by some turn of events that compels us to seek an account of things. As we come to understand it, in this explanatory sense, the world more truly becomes our own, one in which we can partake with confidence and comprehension.

If no change occurred in the world, or if the world were of such perfect order and if whatever is, is all there is, if the character of nature and its things were so constant that each event was not only whole unto itself but a portent of its own continuing wholeness, we would not need explanation. But these are not the conditions of *ANW* existence. The world is a world coming into being, or going out of existence, as full of discontinuities as of harmonious continuities. It is not a world of mere replications of events already encountered. Because this is so, there is a further need for models to inquire into. The development of explanatory systems is the movement toward an understanding of what cannot be read from the face of nature as it appears to us in its immediacy.

RULES FOR CONSTRUCTING EXPLANATORY ANALOGIES

If these conditions oblige us to seek explanations, how are they to be achieved? By reflection, of course, upon the descriptive model presented, in order to come to some agreement on what cannot be observed but could provide us with a more complete image and thus a fuller understanding of what has been described. Thus, to set forth the process of explaining is to set forth the processes of using models and analogies in order to arrive at theoretical and hypothetical completions of the events we are examining.

We need to consider what more is intended by explanation, and what understandings explanations provide that no other phase of the process of thinking does, and where, in the entire process, the explanatory phase fits. The more adept we become at constructing and properly using models and analogies in our inquiries into the worlds of things and concepts, the simpler it becomes to derive or develop explanations of events in those worlds, for these are already built into the models when they are adequately (or even awkwardly) constructed.

Transformation of features and functions.   In order to develop an explanation of anything, it has been argued, we must first have transformed that thing into something that can be more critically observed than the original event itself. But such a step is only the first task. In addition, as closely as possible we must construct the model so that it will behave, either identical with or similar to the behavior of the thing itself, under the particular conditions we have thus far been able to observe. To this we must finally add an additional symbol system by means of which we might read out of the model the behaviors we are attempting to understand, and to observe others in ways that only a model can make available to us.

The more descriptively faithful the elements of the model are to the textures, the structures, and known behaviors of the real event (in the fuller, not the literal sense), the more likely the model is to make an understanding of it possible. And the more likely we are to be able either to observe or to deduce what things or behaviors in the real event might be said to derive from, or produce, what other activities.

Sometimes the model can be made to appear almost an actual miniaturization, or enlarged replication, of the thing being modeled. More often, however, it is not all the actual features that enter into the model, but only certain behaviors that are being reproduced in forms other than those of reality. So, for example, as it has been pointed out, Kelvin's tide predictor does not resemble the tides of the seas. It contains specific symbolic instruments that are analogies of the tides and that rise and fall on numerical scales, much as the seas rise and fall in their seabeds.

Selection of data and invention of the analogy.   At least two traits must be present in any model of explanation. First, the selectivity and organization that is involved in the construction of a model. And second, the choice or invention of the analogies that will symbolize those events that could not otherwise be dealt with (the actual tides of the sea). By means of selection we have isolated those aspects of a given event that recommend themselves to us as being of special importance, and for which we seek an explanation. At the same time we eliminate those parts that, at least for the moment, seem to be of no great promise or significance in our quest.

But the second trait, that of the choice or the construction of analogies, is more complicated. Because all we would like to see cannot ever be seen (concepts, electrons, molecules, atoms, quarks, numbers), we are left with no alternative but to construct a manifestation that would serve as an analogue of that thing. We must, as has been said, give concepts a "local habitation."

Now, there may be some difficulties in reproducing the tangible aspects of things in the world, but they are not so insurmountable that they cannot be reproduced in a way that would satisfy the conditions that would make inquiry possible. Yet when it comes to the development of analogies, the difficulties really mount. It calls for imagination, a genuine inventiveness in the construction of some *thing* that will behave in ways we suspect *both* the observables and the unobservables behave. The greatest problem arises from a recognition of the fact that we can never be certain that the analogy will hold. Often either there is too little to check it against, or the analogy is purely theoretical, with no substance whatever to examine as being that from which it is derived. Here we may have, as the referent, only human imagining of imaginary things. Nevertheless, ephemeral as this may appear, it is a significant source for analogy constructions. Intuition is at work, of course, but more than intuition is needed. We need to know what explanations provide, for these expectations will guide us.

What is derived from the explanatory functions of analogy?

Prediction. Sometimes we seek to explain a given event and its behavior in order to be able to make predictions about its structure or its later behavior. In such a case we construct a model in which the elements are as nearly equivalent to the elements of the thing as we can achieve. As we approach closer and closer to identicality, we are able to predict from the model what is likely to happen in the thing modeled. In pursuit of this identity it must be recognized that the notations of the negative side, that is, where nonidentities are clearly marked, are as important as the notations of the positive, for the presence of some known factors enables us to make predictions about consequences when these identities are not present. This combination of the positive and the negative characterizes the analogy. Thus, for example, if we were to build a model of the moon by analogizing it in certain of its aspects to the earth, we would recognize that we do not include in the model the atmospheric conditions that exist on earth. As a result of this, we were able to predict that life as we know it on earth would not be encountered on the moon, for in the absence of atmosphere, life could not be sustained.

Explanation through analogies of similarity. Sometimes, however, we build analogies that are not recognizably matters of identity, but rather of similarity. This demands a little more of both creators and receivers of the analogy. Suppose we analogized the known properties of light and sound for purposes of explaining the behavior of light.[3]

---

3. I draw here from Mary Hesse, *Models and Analogies in Science* (South Bend, Ind.: University of Notre Dame Press, 1966), p. 60.

The elements we would include in a model of sound would be loudness, pitch, echo, mode of detection, and manner of propagation. It is not hard to select what would be similar to those in light. The loudness of sound would be analogous to the brightness of light; pitch becomes analogous to color; echo to reflection. We analogize that sound detected by the ear is similar to light detected by the eye. Sound propagated through air is, for us, similar to light propagated through the "ether." Now, as with models in which identities, positive or negative, are strong and clear, observations of models with defensible similarities in one make it possible to make predictions in the other. If we accept the analogy between pitch in sound and color in light, it becomes possible to predict aspects of the behavior of light from observations of the behavior of sound in various situations. But this, it must be recognized, calls for some logical as well as psychological persuasion. Can we justify that there is sufficient similarity between sound and light so that the relationships among the elements within the known model can be translated as also being warranted as a description and possible explanation of the matter we are exploring? We shall note later that some practical differences appear in the construction of analogies in history and in the arts, even while the principle of construction remains constant.

The persuasive quality of analogy. Going still further, we construct a model in which persuasion is even more heavily involved, for the similarity between events may have little empirical data to support the claim. In sociology or in political science, we have often found the family used as a model to explain the behavior of the state. Family rules, traditions, histories, and structures are known to determine the actions and relationships of each family member. From this model the state is projected as a kind of nation-family, and the explanations and predictions of the behavior of every citizen in the nation are drawn from their (analogical) behavior in the family. But however clear and persuasive our analogy, we have to remember that it remains just that, an analogy, and therefore ultimately a persuasive instrument. This is more carefully examined in the two succeeding chapters.

IDENTITY AND SIMILARITY IN EXPLANATORY SYSTEMS

The dilemmas.   Suppose we tried to construct an absolutely identical model of an event in its context of operation. Would we also have to construct a tangible event to be called the *cause* that connects events and maintains their processes? Many have done this, of course. In seeking to explain thinking, for example, the brain has been postulated as the causal organism. Others have treated the even more complex neural structure of the whole body as a causal fact. But in order for this to serve as a model for thinking, we would have to demonstrate the identity between brain function and the thinking we are trying to explain. What we are doing, however, is offering an explanation on the grounds of an already accepted explanation, which yet remains to be demonstrated. The supposed identity turns out to be a promise, a stipulation. Unhappily, it only heightens the dilemma, for causality is an explanatory principle, not a fact of nature.

Computers, or "thinking machines," are offered as similarity models. They are analogized to the working of the mind on the hypothesis that electrical impulses induced into a machine programmed for their reception and designed to respond according to the rules of that program are similar to the "impulses" that flow across the nerves and fibers of the human organism. These produce behavior reactions among elements of the organism "programmed" to perform certain acts in response to certain stimuli. Accepting this assumption, we predict, analogically, that if certain reinforcements in the machine produce certain accuracy and speed of specifically designed responses, similar reinforcements in the nerve centers of the human body will increase speed and accuracy of responsive behavior. But the question of validity in what we claim as similar is just as thorny, perhaps more so, than the question of identity.

For the fact remains that when we deal with mental acts, we are dealing with intrinsically undefined operations awaiting definition. The relationship ascribed as existing between brain and mind remains purely hypothetical in this definition. Although we can observe the public event called the brain, we cannot observe the private event called thinking until we agree on the manifest evidence of it. If we can observe the electrical connections within the computer, and can also observe the connection between neural synapses, we cannot observe the relationship between those public synapses and the private event we call thinking. It is the dilemma in John Locke all over again. Though we can, indeed, observe how chalk leaves its trails of dust on a tablet, can we truly observe how stimuli, in any sense, "write" on the "blank tablet" of the mind? At best, therefore, when it comes to a consideration of the act of thinking as model making, one of whose purposes is explanatory, something more than identity or similarity may have to be introduced among the rules.

Identicals and similars, though descriptive, derive from explanatory purposes.   Perhaps in this quest we have been assuming more than we should. Perhaps it is not enough to look intently at phenomenal events in order to describe them with greater and greater precision. For even the most faithful of denotative descriptions contain ascriptions that we all too often claim are completely objective. If it is more than mere recall of something memorized, the care we show in our descriptions already shows evidence of our "mental" intrusion. Descriptions are, curiously enough, generalizations, and generalizations do not reside within the data being described. They are human constructions, intended to help us make later judgments of identity, similarity, or dissimilarity.

We have here an old dispute, that of distinguishing between what nature actually presents and what the mind ascribes as connections, sequences, and influences among the data nature presents. As Rescher points out, nothing in water can *lead* the mind to see in it its power to become solid on certain occasions. We see water, then, we see ice. And *we* propound a law, after further investigations, to explain the transformation. The law contains hypotheses of connections for which no real evidence exists, but the law makes it possible to understand why water becomes solid. Thus, the explanation is about a series of descriptions, but is not itself a description.

If we are to understand the thinking process, it might be wise to look more closely at how such laws, or generalizations, are made.

Models operate as constructed laws used as explanatory principles. Laws of nature do not exist as consciously learnable events for cats or dogs or giraffes. Below the level of humankind, behavior is instinctive. Evidence of what is not present must take the form of some tangible clue, which is. (Piaget's studies in infant and early childhood behavior show that this is also the case for humans at this age.) But for humans, symbols suffice as evidence of events not present, events yet possible, or events that have never existed and perhaps could never exist. It is from such symbols, drawn into logical connections with one another, which have reference to the evidence, sometimes directly, sometimes indirectly, that humans construct a complete world whose purpose it is, now, to explain the real world they face.

The description itself, I have said, becomes the subject matter for the explanations constructed, the laws hypothesized. Of themselves these phenomena of nature are just that, things and other things. It is the mental act of describing them in certain ways that makes them eligible to become elements of laws hypothesized and gives them the functions they come to have.

But at the moment that this activity begins, this observation whose intention it is to develop from the primary domain a secondary symbolic domain, by means of which inquiry will then proceed, the thinking act has begun. When the symbol system is given a logical structure so that the whole is established as having an internal relationship among its various parts, we have begun the construction of a model for explaining the very data that the model has analogized. In the model the whole organized set of events is made manifest. The entire picture, with no breaks in continuity, is present to us. In that whole, the elements that do not appear in the primary domain, but are entered into the secondary, are the explanatory elements. These fill out the "picture." They symbolically complete the career of an event in the context of its existence and its functioning by filling in the missing places in the primary data we observe. Thus, within the model we are able to see an event in its wholeness. What we have added to the model that is not in the material modeled enables us to give an account of that observable data of the primary domain. And this account becomes the explanation for why that primary data is what it is, and what we may expect it to become at some later time in its changes or development. (Which is, after all, just what prediction is.)

The Uses of Structured Models and Analogies

THINKING AS OPPOSED TO MYSTIFICATION

There is abundant evidence that in almost every region of experience we continually struggle between thinking and some form of the mystification or mythification of experience. Perhaps it is because at heart we are still possessed by the notion that thinking is a mysterious power endowed upon us. Certainly it is all too commonly held that some of us are born with the power; some of us are born with an abundance of the power; and some, perhaps too many, are born with little or no power to think. Such folklore ought not to be taken seriously. But it is just these attitudes that make the effort to learn to think so much more difficult. Even the genetic approach to the problem, which is the best face we can give to a demystification of such beliefs, more often than not begins with some innocent assumption that it then tries to rationalize into acceptable evidence. It, too, offers a model of man in which these assumptions of inherited thinking power are hardened into irrefutable, unassailable, or unexaminable basic conditions.

But mystifying the thinking process, that is, construing it as a mystery beyond grasp or seeing it as some miraculous manifestation, achieves only the goal of closing the door to further inquiry. We have no alternative but to treat all evidence as evidence of miracles at work, or the mysterious manifestations of fundamental mysteries. Growth is a miracle, human consciousness is a miracle, the world we live in is a miracle. The model with which we began has ceased to be a model at all. It is a full-fledged mythology, beyond grasp of reason.

EVERY MODEL CONTAINS AT LEAST TWO SYMBOL SYSTEMS

The recognition of and attention to this fact is the best way to prevent the mystification or mythification of the thinking process. One system contains the symbols of whatever it is we are trying to explain. This is called the *explanandum*. (In our earlier terms it is the description of some event.) The second system contains the symbols that make up the explanation. This is called the *explanans*. If we are able to keep these two terms clear, and recognize that each has certain characteristics and limitations, we find it easier to discern when reason is being violated. For if a model is created that has no explanans, we are being asked to accept the suggestion that the first symbol system (the description) is self-explanatory. This can only end up as a conviction that nature doesn't need to be explained.

If the model (say, for example, an astrological chart) has no explanandum; that is, if it contains no symbolic statement of matter to which we can address ourselves beyond the model, we are in the presence of a kind of solipsism, where the world exists only for each individual as he or she individually perceives it, and no further communication is needed. The individual does not even need to set it forth for others to contemplate or examine.

Consider this sentence: "The break-in at the Watergate complex and its attendant discovery mark a watershed in the history of the American Presidency." The first part, ending with the word "discovery," is the explanandum. It is the matter to be explained. But it shows evidence of some event in experience that has been set into a symbol system, where an analogy is already playing its role. Clearly, it is treated as if it were a burglary, and we are led to anticipate a fuller description that will fulfill the whole conception of a burglary. (Was it *literally* a burglary? Most people have held that it was. But others have called it a mindless prank intended to find something that would embarrass a candidate and his party.) We can resolve the argument, not only by summoning further evidence for either view, but also by confronting the primary conflicting analogies that have been employed to describe the event, to see which analogy is more faithful to the events that actually took place.

The second phase, beginning with the word "mark" and ending with the word "Presidency," is the explanans. It provides that larger context of events organized within a secondary system of concepts that enables us to understand the meaning of what is being both denoted and connoted in the first phrase, but is not specifically derived from it. And this, too, carries a metaphor, the metaphor of the "watershed."

This latter metaphor, I have said, is not derived from the direct observation of the events referred to in the first system, in the explanandum. It is, in a curious way, an idealization of some larger event that, on the face of it, has only indirect connection with the events referred to in the first phrase. It transforms one element that is only implicit in the first phrase by placing it into a context in which history is construed as a swiftly running stream. Thus, whatever the outcome of the dispute about pranks or burglaries, the meaning ascribed to it by the second system, by means of the analogy used there, is that the whole "course" of the American Presidency has been altered and now will "flow" into new directions and take new forms and new limitations.

We are mystified when there is no explanandum because we do not really know what is being explained. We are mythified when there is no explanans, for we are being asked to accept the event described (the break-in) as something that nature produces, for which no explanation is needed or possible.

To be able to identify and distinguish the two, then, is evidence of the mind at work. But the identification and the distinctions are first made of the analogies employed. We examine them in order to test the empirical veracity of the explanandum, and the logical, heuristic value of the explanans. Moreover, the second system, the explanans, makes possible whatever understanding we have of the first. As Max Black has written, the identification, similarities, or meanings of that first system are *created* in the second, not presupposed.

RULES FOR THE DEVELOPMENT AND USE OF ANALOGICAL MODELS

A model developed within one pursuit, for purposes of exploring and explaining one of the domains of human interests, say, one clearly identified as scientific, however persuasive in itself, is not likely to be suitable to another, say, to a literary mode, unless a transforming operation has taken place. The models employed in sociology are inadequate, even misleading to the physical sciences without some careful altering to take into account the characteristics of the data being dealt with, and the purposes involved. Simply to use one model, untransformed, in another arena of inquiry, is to produce what is called the *ignoratio elenchus* (an unguarded or an unwitting shift in goals sought.) Their structures and the purposes for which they are used determine in large measure the relevance of the models employed, for they must show evidence of the specific explananda, that is, of the matters to be explained. So we need rules in order to distinguish tolerably absurd from clearly misleading or arresting analogies; and such rules would be tests for the adequacy of the relationships between explanans and explananda. We already have many clues in what has been said thus far, but now we need to be more explicit.

Imagery in the explanans.   The clarity of the image created by an analogy is critical. The image is, however, not the model; it is what the model is able to evoke as a perceptible or a mental construct made tangible. By its means we are able to suggest more clearly, and to test more closely, the validity of the links propounded between what in the world we are trying to explain and the model by means of which that explaining becomes possible. No precise rule for such a construction can be given, of course, lest we add to the continuing danger of substituting the model for the reality. The best that we can say is that the imagery to which we finally give our complete attention must reflect the logical quality of the events being explored. So, for example, the attempt to explain, or account for, the traits and conditions within which light moves ought not contain images of divinity. However tempting it has always been to imagine a god who carries bolts of light in his right hand and throws them through the heavens, or a god who carries lightning shafts in his chariot as he rides across the skies, little can be derived that will explain what we have come to describe as very likely true about the behavior of light.

The imagery of a chariot that bears the sun has long had great appeal, and perhaps, within a specific context, it does not stretch too far into absurdity, though few today would be beguiled into seeing anything literal in it. The knowledge that is our reservoir today has transformed this imagery into something quaint, or, in the hands of a writer such as John Barth, something witty. But such imagery denies the possibility of a physical explanation of the behavior of so physical an event because it is not a genuine description. Or if genuine, it is a description without a testable reference. To take it seriously, history has shown, is to be obliged to direct attention, not to the sun, but to the "sun-god." In such a case, both description and explanation would have to be of gods, not light. This is just what an *ignoratio elenchus* is. Thus, the imagery of the explanans (explanation) must at least embed the imagery of the explanandum (description), and be in harmony with those qualities and traits.

Excessive imagery.   The illustration of a chariot driven by a god, and bearing in it the sun, is too obvious for most of us to take seriously, when the concern is for a scientific explanation of the movement of the sun. But more subtle mixings of phenomena in the construction of a vivid image exist, and we must be alert to them. The key to the choices we make is to be found in the purpose we have established or accepted for our descriptions and explanations. It is all but impossible to eliminate some unexpected presuppositions; for example, when we develop an analogy for the explanation of human powers and human behaviors. So, for example, it has become conventional in the modern world to accept the imagery of the human being as a machine. From this, we embark upon a quest for the most persuasive possible machine-image. Today this is a machine that operates on electrical energy. (In another century it might have been Frankenstein's monster. And since images provoke richer images, I wonder what will it be in the 22nd century?)

Now, any phenomena can be examined in the "filter" of any other phenomena. So it is perfectly plausible to consider a human being from the model of an electrically driven machine. But we must be alert to the fact that the "filter" allows only certain events to be seen; it "filters out" others. Thus, the vivacity of the image with which we have begun, and the model we have constructed from it, eliminates other characteristics that might have been accepted as "native" human traits and powers. Introspection, for one thing, does not exist as matter to be considered within the model of the machine. Either it can be explained in such electromechanical terms, and it apparently cannot be, or it is identified as a superstitious idea to which we foolishly insist on clinging.

As we make a choice about the model to construct and begin to develop descriptions and explanations of the world by its means, we need to be aware of what we have mixed—what we have included in our descriptions and explanations, and what we have excluded. This we can do only by the painstaking act of comparing analogies used, and considering the consequences of each against the event to be explained. Thus we compare the chariot of the gods with the waves of the oceans.

The connecting links within a model.   Because the act of thinking culminates in understanding, recognition of the connecting links within the model is imperative. For they are designed to show or suggest the logical consistency, that is, the relationships which empirical events themselves do not show. Without these, descriptions are incomplete because they are static representations; and explanations are inadequate because they refer to no other conditions than the events in that static model.

The analogy we choose must contain within it, then, a clarity of logical connectives, for they are being proposed as the internal conditions, or relationships within the event now seen as changing, developing, diminishing, and so forth. And they become, when formulated, the explanatory statement of that dynamic or evolving event. There is in this a firm rule for a choice among matters to be used as analogues as explanatory instruments.

In any argument over whether the electrically operated machine is a better source of analogy than an introspective analogy, the preference for the former is found in the fact that it is easier to account for causal behavior in an electrical system than it is in terms of an "eye turned inward." One can more readily explain the way in which electrical contact serves as the means for the flow of energy, how cutoffs, or fusions, or bypasses work, than by any account of the "eye turned inward."

This does not, of course, mean that the electrical model is *the* correct model, the only conceivable analogy. It only argues that it at least makes it possible to see manifest evidence of the explanandum, to which the explanans must address itself. Later models, designed as improvements over this, would at least partake of this concern for connectedness. So an improvement in the explanatory model of the human being, if it rejects the electrical impulse model, would reject it in favor of another, which promises as much descriptive reference, if not more.

Relevance in the analogy.   Just as important as the inner connectives that become elements of the explanatory content is the matter of the relevance of that analogy to the matters we seek to explain. The most secure form of this would be an analogy constructed of the same matters as that which we are exploring. But this, unhappily, is not always possible. In fact, in some inquiries it is never possible. In place of the features of the event, therefore, we look for relationships that we suspect, or know, obtain within the event to be explained. Now, sometimes these can be similar, at the phenomenal level, as when we choose lines and crosses and profiles of buildings as symbols for a road map. But more often, they are more abstract, as abstract as mathematical systems. Why choose, as was shown earlier, the behavior of

The ed has been worked already out posted for do.

waves of water as being more relevant to the behavior of light than the image of the sun-god riding his chariot across the sky? Probably because our concern is to develop a physical explanation of a physical event. (If we are concerned with some emotional quality as it appears in one's vision of what worlds there are, then this guide-rule is less forceful. Here the chariot might well create an image, not of light but of "luminosity.") In terms of the physical world, it is more likely that we would demand a model whose phenomenal characteristics can be further explored. Water, then, is more relevant in our quest, for it makes possible further investigation of the structure of the analogy itself, and further possible a test of the behavior of light for the insight that analogy has made available. What can we test as relevant in the sun-god analogy? The very term "relevance," in this sense, is revealing. It comes to mean a congruence in the qualitative behavior of determinable events.

Categorizing by means of analogy.   Consider again the argument that the events in nature do not come to us naturally categorized. Nevertheless, as we grow and learn we do find that the world has already been sorted out for us, and we learn as we learn these sortings. Nothing so demonstrates the principle of social continuity among the generations of humankind as this apparently simple fact. None of us begins our lives at the beginning of a world. We learn what others have endowed us with, into whatever stage of civilization we are born. But what we do not recognize so easily is that we have inherited the root analogies that others have developed, put to more or less effective use, organized the world by means of, and then left for us to further. "The world is an ongoing business," William James once wrote. But it is a "business" built from the analogies or root metaphors of the past.

Our systems of quantification; our categories of function; classifications of worth, that is, of value and of disvalue; what we deem possible and impossible; our conceptions of order and of disorder, of piety and impiety, of loyalty and of disloyalty; all derive from the analogues we inherit in the language and culture into which we are born. Nor is this all. Our systems of indexing, our ways of distinguishing types of organisms, our conceptions of the nature and structure of the universe, our preferential societal organizations, and our economic classifications are all derived from the analogies that minds before us have constructed and put to use to make clear the powers and potentials of the world as a whole, and in its all but infinite parts. (It is, indeed, the mark of Darwin's creative mind that he reclassified much of the world by giving new form to an old analogy.)

Such distinctions, then, as we recognize we are using them, can be

probed for the analogies that lie beneath them. It is in such inquiry that revolutions of every type develop. For, to discern the underlying analogy, and to challenge it, is to challenge the most deeply held faith to which we have given ourselves.

We still find all about us a commitment to the craftsman's analogy, where the world has the value a person gives to it as he or she puts hand to task. The analogy of the garden helps us to sort out the fertile grounds of existence from "our gardens grown rank with weeds." We talk of hierarchies of authority without being aware of how the ancient Egyptian pyramids have influenced the way in which we sort out person and actions in our social and economic, our political and religious lives. We categorize the various institutions that comprise a whole culture in the terms of an organismic analogy, identifying some as the "heart," others as the "muscles," still others as the "major arteries" through which flows the "life stream" of a healthful national existence.

We consider the world in terms of analogies of scales and of balances, and classify events as they contribute to one side or another in maintaining equilibrium in living things, physical or social.

If nature does not come to us already classified, but if somehow we come into a world already classified, we must look into the analogies all about us in order to find why this sorting system is employed and not some other. For every culture is some analogue of an envisioned world wrought in some human imagination.

Analogies as organizing concepts.   The last point to be made concerns what might be considered the creative or the constructive function of thinking. Creativity is understood by most to be the unexpected bringing of things together that no one else has done before, and showing that in doing so, novelty and richness have resulted. But nothing is left so much in a perpetual state of mystery, of mystification, as creativity. Somehow, some individuals seem endowed with a special capacity for doing the unexpected, for seeing in the world what others have not seen, for bringing together things or thoughts that others have not the power to do. We are grateful for what they have made available to us, recognize the enrichment with which they have endowed us, and continue to wonder how they did it.

But if analogies make it possible for us to give names and distinctive notations to things in the world, to sort things out in larger or smaller groups, or entirely different ones, so that we can deal with them with an economy of intelligence, then it is analogies that we must alter if we seek to reconstruct the worlds of our experience. The altering or substituting of one analogy for another provides us with a systematic basis

for such new organizations and allows us to see the consequences that
would arise from acting upon that new organization. To take the structure of a garden, as we understand its processes of growth, and to apply it to a political system is to mix things together that nature itself
does not recommend, but humans do. To apply the knowledge of the
human organism as an organizing analogy for social, political, and
economic behavior is to see in that behavior what could not otherwise
be seen. To take the analogy of the balance scales and apply it to cultural behaviors would oblige us to look for checks and balances,
weights and resistances in all things. To replace this last particular
analogy with, say, an analogy predicated on a football game (which
has become a vogue today), would make it possible for us to organize
the activities of any society within the strictures of teams, rules for
play, aims of the game, ways of scoring, judging achievement or
failure, and identifying coaches, players, stars, managers, substitutes,
and the like.

The organizational possibilities of the things, the functions, the
institutions in nature and society are as wide, not only as analogies
available to us, but as analogies that may yet be constructed.

To prefer one analogy to another, one model to another, is not in itself proof of thinking. It may well be nothing more than proof of the
depth and enduring quality of those very beliefs that make thinking
unnecessary. Only when we turn in upon the models themselves does
thinking begin, and it continues for as long as we follow them out into
their consequences in experience.

At this point we have taken "thinking directly in hand," and in the
reconstruction of the model, whole new dimensions of data before us
are likely to appear. For room has been made for them in the new
model being constructed. (This is, in simple terms, the argument
T. S. Kuhn presents as the continuing revolution, which is the *construction* of new paradigms, or models, and analogies, and metaphors,
which in our terms *is* the act of thinking.)

3 Models and the Act of Thinking

The traits, the elements, the functions, the variety of models, and the results they produce in different disciplines. Hard and Soft models.

The previous chapter showed how models, constructed in the act of analogizing, function as the thinking process. We focused on the acts of describing and explaining the way the world is and the way it behaves, on the explanandum and the explanans phases of the model. Now let us look more deeply to discern forms common to the variety we encounter, and to set forth further why they are identified as thinking, why it is argued that the absence of models must mean, logically and empirically, that thinking is not going on.

In recent times, three major criticisms have been leveled against what appears to be the flagrant use of the concept of the model. They are worth noting because they provide an opportunity to make clear its functional character. The first criticism is that at best a model can only be an artificial, however psychologically satisfying, means for resolving problems. We use models while waiting to replace them with direct and immediate evidence. As these data appear, either little by little or suddenly, we are able to abandon the model and address ourselves directly to the matter we are seeking to explore and explain. That we seek to address matter more and more directly, of course, is true, but that we can do so without models is what is at stake. We will look more closely at this later in this chapter.

The second criticism, less insightful perhaps, is that the term model is so widely used that everything becomes a model. Now, if everything in the world is a model, then there is no reality beyond the model, and there could be no sufficiently clear and discriminating use made of the concept, for there is nothing to test it against.

The third argument holds that the ubiquity of models and the dependence that models have on other models can lead only to an infinite regress, and therefore there could be no solid base from which to go forward in inquiry. We would always have to go backward to some previous model, and the one previous to that, and so on.

Let me offer some simple analogies that, at least in principle, contain implications for answering all three criticisms. Some more precise analysis of the first has already been offered, but it is extended here.

In a sense, anything can become a "dangerous" or "deadly" weapon. People have been convicted of assault with a "deadly weapon"; read further, and the weapon turns out to have been a piece of wood in the hand of an angry man. The wooden slat was certainly not constructed for such a purpose, as a gun or a sword would be. But lacking a more effective instrument that he could use with safety to himself, a man seized upon the block of wood and went whacking away at his enemy. The block of wood suddenly appears as an analogue of a gun.

A large piece of branch is torn from a tree. A farmer comes upon it, strips it, shapes it, smooths it, sharpens one end of it, notches a handle to hold at the other, and decides to use it to create furrows for seeding the ground. The branch has been transformed into a farm instrument. But after he has used it and observed its effects, he recognizes that he might have created a better instrument. This is the critical point, where reflection enters. He might have examined the soil by that time, considered the seed he was planting, surveyed the size of the plot of ground he was working, thought of the days it would require to complete his task, and on and on. He judges that he might shape a better instrument, one that would make a better furrow, in quicker time, to a more even length, and would not disintegrate too soon. He had picked up what was available, and examination has revealed new possibilities. (Indeed, is not civilization a history of the development and improvement of tools in just such ways?)

Everything about us is available potentially, as a model, depending upon how clear and detailed is our plan to use it, and what our purposes are. Some means are immediately recognized as inadequate. Some we have no alternative but to continue to use. Some turn out to be surprisingly effective from the first. But in every case, a model is not simply something lying about. It is a functional instrument, constructed for the accomplishment of some specific task. The earth does not furrow itself. We need to furrow it, and we need a tool for doing so. Nature does not think itself into a resolution of perplexities. We do that. And we need tools, physical and conceptual, hard and soft, by means of which to do so. Nor do we need to go behind the tool to find some other tool from which this tool was made. We begin with some task, whose dimensions become apparent in our initial efforts with primary means. We shape a tool and then reshape it again and again as experience shows us what is left in the furrowing that this first tool now makes us aware of, but is not itself capable of accomplishing.

In this we find the answer to those who fear the infinite regress of looking for a model of the tool that is a model for the tool to be made, and so on, back into obscurity. We pick up what is at hand, to use it for what is immediately demanded of us. So, too, do we pick up the concepts that are part of the furnishings of our lives; and we use them in their immediacy to meet the challenges confronting us. In the latter case the "matters" are ideas, metaphors, and linguistic forms that have been, in a sense, "floating" about when we were born. We need not go back any farther than that, as the primitive does not, to begin with, go back beyond the stone he finds lying near him. What he does is to evaluate its value for the needs he seeks to resolve. At this point thinking has begun, as we come to evaluate other models, other ideas, other paradigms that our civilization has left lying about, and we move forward to reshape them in the light of their recognized shortcomings when the tasks to which we apply them demand that we reconstruct them. Those beliefs and concepts that were models for previous generations of striving are, for us, at the outset, "primary rocks" of belief, just as the stones were the results of the workings out of nature at some previous time. Both come readily to hand, to be used when some need arises.

The Uses of the Term

Yet a good deal of ambiguity will always remain about this term, this concept called model. It has become so much a part of our everyday language that more often than not it appears more as a sound, an expression of a general attitude than a specific notation. We talk of model buildings, or buildings modeled on other buildings. We talk of dresses being model dresses. And those who wear them are called models. Some models, then, are archetypes, from which other things are built; and some are idealizations, whose purpose it is to give us a complete vision of something.

We talk of statues or sculptures modeled in clay, steel, or bronze. At the same time we refer to the act of shaping, and to the material used in that act, as modeling, and as the basis of the model. We call children's toys models: model airplanes, model cars, and the like. Yet we recognize that when a child plays with them, he is likely to learn about things beyond the models, things that they are models *of*. Clearly, there is a heuristic value to models and to modeling.

Taken all in all, models would then be archetype idealizations molded, or constructed, out of some material that can be handled directly, examined more closely than could the events they model. They make possible investigation and study of things that the world would not permit, as has already been abundantly argued.

From this rather ordinary way of talking, in which we have collected the various activities that surround the making and using of models, we might offer the more stringent recommendation implied at the beginning of this chapter, for a more precise and limited use.

Nothing in the world is, of itself, a model of anything, or for anything, until it has been deliberately established as such by somebody. This could be done simply by being introduced as a model (which is a linguistic or an ostensive action; that is, someone simply points to something and says, "That is the model, just as it stands"). Or it can be taken in hand, as it were, and modified here and there, to serve whatever purpose we have in mind. Or we can construct something in a sense altogether new, for given purposes, and indicate that it is the model of something, for some purpose to be achieved.

But whatever the purpose we have in mind (play, selling, building, display) and whatever the content of the model (wood, steel, clay, words, sound, light and shadow on paper, pictures on a page), models have a singular and characteristic structure. Whether the model's form is idealization or the representation of reality as closely as it is possible to achieve, it performs the functions that minds determine, and includes a conceptual structure in each of its variations. Models, then, are mental constructs developed for resolution of empirical or conceptual problems.

Let me make explicit what is implicit in the previous chapter, and in this one to this point. When I speak of a model, I shall be concerned with both the experiential and the logical relationships of matters we encounter, given some manifest form for examination of physical or mental events of the past, the future, or the present. When I address myself to a model, I am addressing severally: (1) actual events perceived or perceivable, (2) brought together by some theory or hypothesis, (3) from which might be inferred meanings and relationships that could not be discerned from a direct examination of the events themselves. Such inferences derive and are tested partly in a symbol system of logical relationships, and partly by the observable matters that have been symbolically transformed to become the descriptive elements in that model. Thus, in the strictest sense, a model is never simply a representation of something in the world, nor simply a logical or mathematical formula devoid of any experiential content. It is a deliberately constructed whole of some experienced event that of itself does not show such wholeness or unity.

our necessary Laws
R mental
creations.

Events and the Perception of Events

But why models? This question arises again. Those who have argued that models, at best, are simply psychological aids to investigation also argue that to theorize about these things distracts from the inquiry, and all too often misleads us. It would be preferable, it is argued, in the name of greater accuracy and intellectual clarity, to examine events with increasingly greater diligence, and develop formulas for treating them. In so doing, we would avoid being misled by imagination and seeing only desired outcomes.

Several assumptions behind such a view need to be examined. The most important is the fact that events in nature appear to us as one thing after another, for the so-called innocent eye sees things as particulars, not as classes. If we do not know class identifications, we do not see things as members of classes. Of themselves, events have no correspondences to one another, no relevancies, not even similarities. Unless we provide them, they are not there. If things in nature, in experience, are to have links to one another, and observable tendencies, these must reside within the context of some *invented* perception of completeness; that is, by means of a model that gives them these attributes. When we see such relationships we have already been viewing them from within the context of some construct, or model, which has created those relationships. We are deluded into an anthropomorphic mistake when we think we can observe nature so directly that we need bring nothing to our observation except a completely open mind. Neither logically nor psychologically are eyes innocent in this way. If we are to foster the economy of intelligence, it will not be by ridding ourselves of imagination, but rather by developing the means of using that imagination with greater force and flexibility, with greater awareness of what its constructs allow us to see, and what they prevent us from seeing, since inclusion of some things into a model necessarily entails exclusion of others.

It may be true that the uses of models for observing and describing, for explaining and interpreting the things in our experiences, are at the outset intuitive or unwitting acts, as using language begins as an intuitive act. We use models before we even know we have them. Within some model the events we see are symbolized. Even the interchange between things we see, as we are able to "follow out" the logic of the symbolic relations, is embedded, symbolically, in the model. The events of the past *are* history because they are, as we contemplate them, evidence in symbolic forms. We "grasp" the logic of relationships between these symbols because they reside in the model. The anthropologist Levy-Bruhl goes so far as to say: "All of us, learned and unlearned, sense that we live in an intellectual world whose frame is made of necessary laws and fixed forms *that correspond to concepts in our minds.*" [1] We can better understand this when we remember the distinction between the physical and intellectual worlds. Our *necessary laws* are mental creations.

In the physical sciences the laws of nature are generalizations about the behavior of constructed classes of things in situations that have been marked out as identical or similar. The structure of these classes, their sequences of appearance and forms, their attributes of identity or similarity with other events, all lie in some model that we have either absorbed without being aware of doing so, or have constructed specifically for the purposes of a given inquiry. Without some model the world of things would, undoubtedly, exist and would be sensed in some way, but it would have no meaning.

It is one thing to be warned against a too rigid, too diffuse, or too limited a model that we might employ in mental acts we undertake, but it is quite a different thing to argue that we can think without the employment of a model. For it is some model that gives to the world qualities it does not otherwise have, certainly that could never be discerned. Nor is this a dissolution into total subjectivity, because the models themselves are public in form, and are themselves examinable.

The logic of this activity must be considered. Even when we explore things directly, without any artificial instruments, we intrude ourselves into that activity. We see from whatever position we are in, by means of whatever visualizing instruments we have available (our habituated perceptions first), and we report it in a language that is also available to us. When we begin to discover that the language we have is not appropriate to the work we are performing, the very observations we make about that appropriateness or adequacy are already the beginnings of an alteration, not of the world of things, but of

---

1. Italics mine.

the models that give us our perceptions. Our earliest language competence has, in a sense, begun to corrupt our "innocence." It gives us
a sophistication that no other living creature has. Indeed, many
have argued that language *is* a form of vision, and that our first perceptual models are linguistic, or that our language is our first visual
model.

It is important to note that the model makes possible the establish-
ment of psychological "distance" between ourselves and what we are
examining. This makes it possible to be more economic and more intellectually firm in our investigations, to avoid being drawn totally into
subjectivity, or totally reduced to a passive element in a stimulus-
response situation.

The only time that models of some kind are not in use are those
occasions when no thinking occurs. Dewey has argued that in such
cases, however, we do not even experience. We simply undergo. That
is, when we are not engaged in any activity of explaining, when we are
doing nothing more than pointing to something, no discriminated
perception of events is required, no models are in play, and no experiences of the world are had. And if the thinking act is, indeed, the
modeling (or the analogizing) act, the only differences to be noted
among individuals who are experiencing are differences between
ranges and degrees of awareness made possible by the models that are
in use. For, even when we seem to be looking at an event directly, with
no apparent intermediary, if there is understanding, there is an act of
organizing that event within some class of events to which it is held to
belong, or to which it might belong.

Such a thesis makes it possible to understand the nature of errors in
thinking. Errors do not occur, that is, we are not misled by the use of
models because we employ them for inquiring into things rather than
coming directly at them. Errors occur when we either use an inap-
plicable model that will not explain what we seek to have explained,
that misrepresents events in the explanandum, or when we use the
model badly and thus produce an inept explanation of the event. But
without any model we are rendered incapable of drawing logical inferences about the data we are examining. We do not make errors in
such cases. We just do nothing.

To go further. A model is *not* simply an interim device for examining the world, to be cast aside when it has performed its purpose so
that we can get on with a further exploration of some thing in the
world. The model-use *is* the act of investigation. It may well behoove
us, then, to be conscious of models, to be alert to their limitations
and prepared to rectify their inadequacies when alterations in events
that cannot be explained by a present model suddenly become evi-

dent. But to talk about modifying or improving a model is very different from talking about investigations without any model.

Yet it must be acknowledged that all the above arguments, which attempt to support the irreducible role of models in the thinking act, are not likely to persuade those who continue to insist that we can look at nature directly. If you prefer to believe that all thinking is a matter of stimulus and response, and thus a matter of electrochemical movement through the nervous system and the brain, then you can conclude that you are actually looking at "the thinking act" when you take a brain scan and read it out on some graph. But it must be apparent that even to believe this is already to have accepted some model of the behavior of brains and other things in the world experienced.

The Functioning of Models
in Disciplined Inquiry

Inevitably models contain within themselves distilled or exaggerated representations of the subject modeled in its explananda. Sometimes the subject is not known (as, for example, the specific shape of a molecule), but the source, or mode, of its behavior is known or suspected (heat). In the first case we have a model whose explananda are of some observable, or partly observable, subject. In the second we have explananda as substitutes *for* something that is not known, but for which we have constructed, in a sense hypothesized, data. The important point here is that we recognize the model is never simply a replica of something, or a synonym for some symbol (word), but a deliberately, selectively constructed representation, an analogue of some substance or event, present or suspected, for purposes of exploration, explanation, or prediction.

Now it must be recognized that every discipline, that is, every systematic approach to exploring some aspect of human experience, is a model-making and model-using activity. This means that every discipline is the maker of its instruments of exploration, increasingly critical observation, description, explanation, judgment validations, reasoning modes, and evaluation methods of whatever assertions it concludes with. And every discipline is recognized in the use and testing of those instruments. Sometimes those instruments include hardware, such as scopes, finders, probes, counters, sensitizers, lights, and the like. Sometimes they are exclusively software: concepts, ideas, theories, hypotheses. Inevitably, however, they are a combination of these. But whichever they are, they have reference to experienced events, and they are the means by which we explore the events beyond the model. The conclusions reached, identified as the findings of those disciplines, are inextricably bound up with those instruments.

Thus, each discipline is distinctive in the models that make its specific inquiries possible, certainly in that part of it that contains a description of what is being investigated. Even when a given discipline borrows models from another discipline, which is always taking place in the explanatory phase, a given discipline retains its own distinctiveness by transforming the models borrowed from some other discipline into an instrument relevant to the purposes that direct its specific activities. For what is described in one discipline becomes a metaphoric description in the other. In this way we can argue that physics has not become a branch of mathematics, but has borrowed mathematical models in order to pursue its own quest for describing and explaining what there is. Behaviorist psychology is not simply a branch of engineering, but has borrowed some instruments of mechanics and transformed them in order to make them applicable to the purposes of explaining human behavior. The great danger, of course, lies in the fact that descriptions derived from unguarded use of this model could readily produce absurdities, for they are not seen in their metaphoric character. The brain is not really a switchboard.

The Contents of the Model

At the generic level, the process of thinking presented is the same in every inquiry, however it may differ in the particulars imposed by the distinctive purposes we may have for given data, and however different the data we are examining may be.

Thus, every model will contain:

1. A symbol system that is either a representation or an analogy of the data to which it addresses itself. There will be dramatic differences in this phase of the content of the model, depending upon whether the referent of the explanans actually exists; whether it has existed and we have only fossil records of its existence, or records of it only in verbal form; or whether it exists only in conceptual form, as in philosophy and in certain of the arts.

2. A symbol system that permits a conceptual manipulation of events that are not otherwise possible of manipulation. Such a symbol

system will be just that, a *system*, bound by a logic or grammar (sometimes called a syntax) that allows for the making of deductions, inductions, recommendations of conclusions that would otherwise not be justifiable, and inferences about the behavior of things that could not otherwise be made.

3. Some explicitly or implicitly stated rule, or law, as part of the explanans, by means of which the symbols of events are given meaning within a context of meanings.

4. Some hypotheses that enable us to go beyond the data given and allow us to set that data into a larger context of inquiry by means of which we can consider an event in the widening setting of events that affect it, and are affected by it.

If we accept this basic structure and function of models, we may better understand the distinctiveness of each discipline within the unity of the thinking process. Moreover, it will have the added virtue of justifying consciously what we often do unwittingly, that is, borrow specific, successful models from one discipline and transform them into effective instruments of thinking in others.

The Construction of Models: Purposes, Inclusions, and Exclusions

SOME PRINCIPLES

What, then, of the construction of models? What kinds of model constructs might we distinguish, which will give us some insight into this important matter, in order to understand how the thinking act constructs itself, as it were.

All models, of any type, are constructed and used in the same way, whether they be in the fields of the natural sciences, social sciences, or history. And the development of increasing skill in this process of construction becomes simultaneously an improvement and deepening of the thinking skills.

Certain principles of construction of the explanandum phase of the model are apparent:

1. In every case some actual evidence in some domain is required, which can be explored in increasing depth and with greater refinement.

2. In every case we need to check what is observable, that is, the matter we hypothesize as being potential evidence of what we are seeking to understand more fully and explain more justifiably.

3. In every case we need to propound dependable correspondence between the observable and the hypothetical.

4. In every case we need to go from the relationships between what is known in the model to the hypothesized relationships in the matters for which we seek answers.

5. But in every case, what we know about the matters constructed into a model that give us a basis for knowledge about other elements in the same model are not to be treated as absolutely true about the matter being probed. Simply on the basis of this correspondence, that truth is determined in the primary data alone. The model enables us to get to that domain.

DIFFERENT EVIDENCE IN DIFFERENT DISCIPLINES

In a sense, it is easier to learn how to construct models for explaining the behavior or structure of physical events than for those in the field of the social sciences. For in the latter we are often called upon to explain purely theoretical events by means of purely theoretical models. That is, in neither case, of explanandum or explanans, is there the same *kind* of direct evidence available as there is in the exploration of the physical events of nature. But, understandably, in order to bring a discipline closer to the strength of the natural sciences, researchers will construct a model from selected observable events that will be used to explain such unobservable qualities as, say, "motivation," "aspiration," "inspiration." This does not mean that it is not possible to develop a model that will provide a useful explanatory system. It only means that the model is that much more vulnerable to the probings of other inquiries. Skinner's model for the explanation of human behavior, for example, does not show weakness in the structure of the model he has developed (the behavior of computers, or of pigeons and mice, in response to stimuli introduced into a situation), but rather in the acceptability of the correspondence between human perception and behavior and the recording capacities of his machines; between the perceptions and responsive behaviors of pigeons or mice, and those of human beings.

Yet the *principle* of the employment of evidence in the construction of models, and his application of these, are quite similar to the development and application of the model of the water wave in order to explain the behavior of light and sound. But because there remains the question of the warrant for the one-to-one correspondence, the claims to being scientific, in the sense that physics is the paradigm, are continuously vulnerable. In fact, nowhere does this vulnerability show as much as it does in the field of psychological inquiry and of psychological explanations. That field remains constantly divided because the fundamental models of the explanation of human behavior of one group of psychologists are challenged by another who argue for other basic models, and this, because there is no agreement on the data of the domain and thus on what shall constitute evidence for the explanations.

Imagination in Model Construction

This problem of the vulnerability of models, in terms of the explanations they provide, leads to another important phase of model construction. In the continuing disputes among psychologists and within the social sciences, it is easy to understand the empiricist's impulses. If we could limit ourselves to what is observable in nature, to what can actually be measured in some way, to "hard" data, and to allow for no theorizing lest imagination lead to mythification, we would allow ourselves to be directed by what nature alone reveals in its proper time. If we treated only what is actually evidential, we would be on solid ground in our inquiries, for our explanations could constantly be checked by hard and observable facts. The trouble is, however successful we are in reducing the theoretical and the imaginative to substantive states, by treating motivation not as a purely conceptual or mythic-type affair but in terms of observable behavior, they reappear in definitional problems, demanding to be given some accounting.

If, in the final analysis, we are seeking to explain and describe, to explore and interpret whatever is experienced, we must at least acknowledge the wide ranges of experiences that are possible, and indeed quite likely to be built into a model. It is obvious that we experience things in terms of how they look, how they feel, how they sound. But we also experience in a great many other ways. Certainly we encounter, or are concerned with, relationships observed, felt, even intuited in an emotional or purely theoretical sense. We can observe relationships between water and fire, but not between molecules of water or of light. We can experience, in some emotional way, family rela-

tionships or civic relationships, though we do not actually observe
them. We can "grasp" relationships between ideas, though these are
never matters that can be observed. Nevertheless, observed directly
or imagined in some way, there comes a time when they need to be
described and explained, and thus there comes a time when we have
to construct some tangible model by means of which we can do this.
In so doing we discover that not every analogy, or analogical model,
is a model of the actual features of one thing used to explore and explain the actual features of something else. We build analogies that
may be observable in the model, since it is our purpose to do just that.
But we do so in order to explain what can never be seen. Such analogies are theoretical, and the best we can use them for is the construction of hypotheses, but never proofs of what we are saying about some
explanandum.

Hard and Soft Models

The tactic of developing a classification system has a practical purpose. Empirical classifications make observations and explorations
of things more effective to the extent that they make it possible to
establish identities, similarities, and differences in events in nature.
Logical distinctions transformed into a classification system are designed to improve the ways in which one thinks about the concepts at
work in the explorations of things. This is the only reason for the
rather broad classification I make here. Its purpose is to direct attention to the thinking processes that are involved in the examination of
descriptive and explanatory systems at work in the various inquiries with which we are concerned—into the behavior of things,
groups, individuals, and the features of the cognitive processes employed in those various inquiries. I make no greater claim for this classification than that it will aid us in the development of our own
thinking processes.

Let us call those models in which actual phenomena are being
symbolized HARD models. And let us call those models in which there
are symbols of purely theoretical or hypothetical or conceptual matters, of imagined characteristics of some event of our concern, SOFT
models. (I have avoided calling these alternately *strong* and *weak*,
because even so-called Soft models can have very strong consequences and determinations on the explanations we offer about the

various experiences we are attempting to explain.) Now, between the hardest of the Hard models and the softest of the Soft models, we can establish a spectrum. For example, a road map, drawn to scale and containing symbols for every feature of the road system between, say, Boston and Chicago, including the different widths of road, alternative routes between intervening points, detours, roadblocks, rest stops, restaurants, waterways, mountain ranges of different heights, and so on, might be considered on one end of the spectrum as a Hard model. A model for reading a poem in order to be able to trace the meaning and connotations of all the metaphors used, the effects of the various rhythms and rhymes, the quality of the tension of feelings produced by the various techniques of writing poetry, and so on, might be on the other extreme end of the spectrum, the softest of the Soft models. Between them, on a line that could be extended in either direction as we became aware of more concrete ways of producing a model of concrete events or developed new symbol systems for exploring and explaining the realms of cognition reaching farther and farther back into the non-cognitive, there could lie all those models that mingle the stubborn data to be accounted for and the seemingly ephemeral ideas used to organize those stubborn data and give them meaning, focus, and determination. What would indicate where on the spectrum they lie is the emphasis given in the particular model to the factual and to the conceptual.

THE QUALITY OF EXPLANATIONS PRODUCED

The point of this suggestion is not to argue that the harder the model, the more likely it is to be valid; and the softer, the less likely. It has two other purposes.

First, it enables us to distinguish between the claims we make as to "true" explanations and those that are neither true nor false but simply "justified."

Second, it makes it possible for us to distinguish between conclusions for which empirical evidence can be offered, and conclusions that, being only logical, derive from the internal rules, or the syntax of the model, and remain at best hypothetical or theoretical.

The force of this can perhaps best be seen when we find ourselves analyzing some description or explanation of the kind of research that we call "purely conceptual." When an analysis is made upon the cognitive powers of God, for example, the Soft model that is used may well end with persuasive arguments as to the meaning and extent of God as infinite knower. But claims to demonstrability cannot possibly be submitted to the kind of test to which we submit the road map. Indeed, in the God problem, there can be no empirical test as to whether the model is faithful to the event.

Or suppose we were reading a work in history, whose focus was on the causes of some war that occurred several centuries ago, say, the War of the Roses in England. In this case much evidence exists, and must be exploited in the construction of a model of explanation of that war. But in the writing of history, as we shall see in chapter 6, the records of that event alone can hardly be considered sufficient to provide an explanation of the event. Some conjecture must be included as to human intentions, perceptions, aspirations; why certain tactics were employed here and others there; what visions were entertained for which there may be some actual evidence and more that is derived only inferentially; and what visions for which there is only negative evidence. We must make place for beliefs held, *how* they were held, and what motivating force might have been at work. (That is, how do acts for which we have evidence square with what might have been reported?) Here, building an explanatory model for the War of the Roses obliges us to look for some event in the present. But this would always leave us with little chance to establish a complete point-by-point correspondence between the explanandum and the explanans. However logically complete such a model might be, however persuasive and internally consistent, however illuminating to our understanding of that war (and from it, of other wars), the fact remains that as a model it is very close to the Soft end of the scale. Its conclusions can never be much more than justifiable. If some actual data can be held to be true and proven, the explanations of them derived from this analysis can claim very little truth, however meaningful they might be in other ways.

So, knowing the quality of the model to be very Hard or very Soft, or some more or less clearly noted point in between, allows us immediately to know what status to assign to the explanations. To know, at a glance, how to distinguish a Hard claim, however weak, from a Soft claim, however strong, provides us with an intellectual security in dealing with the reports we constantly encounter about the nature of the world. To be able to entertain a myth and never be persuaded to treat it as anything but a myth is at least to allow us the full enjoyment of that myth. We can surely appreciate its inner rationale and the function or force it plays in the lives of people, even when no question of its truth arises. If, for example, astrology is absurd when measured against the Hard end of the scale, it is not so when measured at the Soft end. At least we can understand its effects on its believers, while recognizing its lack of any truth claim.[2]

THE CATEGORY OF THE MODEL
AFFECTS PRECISION IN THINKING

The Hardness or the Softness of the model defines the temper of thinking about experiences. But it must be recognized that nothing that is examined and explained is exhausted by any particular model that has been used. We can always choose to look at the same event by means of some other, harder or softer, model and discern new or different meanings, features, relationships in those already familiar events. Indeed, this is precisely what takes place in our endless quest for wider and deeper understanding of human experiences. The same substances in nature and the same concepts can be explored by different models, and from this exploration entirely different awarenesses are wrought, completely new understandings are developed, new features are recognized.

Thus, the same record of events may be treated by what we recognize are historical models, by psychological models, by sociological models, by anthropological models. And each one provides us with completely different, though perhaps congruous, sets of descriptions, explanations, interpretations.

Even the Hardest Model
Has an Analogical Basis

Some further comments can be made about the hardness of Hard models, consistent with what we have said about the role of analogies in every form of model.

Max Black has offered some very important and illuminating distinctions about the various forms that models are given. He distinguishes between Scale, Theoretical, Mathematical, and Analogical models. Others have added Visual and Linguistic. Still others have di-

---

2. Bruno Bettelheim's explanation of the role of fairy tales, analyzed within the psychoanalytical model of human development, is a luminous example of this. See his *Uses of Enchantment* (New York: Knopf, 1976).

vided models only into Representative and Analogical. Each classification has considered the kind of data explored, the purposes that can be attained in inquiry, the types of correspondence to be looked for between the model forms and the materials being investigated, and the status of the conclusions to be derived as a result. All these distinctions have genuine worth and add to the clarity of understanding the specificities we can expect from their employment.[3]

I have a different task here. It is the task of showing how it is that even in the hardest of models the presence of some analogical base tempers that hardness so that none can ever be read as providing us with such an absolute and precise conclusion that further inquiry is no longer needed. Indeed, this logical involvement of the analogue has provided the grounds for the many scientists who say that if we are looking for complete exactness in the sciences, complete precision in the models they construct and use, we will be looking for what never was and what could not possibly occur.

Every model that we use, from the most detailedly representative to the most exclusively imaginary, is basically constructed on the predicate of some analogy that has been posited between the internal relationships of one event and the internal relationships of some other event we are trying to explain. It is certainly true in the biological sciences, say, in the development of the double helix model to explain and predict the behavior of those chromosomes that are the bearers of the genetic traits of human beings.

A picture, though it is called a representative model by Black, is still an analogue of what it has depicted, as I have shown. The map is an analogue of the terrain; the double helix, an analogue of the behavior of the chromosomes of the body. And when the model begins to show some inadequacy to the task for which it has been constructed, it is to the analogue that we first look. If changes are to be made in the model, or if the entire model is to be abandoned and a new one developed in its place, it will begin with a change in the basic analogy from which the first model was first developed.

Newton's model of the universe is, after all, constructed on the analogy of a "perfect" clock. From this point, every aspect of the model, its laws of the behavior of energies and masses in the universe, of motion, of direction, all reflect that clock analogy. Only when that is changed, as for example, into an analogy of randomness, say, of the random behavior of popcorn being slowly heated in an enclosed container, do we begin to see an entirely different kind of world. The

3. Max Black, *Models and Metaphors* (Ithaca, N.Y.: Cornell University Press, 1962), chap. 10.

behavior we now observe and attempt to explain is the behavior of particles in a popcorn world. And wasn't it also the behavior of an analogical clock that was central to Einstein's new theory of relativity?

All this, in the physical sciences, in what would appear to be the hardest of the Hard models. The fact of analogy disabuses us from looking for absolute and ultimate answers, beyond which there would be no answers. In the softer models the tentativeness is even more obvious.

In the social sciences, in sociology, for example, the borrowing of a mathematical model on the grounds of the possibility of producing stronger and perhaps harder conclusions and predictions about some problem in societal affairs brings about the development of new analogies. The use of instruments usually employed in one domain of inquiry is analogically transformed into a model useful in another domain. As complex as this becomes, the simple fact is that continuing examination of the models of exploration and explanation culminates in the manifestation of thinking in newer, more creative, more concentrated ways. And it begins with consideration of the analogical content of our models.

Summary

Let me conclude this chapter by discursively setting forth some conditions and procedures for the development and use of models, whether they be scale, theoretical, mathematical, linguistic, or any yet to be invented, acknowledging in advance that this is a series of general recommendations that would take on differentiation when the traits of whatever it is we are attempting to explore and explain differ.

PRIMARY DATA

In principle, there will be a field to be investigated that, in terms of our familiar models, is observed to have some regularities, and some facts have been established in previous investigations or experiments. By means of that already developed reservoir of models we recognize what some previous theory, or set of laws, or procedures, some earlier analogies, have made available to us. Thus, every investigation is, in

some sense, prepared for, either in primitive or sophisticated experience. This plus the data become the subject matter of an inquiry.

CHANGEABILITY IN THE MODEL

For some reason, either because of a desire to know more about
behaviors, meanings, or relationships, or for purposes of extending
knowledge or clarifying what is already known, we seek sharper, more
discriminate descriptions, explanations, or interpretations of the
matters of this original field; in short, improved, and thus altered,
models.

The above are conditions for the construction of models. The phases
of the procedures for their development and use include the following:

1. We identify or construct a less problematic context of events
that we can demonstrate to be representative of, or analogous to, the
original domain, but that is more susceptible of being described and
observed. This description and observation becomes the analogue and
presents to us greater specificity in the domain to be investigated.

2. We must assure ourselves that the laws of the behavior of the
events in the model are coherent with, or correspond to (are analogous
with), the laws that might be employed in the investigation of the
new matters. The firmer the relationship of similarity between the two
domains, the more likely the explanandum in the analogy will be to
provide a faithful description of the matters being investigated. And
the more likely will an explanation of the model be also an explanation
of those matters.

3. The examination of the assumptions on which the model has
been constructed is more readily available to us than is a similar investigation of the new material of our concern. In this way, by
strengthening the warrant for those assumptions, we strengthen the
context of meanings of the original domain.

4. The inferences we are now able to draw in the model, as to what
things are and why they behave or appear or mean what they mean,
by means of the rules of correlation we have constructed in phases 1
and 2, now become applicable to the domain being investigated. What
we examine *directly*, then, is the model; *indirectly*, the original or
primary domain whose traits and functions have been analogized in
that model.

As Black points out, "the key to understanding the entire transaction [of thinking] is the identity of structure that in favorable cases
permits assertions made about the secondary domain [*the model*] to

yield insight into the original field of interest [*the matters in nature or in experience which we seek to explain more clearly and to better understand*]." [4]

Now these stages of the mental acts involved are very general and cannot be reduced to the specificity of a formulated set of steps to be followed. It must be evident, however, that if thinking is to be applied to the hard matters of the things of the world, specific recommendations for analogy making and model construction will take on different forms than if we are concerned with what we have called the soft matters, matters of the imagination manifest in philosophical, poetic, or fictional talk, even of much of historical talk. We cannot claim, for example, that the feelings and visions expressed in poetry, because the logical development of ideas is impeccable, speak with the same quality of hardness about their domain as the models of the sciences speak about theirs. Yet, though we can distinguish these qualities in each of the domains, the processes of thinking in each are recognizably one process.

One final point about what it is that makes for Hard and Soft models in thinking. It is not really the case that Hard models refer to strictly observable data in the world of things, and Soft models concern themselves with purely conceptual matters such as visions, fictions, metaphysical postulates, or mathematical figures. It is, rather, that because of their objectifiable states, we get to know the matters of one domain, or field of inquiry, more familiarly and more often in terms of measurability. Models with which we are very familiar enable us to examine even the most private of private domains. It is no accident, therefore, that there has been a constant increase in the use of electrical models in order to attempt to understand motivation and compassion. Nevertheless, we cannot eliminate the role that observable data play. Matters that are either directly or indirectly observable provide us with symptoms of their behavior with a greater clarity than do the matters of loyalty, indulgence, or idealization.

Thus the concluding point: The use of models is an irreducible fact, nature and humankind both being what they appear to be. To attempt to deny their use, to deny the necessity of "seeing" what we are about, is to insist that the logical world, and the precepts of logic, are all that are needed to understand the behavior of things and of thought. But even here we must recognize the role of models and analogies, for the "logical" world *is* a model for examining the world of experience, beginning with its acceptability as an analogue.

---

4. Black, *Models and Metaphors*, p. 230.

mental embroidering

4 Metaphor and the Act of Thinking

By "laying" one context of knowledge over another, new knowledge, new perceptions, and new expression become possible.

The simplest proof—for the claim that the act of metaphorizing (as a mode of analogizing) is one form of the act of thinking—is the fact that, as circular as it may sound, the employment of metaphors as literal truths shows evidence of a fixity of belief that requires no further thought. The dead metaphor in communication is revealed in several ways. It is shown when we parrot ideas or beliefs without understanding what they intend. It is shown when the metaphor is held as a literal statement. It is apparent in the myths that dominate us. The live metaphor is one that is newly created when the occasion demands, or consciously considered at the moment of its use. In this it is like the person who looks at the world through rose-colored glasses but is conscious of the fact that the glasses are tinted, and that the tinting must be taken into account no less than the character of the world that the glasses make possible. Not to recognize metaphors, but to speak or write them, is to be used by those metaphors and to be entangled in them. To recognize them is to use them, consciously alert to the influence and consequences of their use. In this, metaphors are like stethoscopes. They are there, both metaphors and stethoscopes. They have uses. They can be employed for the purposes for which they have been created. But in and of themselves, both are inert. Wearing them or parroting them does not guarantee an understanding of them or of the world they have organized. But they look or sound impressive, even though they are dead in our mouths and in our minds.

But this only begins our analysis of the metaphor. We need to examine its form, its inner structure, the ways it functions, some traditions about it, some fallacies that cluster about its use, the dangers of its misuse, how it is to be discovered, and what its limits are.

Tradition has led us to expect that the use of metaphor is evidence of poetic or artistic thinking. So widely is this held that there is a stan-

dard caveat against its seductiveness: "There is no room in the laboratory for the poet." There is no place in science for the use of metaphor,
meaning fanciful thought, if we are seriously in quest of knowledge
about the behavior of things and people. But it is no more possible to
keep metaphors out of the laboratory than it is possible to conduct any
kind of inquiry without the use of models. For metaphors, as a kind of
analogy, are an element of any model. What appears on the surface to
be a fanciful or extravagant mental embroidering is better understood as an imaginative yet logical way of employing familiar matters
in order to discover what lies beyond the familiar, of seeing similarities
and dissimilarities.

Yet somehow, metaphors (even though they are acknowledged as
types of analogies) seem to go too far.

There is another way of distinguishing between models, analogies,
and metaphors (other, that is, than the one made in chapter 1). All
boys are males. All male children are human beings. On the other hand,
not all human beings are males, and not all males are boys. This is, I
suggest, analogously the relationship between our three terms. All
metaphors are analogies, but not every analogy is a metaphor. All
analogies are models, but not every model is (except when we are
talking very loosely) an analogy, though every model will contain
analogical elements as its base. In the previous chapter I tried to distinguish, and then to relate, models and analogies. Now let us turn to
more critical consideration of the metaphor, its grounds, its functions,
and its uses.

What Is a Metaphor?

The dictionary says that a metaphor is a transfer. That is, it is a
figure of speech by means of which we denote one kind of object, or
idea, by means of another, generally because of some analogy existing between the two. Webster suggests "a volley of oaths" as an illustration, implying something like the fact that oaths came out of the mouth
like a volley of shots comes out of an automatic rifle fired rapidly.

Now every metaphor is an analogy, with this distinguishing trait:
Metaphor deliberately makes use both of certain similarity in proportions *and* an emphasis on the observable differences. This lends to
every metaphor a quality of the absurd, for that difference is, in a
sense, winked at. "The computer is a brain" is analogy. But, "In him
one hears the clank of rust" is metaphor. Inevitably, there is wit as

well as absurdity in metaphor; the wit that stirs us when the familiar
is violated. For what is absurd is what does violence to our habituated
expectations.

METAPHORIC AND LITERAL CONTEXTS

The alternative to a metaphor is a literal statement. Instead of talking about one thing as if it were another, why not talk about the thing
itself, directly, in its own terms, or nature, or function? That this is
possible would be absurd to deny. But put so simply, we are led to the
conclusion that literal statements and metaphoric statements are both
concerned to say the same things and that, therefore, the former has
the possibility of being true, the latter simply imaginative or fanciful.
But this is not the case. Presuppositions are at work here, about the
nature of language, the nature of thought, the nature of nature,
which need to be accepted; lacking these, the *opposition* between the
literal and the metaphoric would disappear. The fact is that what a
literal statement does and what a metaphoric statement does are
quite different. One is not simply a substitute for the other. If they
were, sooner or later all our metaphors would be replaced by literal
statements as we moved closer to the empirical truths of the world.
But this is not the case. On the contrary, our quest for truth more
often than not leads us into the quest for better metaphors *by means
of which we see more in things than a literal description of them will
afford us.*

A literal description states what is true but rarely exhaustive of possible meanings. When we move from the literal to the metaphoric, we
change the context of our inquiring. In making the transfer we "see"
more in and of any event than we do when we concern ourselves
only with what is literally present to us. In such a movement we are
saying something quite different from what we say literally.

The difference comes to this. Each describes an aspect of some
event. But in a literal statement we are describing that event, first,
as an isolated event in which the tangible is the total context; and second, in the language of denotation. Thus, if an explanation of that
event were offered, it would have to be deduced from those denotative sentences. We explain a book, for example, by saying that it is
written in the English language, has a given number of chapters,
covers such and such a subject, and is produced by someone who is
or is not an expert in the field. No other explanation is given, and none
is required at this level of inquiry.

The metaphoric statement, however, involves a transfer from one context of thought and knowledge to another. As such, it is, as Max Black has said, an "interaction" between two contexts. It is the deliberate use of what we know, or know well, to probe into something about which we know little or do not know at all. We examine something unfamiliar or unknown to us within a context of, or by superimposing upon it a "map" of, what we already know. By doing so, we no longer perceive the event in isolation, as static, but as a component of a widening, changing, series of events to which, we are suggesting, it belongs. The examination of events in isolation is always but a step in a wider or widening inquiry. Growing understanding of any event is always a matter of broadening the context of inquiry of that event to see its role relative to other events. Moreover, even to see an event in total isolation, in total arrest, requires us (1) because things change, and (2) because of the character of the language available to us, to impose contexts if the limited event is to be understood.

The failure to see the way in which contexts of inquiry are developed and employed leads us, in our innocence, to see the literal and the metaphoric as being alternative ways of saying the same thing and, thereafter, to eliminate the one so that the other alone will remain as the more accurate. But to confuse the two is to create more than confusion; it creates serious error, the error of ascribing tangible or physical reality to what is intrinsically purely conceptual.

METAPHOR AS "FILTER"

In the transferring movement, one context is deliberately replaced with two, the second functioning as a cognitive ground for considering features in the first. In the interaction of the two contexts a new organization appears, giving emphasis to certain features and deemphasis to others in the primary domain. Thus, a metaphor, like a model (as I have argued in *Education as a Discipline*), becomes a kind of lens (Black uses the notion of "filter") by means of which the familiar is seen in new light, new organization, new interrelationships of meanings. Terms and concepts that are normally understood as belonging to one context become the means for speaking of the other.

From such a view of the operation the metaphor as cognitive act becomes very apparent. The thinking process manifest as the use of metaphors is that which is involved in the construction of the interaction between two contexts now treated as a single, larger field of perception, but whose specific distinctions are not completely erased by that interaction. When they are, the metaphor ceases to exist, and we have once again something that sounds like a self-enclosed, exhaustive

literal statement. But this, on the face of it, would be a fallacy because the claims made now about the primary subject should be
demonstrable in that extended denotative sense, and they are not.
(How absurd it is to read literal meaning into the statement "She
came home in a bucket of tears.") To read Plato literally, for example,
means to read him as intending a direct description and concomi-
tantly entailed explanation of the world he saw. His myths must either
be dismissed as mere dramaturgical but logically unnecessary effects,
or he was dominated by an idealism in which not irony but anger was
the underlying quality. The arguments that constantly abound, as to
whether Plato was a fascist or a communist, both result from this
literalist insistence. But to read the metaphors as metaphors is not
only to be alive to the witty connotations of his writing, but to be enabled to understand more fundamental intentions of the critical interpretations that infuse his work.

Thus, the basic characteristics of the metaphor: We view a given
event by embedding it into another context that serves as the means
(the "lens" or "filter") by which the matter of that event is given other,
newer meanings by extension, by new emphasis and deemphasis, as
the new context makes available. From this act of thinking inferences
other than those to be made from denotative descriptions (syllogistic
deductions) are made possible about the primary matter. In this sense
the literal and the metaphoric are not so much opposed to one another as that the second is a legitimate extension of the first, by means
of which we see more in the event than could otherwise be seen.

Forms of Metaphor

The transactivity that is metaphoric thinking, this transfer of language and concepts from one context to another, has been called
"crossing sorts of things" with one another. Now, what kinds of
things can we cross with one another, and in what ways? The answer
to these questions gives us the forms that metaphor takes.

Aristotle has written that we may cross particulars with generals
and generals with particulars. More specifically, we may cross species
with genus, genus with species, and species with species. We may
cross the name of a class of things or ideas with the name of a particular thing or idea. Operationally, we may cross ways of doing things
generally associated with one kind of event or idea with the ways we
do things associated with other kinds of events or ideas. We may cross

the employment and the consequences of sensing with one another. We may cross states of being with one another—the animate with the inanimate, for example. Turbayne offers some distinctions, others have added to them. To illustrate:

1. We sometimes call a genus by the name of a species. We treat the university as the same sort of thing as a building on the campus. (Synechdoche)

2. We give a thing a name that belongs to one of its attributes. We say that "the White House has said" instead of "the President has said." (Metonymy)

3. We give to something with no name the name that belongs to something else. We talk of the "drama" of history. (Catechresis)

4. But we also apply the term for one sensing activity to a different sensing activity. We speak of "seeing" a meaning, or "hearing the anguish of his words." (This Wheelwright calls an example of *plurisignation.*)

5. We apply the quality of one event to an event of a different kind. We talk of the lyrical quality in the architecture of a church.

6. We apply a kind of action performed in one form of experience to a very different kind. We talk of probing a theory, a philosophy, an idea, of ferreting out some information. These are variants of anthropomorphism or, as Ruskin calls it, "pathetic fallacy."

Let this list serve as a suggestion of how diversified metaphoric forms can be. It should be possible for us to examine them to see if we cannot distill a fundamental set of traits in metaphors. It also should enable us to recognize when metaphors are being used even if, for the moment, we cannot be sure because we do not see the specific *as if* recommendations being employed; even when they have become so conventional that we simply assume them to be literal denotations.

The Relation Between Metaphors and Models

The fact that every metaphor is the symbolizing of some perception that appears essentially private is what renders it suspect to those who seek objective truth. Two problems confront us here.

First, the metaphor appears to do more than we require in our quest for a description and an explanation of what there is. It distracts by excesses of imagination and subjectivity.

Second, it provides distracting explanations, when it provides them at all, for it is held to be only a psychological tactic whose purpose is persuasive and not cognitive. Indeed, it is never hard to find evidence of such digressions in inquiry and in communication about that inquiry that are traceable to glittering or overly dramatic metaphors. But it is equally never hard to show that such digressions are not so much the result of metaphors but the misuse of metaphors, or the use of misleading metaphors in place of metaphors that are genuinely equal to the task at hand. For the metaphor serves a model function, sometimes Hard, more often Soft, sometimes Strong, all too frequently Weak where it should be Strong.

We have already seen that in order to investigate matters in the physical or conceptual worlds we need a model that is coherent and consistent; that is, correspondent with the event being investigated. In this concern, the simplest definition of a metaphor would be that it is treating some primary event as if it were something else, something more familiar, or simpler, or more immediately available to us. This characteristic it shares with analogy, the class of conceptual events to which it belongs. And in this sense, every model employed to examine something beyond itself, in some primary domain, is, loosely speaking, on the verge of becoming a metaphor of that primary event. The congruity between the two should be clear, or there should be a reasonableness about it. But this alone is not sufficient. The metaphoric, chosen or created, should have heuristic value, making it possible to envision in the primary data what is implied in the metaphor itself. ("The mirror of history" becomes "cloudy" or "distorted" or a "one-way" mirror of history.) Thus the metaphor must have the power to lead on to other thought, to other metaphors or variations to the making of inferences that the primary event, seen in isolation, does not. In short, it should lead us to develop additional visions about that event.

It must be emphasized again that no particular metaphor is *the* necessary one, however sufficient it might be to a specific task. Nor could any one metaphor, however apt, possibly become permanent without running the danger of losing its force and coming to be treated as literal. Nevertheless, in the quest for an exploration, description, and explanation of some event in the world, the models develop from analogies which often begin with metaphors.

Denying or allowing the metaphor to degenerate into the literal sometimes shows more clearly what its positive force is. Turbayne, for example, illustrates how metaphors of great power and persuasiveness have disappeared into some misconception of literality and have come to use us, rather than be used by us. Euclid, Newton, and Descartes, he writes, were all either overpersuaded by their models and metaphors of the universe or their followers read them as literal descriptions of the secret worlds that they alone had discerned.[1] Recently a movement to create a new language of psychiatry began with a condemnation of Freudian metaphors too long read as literal statements and therefore treated as absolute descriptions of human behavior.

All this, however, allows us to move into a dimension of models and metaphors that we could not otherwise get to. Some models, those which are especially Hard, are Hard because they are characterized by having within them elements that run close to being identical to the events of some primary domain. Scientific models designed to make possible explanations and explorations of the behavior of heat and light and water, or of the heart and vascular system, and which reproduce them wholly or in part in the model, often but not always use actual replicas of such events. To that degree there is a literal dimension of the model, which gives it its Hardness. But recognizing the inevitable metaphoric role here, the claim to exclusive Hardness is evidently exaggerated. The most that can be claimed is a relative Hardness.

Logical Grounds of Metaphor:
Identity and Similarity

Cassirer and many others have argued that the very condition of man's language is the basis for the development and use of metaphors and, beyond them, myths. Whatever the world may in fact possess, when we speak of it, communicate our conceptions of it, consider it in any way for any purpose, we are required to employ some language in order to accomplish our task. And because language is a symbol system, both inescapably full of ambiguities and not a direct replication of the events to which it refers, we have no alternative but to contribute quality or meaning that resides, not in the event sym-

---

1. C. M. Turbayne, *The Myth of Metaphor* (New Haven, Conn.: Yale University Press, 1962), pp. 34–45. J. M. Morse, *Prejudice and Literature*, does the same with the metaphors of literature and politics.

bolized, but in the mind constructing the symbol, and thus, to the symbol itself. Such meanings and qualities may be partly sourced in what is present before us. But they also derive from our histories, culture, perceptions, and interest in some past or future state of this event. They are sourced, as well, in a knowledge of the futures of like events, and in specific intentions on our parts. I do not intend to take up the argument about myth origins that Cassirer explores, but I want to argue that the very conditions set forth here about the difficulties of establishing identicality are another factor attesting to the logical necessity of metaphor as an irreducible characteristic of thinking.

There is a more broadly identified linguistic matter to be considered. This derives from the fact of that other dilemma mentioned, that words in our ordinary and our special vocabularies are not limited to single meanings or to such singular uses that their misuse can readily be observed. Now words, singly, are usually not in and of themselves metaphors. But words in a sentence, used as the overlays that integrate two different contexts of inquiry, are precisely what we mean by metaphoric terms. This plurality of meanings of a term is what we understand to be ambiguity. Yet in the quest for precision, we are always being warned against ambiguity, which can be avoided only in very limited areas. This ambiguity is the condition for metaphor, and the power of metaphor. If not all such overlays, or metaphors, are particularly novel or provocative of newer insights, they are still metaphors, however bad. What is needed is to replace the overused overlay, the cliché, with a more refreshing one, in which we mix the heretofore unmixed to make new insights and new understanding possible. Overuse tends to make us content that the metaphor, like the well-used stethoscope, will by itself do the work for which it was created. It is by such overuse that the mind is idled and the thinking act stilled.

Daily conversation is replete with acceptable, understandable phrases that are, when examined, metaphoric, even though their metaphoric character has been glossed over or simply lost sight of. "Grasp an idea." "She turns people's heads." "The test was a breeze." "Prices are going up." "The smile on his face." "He's a very perceptive person." "Talk on the phone." A vast dictionary of such phrases and sentences is available to us in every catalogue of language (another metaphor), the examination of which could become a veritable archeological expedition of the structure of knowledge of a given group in a given place at a given time.[2] This source of metaphor in

2. Cf. M. Foucault, *The Archeology of Knowledge* (New York: Pantheon Books, 1972).

deliberate ambiguity, in plurisignation, will be considered again, especially in chapters 5 and 6.

Functions of Metaphor

The most obvious function has already been shown in the discussion of form, but only in a broad sense. More specific and detailed comments can be offered.

BY INTEGRATING DISCIPLINES NEW KNOWLEDGE IS CREATED

We become increasingly aware of the necessity for creating unities and coherences in a world always tending toward a fragmentation that the advances in knowledge seem to contribute to. It is all too apparent that experts in one field of inquiry are less and less able to communicate with experts in another. And those who are expert in no particular field, who are of ordinary and even above the oridinary mental development yet who have no specialization in any field, appear to be unable to communicate with any of them. Colleges move to forestall the deepening chasms between specializations by introducing what they call "interdisciplinary studies." The intention is understandable and reasonable, at least empirically. Logically, the problem is rarely touched upon. The usual approach is to begin at the achievement end of the cognitive process rather than at the initiatory, process, or task, stages. That is, they begin with an effort to show that the conclusions in one discipline, the findings in one field of inquiry, can be shown to have coherence with the findings in other fields. My argument, as I indicated at the outset of the book, is that all fields of inquiry are unified, and thus integrated at the point of their operations, their originations in the thinking act, rather than that they are all concerned with a basic substance. It can be observed on occasion that several disciplines will actually use models in common, or employ the same metaphors in their individual pursuits. But the real point is not so much that the individual model or metaphor or analogy may be shared by different disciplines to reach their separate conclusions. Rather, the *forms* of models and metaphors that enter into the character and the direction of thinking are the same in every field. And thus, however distinctive each field becomes in its special vocabulary, in methods unique to their materials and specific purposes, in special instruments of inquiry, or in specific findings, what is common to them is the singular, generic process of thinking. This commonality lies, not in the specific models or metaphors used, but in the *act of constructing* models, analogies, and metaphors for the general purpose of extending knowledge and understanding, and for the specific purpose of adding to knowledge of the world of things and ideas.

This is the primary, overarching function of metaphor making, as apparent in common-sense inquiry as it is in the most advanced science, in ordinary talk as in the realm of poetry. The statement, in science, that "gases are collections of mindless, moving particles" is as much a metaphor as is the sentence "Books are windows on the world." "The moon is a ghostly galleon, tossed upon cloudy skies" is no more metaphoric than "those clouds hiding the moon promise rain tomorrow." All show evidence of two contexts laid one upon the other, the events of one perceived within the context of the other.

It is interesting to note that the primary matter and the secondary, separately, might be described to some extent in observational or literal terms (say, e.g., "books" and "windows"). Every discipline is involved in creating an interaction between two fields that produces the metaphoric description. For the language and concepts are now made to serve the descriptive purposes in contemplating the first. It is by this means that the metaphor, as Black has noted, *creates* a similarity rather than simply laying bare an assumed preexisting similarity. ("Books" in themselves, denotatively, are not "windows.") But this must not only be read to mean that the one is simply imposed upon the other in some whimsical manner. Rather, it is a similarity created in the creation of an integrated larger context of consideration, in which the two separate languages are made integral, and the vision that derives shows the heretofore separate matters as one. We see one in the form, function, language, and features of the other. Refer again to Bettelheim's overlaying his Freudian model on the "body" of fairy tales.

There is always, I have said, the possibility that at first these appear absurd, because they are establishing a conjunction between matters not usually conjoined. It takes a little getting used to. But when it begins to take hold, we have presented to us a new description of otherwise familiar material, in which the primary material is seen anew and even the secondary material begins to take on new qualities, the qualities and features of the primary. Thus, the assertion that human beings can be described metaphorically as computers also gives us the sense of computers having human qualities. Cartoons in popular magazines are often humorous illustrations of machines with human dilemmas such as headaches, loneliness, nervous moments, and sexual frustrations.

So metaphoric expressions make possible new information and knowledge. But they do something more. They allow us to see new dimensions in the already familiar. This is why it is said that by means of metaphors we create *re*-descriptions. Tacitly understood elements of both domains, now seen in the overlay, become more explicit in the transaction, in the reorganization, which emphasizes and deemphasizes different elements of the familiar.

EXPLANATION AND THE METAPHOR

A second function of metaphor is found in the role it plays in explanation. There are some perplexities here, however. Every metaphor, I have said, creates a new explanandum, a new description of the familiar, or of what has not been observed before. The result, as we might expect, is that it provides the conditions for the development, too, of a new explanans, or of explanations where none had been possible before. Except, of course, where no explanations are called for. As, for example, in the arts, which are a quest for expression, it has long been held, and where no explanations enter. (We might "explain" a work of art, to be sure, and find ourselves giving an account of the artist's social-psychological state, but a work of art, as such, is a presentation of the directness of feeling and thought experiences, transformed into a vision in the colors and forms of the painting.)

Only in a quest for knowledge, where the knowledge derived is an explanation of something, will metaphor perform this explanatory function.

Metaphor is not necessarily intended as an explanation of anything, in and of itself. It is, rather, the means by which an explanation, or a new explanation, is arrived at or altered when the relationships between some primary and some secondary fields are altered. The new context of events, being redescribed from some earlier form, now may call for a new explanation. It is very possible to make available a better explanation of Hamlet's dilemma, for example, by a more modern metaphor than the one so much in vogue today, that of "filtering Shakespeare through Freud." Look at Hamlet through the filter of a weakened chromosome structure, and we are in the position of developing a wholly new explanation of his behavior. The data remain the same, as raw matter to be considered, to be sure. But surely a new description must now be made to reflect the influence of the secondary domain on the first. From this, we explain that it is not so much that Hamlet loved his mother in some incestuous way, but that he was biologically disabled and could not generate the physical vigor demanded of him in his situation.

Clearly, we are looking at Hamlet, but equally clearly, we may be "seeing" him for the first time in this new metaphor. New imagery arises, and even familiar language has new meaning. All the data must now be shifted about to suit the demands of the "filter" we are using, and new ranges of meanings of those data come into focus for us.

It is quite likely that the *form* of the explanations, however, will remain the same. We would still be looking for some causal explanation of Hamlet's behavior; but within that cause, we will find ourselves making totally different specific deductions, for our premises have changed.

In the physical sciences, however, one or another explanation may be "proven" to give a better account in the wake of experiments performed, for example, to reveal the behavior of light within each of the metaphoric contexts. What the discussion here reveals, as Hesse has written, is that rationality (thinking) "consists just in the continuous adaptation of our language to our continually expanding world, and metaphor is one of the chief means by which this is accomplished." [3]

REDEFINITION IN TERMS OF NEW CONCRETIONS

The function of the metaphor in creating new organizations among otherwise familiar matters also includes, as I have shown, making possible the construction of new definitions, and thus offering new ranges of meaning to material already fairly firmly defined and limited in its meaning. We come back again to the effects of the deliberate use of the ambiguity of terms. The denotative meaning of a term is applied in a context where it makes no sense, but where its secondary, alternative, or connotative meanings do. We speak of the "attractive" powers of electricity. The denotation of the term "attract" is "to draw, or to draw in, as by some form of suction." It makes sense, then, to say that electricity attracts certain things in the world. Of electricity itself we say that it denotes a fundamental entity of nature. The terms taken together denote a kind of behavior of a primary domain

3. M. Hesse, *Models and Analogies in Science* (South Bend, Ind.: University of Notre Dame Press, 1966), p. 176.

of concern in the world. Now, use those same denotative terms in a wider context, say, in order to describe a person. We say of someone that she has an "electricity about her," that she is "most attractive." By the interaction we are ascribing to a person the qualities and the powers of a force of nature, a kind of anthropomorphism in reverse. Nevertheless, however mundane such a description has now become, there is concreteness of a new quality. If it is more novel to say of such a person that she is as compelling as a "black hole in the sky," and if the description and the meaning are thereby altered, the concreteness nevertheless derives solely from the metaphor.

THE ATTENTION-DIRECTING FUNCTION

Little more needs to be said about the attention-directing function of the metaphor. The structure of a metaphor, even though it is not always consciously recognized, directs our attention. In this, metaphor performs the function of language itself; that is, of directing attention by the fact that the *way* in which we talk about the world, and the aspects of the world that we talk about, both derive from what is intrinsic in the language we use. If we assume that all language, all terms, are stipulative to begin with, then by metaphoric stipulation we are directed to attend to a given matter in a context that extends beyond the context with which we are familiar. (Consider what our attention is directed to when we talk about a table as "distressed.")

Finding the Metaphor

THE DISAPPEARANCE OF METAPHORS

Very often, the difficulty in finding a metaphor derives from its very success. When it has been effective in enabling new understanding to arise, new events to be identified, new ways of seeing to be developed, the metaphor becomes so standardized a way of talking that its metaphoric identity dissolves and it comes to be treated as a literal denotation. A fine example of this is the title of this book. We speak so frequently of thinking in terms of process, and of talking and writing about the "act" of thinking, that in modern times it has been accepted as a literal assertion of the nature of cognition. Yet there is an assumption here open to challenge. The fact is that although it is employed as a literal description, the metaphoric character of "the act of thinking" remains fairly evident, for we are always susceptible to any challenge from any source that would demand more direct evidence of this "act."

But we must also recognize that when a metaphor has become so widely successful that it enters into our daily discourse, something more than just the extension of our language takes place. We may well be embarked upon fostering a mythology of events. Indeed, a dead metaphor, a metaphor transferred into a literal statement, is clearly mythic. So many such terms are now employed in the English language (and no doubt in other languages as well) that it is small wonder that we continue to see spirit in inanimate things, persons in animals, hypostasis, that is, fixed but transcendent images, in the changing events of the world. When this happens, the purpose of the metaphor is lost. Instead of maintaining an openness and a flexibility in our thinking about the world and our thoughts of the world, about our feelings and the modes of expression of our feelings, a susceptibility to new forms in which more of the world's potential becomes available to us, the language of creativity is closed down. In confidence or in weariness, or because of the innocent assumption that there must be a rock-bottom basis for truth, we come to rest on some metaphor that has pleased, illuminated, or enlivened the world for us. Creativity dissolves first into cliché and then into myth. This is all too often the case with ordinary language in our ordinary affairs. This is also, all too often, the case in the workings of our special disciplines. When the Euclidean metaphor of geometry, of the harmony of the universe, ceased to be metaphor and was transformed into a literal assertion about the world, there began the myth of the nature of the universe from which we have still not been able altogether to free ourselves.[4] When the metaphor of the birth, death, and resurrection of love, symbolized in the story of Christ, was transformed into a literal statement about the "Son of God," we began to construct a myth that is even now vigorously trying to demonstrate its literal truth. But the institution built to house and protect the myth seen as literal truth is slowly crumbling because of its inability to demonstrate that this way of talking about man in the world really has literal evidence to sustain it. (In the final analysis, the evidence adduced may well be social, not theological, and certainly not physical.)

Our daily lives abound with evidence of metaphors that have died and become myths, and have fixed us into a way of talking and see-

4. Turbayne, *The Myth of Metaphor*.

ing a world that, had the metaphor been remembered, has no final form but is continuously expanding. What probably has happened is that what was first offered as an explanation was, by its success, transformed into a description in final form.

FINDING WHAT HAS DISAPPEARED

How, then, do we find the metaphor in use in the materials to which we address ourselves (recognizing that to find the metaphor probably means a myth is about to dissolve)? It is probably not so difficult as one would suspect.

The literalness test.   A certain level of sophistication will be required for discovering, and then creating alternatives to, a prevailing metaphor. If we remain insistent in the view that all metaphors are erroneous at worst, or at best charming though temporarily useful fictions, we will have one kind of a problem. If, however, the world as we understand it is viewed as being only partly derived from the data of experience, and partly from the "screen" through which we perceive it, the problem becomes simpler and yet more difficult.

If the only meanings we ever seek are truth meanings, we will, generally, be committed to looking always for the literal; that is, the denotative statements that can be verified in fact, be demonstrated to be the case claimed. If such be so, then what we must do in order to discover some hidden metaphor is to replace every connotative term, every hint of a metaphor, with a literal or denotative term. If the sentence still makes sense, can still be tested and found valid, then we have been able to locate the literary decoration by what it has been replaced with, and we can avoid being dominated by its imprecision or distracted by its ambiguity. Our quest will be for a perfect, self-explanatory description.

Suppose we were seeking an explanation of Shakespeare's melancholy prince. Hamlet says, "Conscience doth make cowards of us all." Is there a metaphor here? What can we replace in order to test the validity of the sentence? For *conscience* say "developed habits of response to given stimuli." (Some such notion is, indeed, entailed in a behaviorist psychologist's explanation of responses programmed into operant behavior.) Can we then replace the original with the statement: "The developed habits of response to given stimuli make cowards of us all" and not only mean the same thing but be more precise about it? Obviously not. *Cowardice* must now also be replaced. Suppose we replace it with the phrase "action brought to a state of arrest, or withdrawal." I submit this is not altogether an unfair restatement. In that case, the literal statement would now read, "Any behavior that is contrary to the developed habits of response to given stimuli brings about a state of arrest in behavior, or a withdrawal from a situation." (Imagine Hamlet saying this at the end of an equally literal translation of the question of whether he should or should not continue "to exist.")

This last, however, is a reasonable statement that assuredly can be tested in direct experience. If the transformation from the metaphor to the literal is accepted, then the metaphoric character of the first is clearly evident. "Conscience" is simply an ornamental reference to behavior patterns that have been programmed, and "cowardice" is a dramatic catachresis for the state of hesitation, or of a tendency to flee. So we have replaced the metaphor and made it a much more valid and literally true statement.

One obvious question arises. Do the two sentences really have identical meanings? If you think they do, then metaphors are words that only obscure the truth. It can and must be replaced by a true and testable sentence. But what happened to Hamlet, and to Shakespeare?

However, even if we suspect that they are not identical in meaning, but rather only vaguely similar, the test made of translating the original into a literal statement does make clear where the metaphor is. What it means that the literal sentence does not, and what its irreducible yet primary meaning is, still can be submitted to test, though we are looking for different things. We are now looking for an interpretation, not a descriptive truth, and that is concerned with connotation, not denotation.

The first test, then, for finding the old and creating a new metaphor is indeed the test of literal translation. What you do about it afterward derives not from the test for finding it, but from some further assumptions in our concepts of man, nature and truth.

Overextension as a test.   The second test for finding the metaphor is the test of overextension. In a way, it has some of the characteristics of the literalness test, but it looks for more than just absurdity. It is by means of exaggeration rather than in seeking a one-to-one correspondence of terms that we locate it. Turbayne asks, in effect, what kind of needles does sleep use to "knit up the ravelled sleeve of care?" [5] Or, I might ask, what dire thing happened to the "eyes" of justice to make them blind? Somewhere Lorenz talks about rats and mice, and ob-

---

5. Ibid., p. 57.

serves that when he placed a number of specially trained mice into a roomful of wild mice, the trained mice were attacked furiously, and only after hard fighting did they manage to regain the safety of their prison, which they defended successfully against invasions by the . . . wild mice. Was it because the wild mice did not have a clear and definitive battle plan? (Anthropomorphism, quite clearly.) [6]

What I have done here is probe into the adequacy of the analogies employed; first, by treating the terms as literal, and then by exaggerating, by deliberately emphasizing or extending toward absurdity a key phrase or word.

Now, exposing metaphors in this way, or in a one-to-one correspondence, does not really show that they are illegitimate. It simply locates them. In doing so we make it possible to see how even the strictest effort at scientific inquiry finds itself unable to avoid the use of metaphors, for we cannot always find a one-to-one correspondence, or ever avoid deliberate exaggeration. What it does demonstrate is how a metaphor becomes, for many, a literal statement, and the model of explanation (the explanans) of some event comes to be read as a description of that event (is transformed into the explanandum). As Turbayne says, "The mask becomes the face." The "lenses" through which we view the world become the world we see. Mask and lens disappear into the world itself.

CREATING METAPHORS

If we have not shown metaphors to be false, at least the discovery of hidden metaphors has the virtue of revealing to us how metaphors are either consciously or unwittingly created, and how they are employed.

The primary test for the application of this metaphorizing act is the test of whether the analogy is adequate to the new field or not. In the sciences, the hardness of the data, of the things being examined, exercises a clearer test of the possible strengths and weaknesses of the analogy. In the social sciences, as shown in chapter 7, the testability is there, but not quite in the same Hard terms. And in the fields of the arts, the testing of the analogies is more purely theoretical and emotional; more matters of logical and emotional satisfaction than of responsiveness to the Hard data to be dealt with. Thus, the range of flexibility goes from the more limited and precise to the more

---

6. A number of such illustrations can be found in K. Lorenz, *On Aggression* (New York: Harcourt, Brace & World, 1963), chap. 3.

unlimited and imprecise, as we move from physics and chemistry to sociology, anthropology, and psychology, to painting, fiction, and poetry. But in every case, some test of evidence, of logical coherence, of emotional-intellectual satisfactoriness, remains necessary. Yet, in no case can we say in advance, or at any given point in the development, that metaphors cannot be drawn from this or that specific field to be applied to that or this area of concern. On the contrary, it is often not possible, in advance of the actual construction and application, except perhaps by logical projection, to know what new forms of the world might yet be discovered and constructed, what new modes of expression might yet be achieved, what new dimensions of understanding about an expanding world can be made possible by the borrowing of metaphors. Until we have crossed the most unexpected sorts of things together, so that one becomes the means of seeing the other, we have no way of anticipating the newer meanings available to us.

At the very point that we are in some way warned against a possible heresy for viewing some things in the world other than in ways now accepted (in the name of scientific truth no less than in the name of some societal standard or religious conviction), we ought at least to suspect that we are in the presence of some metaphor that has been transformed by the frequency of its use into a statement of literal, universal truth that is not to be denied or tampered with. At that point we ought to try a little tampering, that is, finding by means of another metaphor, a new way to see this old matter. Indeed, heresy may well be the only means for fostering intellectual, and therefore, cultural and emotional growth.

As for the actual making of metaphors (and of models and analogies) we shall demonstrate how this is done in the various disciplines in the second part of the book. But surely Aristotle served us well when he wrote, somewhere, that whoever is the master of metaphor is the master of thought.

PART 2

One statement is worth making again to maintain the continuity between parts 1 and 2. I have argued that the models, analogies, and metaphors employed in the thinking act are themselves that act. That if one seeks to understand thought and to learn how to think, one can do no better than to learn how to model, how to analogize, how to metaphorize. Now let us turn from an analysis of general principles and toward the specific. For models, analogies, and metaphors, though they are generalizations of one kind or another, are nevertheless unitary and unifying efforts for dealing with the particulars of human experience. To be concerned with what things there are is to be concerned with the specifics found in nature. To be concerned with what behaviors and beliefs men hold, how these behaviors are to be explained and how beliefs and organizations of relationships influence activities and judgments, is to be concerned with specific events in experience, but always within a unifying context of some model of inquiry. To be concerned with what happened in the past, and to attempt to explain how past events have influenced the world of today is to be concerned with particular events within the context of a theory. And to explain how poetry, or any of the arts, expresses human feelings, or vision, dread or desire, is to be concerned with most particular events in that context we call a "vision" of man or nature or both. Coping with these particulars is what mind is about. It sets about those general tasks by the specific tasks of modeling, analogizing, and metaphorizing in specific undertakings.

The division of the chapters that follow should not be interpreted as a segmented approach to a standard curriculum, or the purpose of the chapters an investigation of the structures of the disciplines examined. I have repeated several times that what we are seeking is the way in which the unitary processes of thinking manifest themselves in the variety of human concerns, which end up as specific disciplines of investigation into further such concerns. I could have chosen other fields (if I had the competence in them), and the same outcome would have been sought. The process is our concern, not the classically organized bodies that comprise a standard curriculum. Thus each chapter is intended as a kind of archetypal demonstration of how analogizing, modeling, and metaphorizing issue forth into distinctive disciplines.

# Poetic Thinking

In which the mental act focuses on the forming of metaphors without concern for their explanatory use.

I wish it were possible to avoid all consideration of aesthetic theory in this chapter. I would much rather go directly to the problem of the thinking that manifests itself in poetic forms, analyze its specific characteristics, and show some evidence of how it has been done and how it might be done. But to neglect this would be assuming more than we have a right to assume. Some small consideration will have to be taken.

Poetry, as all the arts,[1] seems to be profoundly concerned with the "inner" world of our emotions and our contemplations. In *New World of Education* I argued at length that thinking is ultimately a matter of externalization. Nowhere is this better seen than in poetry, where, as Cassirer has written,

> The artist must not only feel the "inward meanings" of things . . .
> he must externalize his feelings. The highest and most characteristic powers of artistic imagination appear in this latter act.
> Externalization means visible or tangible embodiment in a particular medium . . . in sensuous forms, in rhythms in color pattern, in lines and design, in plastic shapes.[2]

This "embodiment," then, is what we shall be considering here, and the impediments to it. For in poetry, models, analogies, and metaphors are not merely *used* for ends other than themselves. They are contemplated, formulated, and enjoyed *in themselves*. They *are* the act of poetizing (forgive this ugly word).

It would seem almost an incontrovertible fact of human experience that as we get more deeply into the investigation of the things and processes of the world, something more than knowledge appears. We not only intensify our efforts in refining our procedures; we find

---

1. If music is your preference, read and listen to the accompanying record of Leonard Bernstein, *The Unanswered Question: Six Talks at Harvard* (Cambridge, Mass.: Harvard University Press, 1976), especially the chapter on musical syntax. His discussion of models and metaphors in music is congruent with our analysis here.
2. E. Cassirer, *An Essay on Man* (New Haven: Yale University Press, 1944), p. 154.

ourselves absorbed and fulfilled in the activities themselves, almost as if they were enough of a reward for us. We not only find or develop explanations for the events we probe; we find arising "in" us a rich satisfaction, often a kind of delight in the act of finding or developing those explanations, that cannot be accounted for by the explanations themselves. Indeed, how can we account for the fact that even a poor explanation or an explanation that we know to be inadequate still gives us a fulfillment equal in measure to one we might get if it were entirely original or entirely adequate? Can we find a physical explanation for the exultation we feel when we have arrived at a physical explanation? Does a psychological explanation fully account for the profound gratification we get from the development of a psychological explanation of things or people's behaviors?

The model for the structure that the architect is to build, the map of some piece of territory, the design for a factory to be constructed, the form of a tool to be used in hammering or digging—each in its own terms arrests our attention to the exclusion of its utility. We see in that model something permanent and distinctive, which has a quality, a power to move, to delight, to arouse, and to absorb. We turn from the event's use to the event. We *play* with, or we contemplate, what otherwise would be used.

We write a declarative, expository sentence, and somehow we find ourselves beguiled by the words, free of their declarative and expository meanings. Our concern with the *use* of the model disappears, and the model itself is our total concern: its shape, its tones and colors, its symmetry or asymmetry, its lines and curves, the sounds made possible by it. Our concern for use evaporates; we find ourselves making a song out of variations of sound. Function is available to us, of course, but it is to form that we are addressing ourselves. The whole action on our part has become autonomous, concerned not with the purpose of the instruments, but with the instruments themselves.

Meaning and truth in art, in poetry, is always a special problem because of this shift. Unhappily, the language of poetry is the same as the language of exposition, of discourse. It makes distinctiveness between these two functions difficult. Poetry, however, is not discourse. Or if it is, the form of the discourse draws us, not the content. We cannot read a poem as if it were a psychological treatise, or a biological or anthropological statement of some human or social process. Whatever understanding we may derive from a poem, it is not the understanding that can be derived from a statement about the structure or function of some event in nature. The models, analogies, and metaphors in poetry, then, have no reference either to Hard external data, nor to the rules by means of which external data may be approached and explored. They are models of illusory worlds, of imagery formed from the instruments and the subject matter of the arts. Poetic models are models of sounds and rhythms, of tonal tensions, of verbal juxtapositions that represent nothing beyond themselves. They are Soft, then, not because they have meaning in the usual sense of that word, but because they have *import:* verbal, visual, tonal, sensuous quality in themselves. They are not actual statements about actual worlds. They *appear* as statements about worlds that we frankly acknowledge as tempting illusions. Further, what follows from this is that the logic of history or any of the sciences has no relevance to them. Every such Soft model has a logic unique to itself.

It is difficult, perhaps impossible, to offer a simple and clear definition of art. How give a functional definition to an activity that seems to exist by ignoring the functional outcome of things? How offer an elemental definition of an activity that seems to defy a reduction to elements, that so often seems not to have elements?

Consider. We use analogies in order to make judgments about the things we experience. Those judgments are embodied in the descriptions and explanations we have constructed about the observed behaviors of things. But we also analogize in order to *express* (externalize) the experiences we have had, are having, or yearn to have. The analogical substance is common to both activities, but in the one it is clearly a matter of use, of explanation; in the other, equally clearly, it is a matter of forming, and of enjoying the forms created. The one is concerned to make coherent the world about us. The other is concerned to illuminate the "world" within ourselves, and the "world" within the world. The forms we create give tangible expression to those worlds in words, in sound, in movement, in marble, in color.

We can make another distinction. I show in the next chapter that historical thinking requires a concern with pastness and thus could not have been written by people without pasts. Art, however, begins with the beginnings of humankind, for this act of forming appears, in its origins, to be an intrinsic human capacity. The act of living entails within it the act of the enjoyment of living, of giving vent to that enjoyment in some formed expression. Listen to Santayana:

> Primitive man, having perhaps developed language before the other arts, used it with singular directness to describe the chief episodes of his life, which was all that life as yet contained. They had frank passions and saw things from single points of view. A breath from that early world seems to enlarge our natures, and to restore to language, which we have sophisticated, all its magnificence and truth. But there is more, for . . . language is

spontaneous; it constitutes an act before it registers an observation. It gives vent to an emotion before it is adjusted to things external and reduced, as it were, to its own echo rebounding from a refractory world.[3]

Whatever we call art, then, is some manifestation of man's shaping those feelings and perceptions that arise from his immediate involvements with the observables and unobservables of his world. It is the expression of his passion before he explains it, an expression manifest in whatever means he finds or makes—language, sticks that produce thunder, his own voice representing what he has heard, his own body as he reenacts his experiences, the colors he finds available to him in herbs and clay, flowers and roots. His expressions overlay representations of events experienced and events imagined, and become metaphors in the overlaying. So he invests the world with his own powers, giving animals human speech, natural forces intentions, the heavens powers he alone can envision. From a realistic point of view, he produces absurdity, an absurdity sourced in his imagination and his passions. He experiments, Santayana says, with the colors and sounds and words available to him, never knowing the effects of his experiments on others who listen or watch him. What he is doing is creating, in imagery, a world he does not see until he makes it vivid for himself and for others. He is creating models and metaphors whose reflections of the "real" world are at once, paradoxically, both imperative and irrelevant. They arise in response to experience but show immediately a formulation of aspects of those external events, the veracity of which he cannot or need not test. The source of the forms of these models is entirely in his imaginative powers, and their force is found in what they make possible for us in an appreciation of the models themselves, and afterward only, of the external world.

The Absence of Explanation
in Poetic Thinking

EXPRESSION

There is in art an autonomy that explanatory systems do not add to or diminish. To try to impose rules for enjoyment from sources outside the event, either from science or from some moral system,

3. G. Santayana, *The Life of Reason, Reason in Art* (New York: Scribner's, 1905), p. 87.

adds nothing and perhaps diminishes the process. Even more than in historical thinking, where imagination plays so great yet so clearly limited a role in the development of explanatory systems, imagination is the entire source of the arts. In this autonomous condition, as Cassirer has said, "the logic of the imagination [has] to be distinguished from the logic of rational and scientific thought, from such concerns as place evidence in so fundamental a position in inquiry." [4]

Art is not to be written about, analyzed, or searched for meaning in the sense that science searches for meaning. One *feels* the effects of art. Any attempt to explain it is already a movement toward psychology, biology, or physiology which destroys the essence of the art. Those who follow such paths will say the most astounding things about a work, about creativity, about beauty, for what they say is derived from outside disciplines. All they see in a work of art is a manifestation of behavior. In the process they wash away the sense of exultation in the work. Even when such analysis is not foolish, it is nevertheless not about art but about behavior, and belongs to some field of science.

The last chapter considered the probability of absurdity in metaphor, absurdity that makes possible particular perceptions of the things and ideas of the world. For the scientist this knowledge of absurdity always lies uneasily, compelling him to diminish it as far as he can. But in poetry this sense of uneasiness disappears, for we know that art is, much as we may bridle at the phrase, a deliberate distortion of the world experienced. In forming such imaginary visions truth is simply not at issue. Purple cows and green skies, animals with three heads, humans with two faces or four arms—these distress only the literalists, and only when they are asked to take them as serious "statements" about the factual world.

Whether we are aware of the terms or not, every work of art is, by its very nature, a metaphor for something, formed by the artist whose intention is to compress, to intensify, to externalize something, so that it can be experienced and absorbed by others. We shall discover that much the same can be said about science. Every model is in some way an analogue whose intention is to compress and to organize data into forms that can be dealt with. The difference is obvious, however. In science the intention is to make possible an understanding of the functioning of the world as object. When the metaphor in art is appealing, when it is persuasive, it transforms nature until we become absorbed in the transformation itself. The world as

4. Cassirer, *Essay on Man*, p. 137.

object dissolves, and we come to see the world of forms and inner tensions that the painter has fashioned. We sometimes listen to disputes among people but find our attention wandering from the substance of the arguments; we become aware of the formed structures that playwrights have allowed us to hear. We see in nature the imagery that the poet has enabled us to see. What we have been warned against in the sciences we seek out as the determining quality in the arts. For it is only in art that, as Aristotle said, convincing impossibilities are preferred to unconvincing possibilities. It is, in such terms, the performance of a distinctive mental act where the world available to us is only matter to be transformed.

What an artist celebrates is his sensuousness, his imagination, his consummation of his world, his powers of identifying himself with the infinite variety of sights, sounds, and movements about him. In short, he celebrates his power to celebrate. The tools available—brushes and color, sound, words, movement—become for him the substance of that revelry. Nor can we deny that ideas are also always substances of any work of art. They are as much matters for revelry as are sound, word, color, or the body in motion. All these things can be cast into idealized symbols. The imagery produced shows that celebration in gaiety or in looming tragedy. Even the simplest ideas become the substance of the most subtle and profound revelry. Hamlet can most simply be reduced to the idea of a man who could not make up his mind. But even within this simple statement is to be found the sheer wonder of the words forming a verbal imagery of "inner worlds," endless in their variety, inexhaustible in their interpretability. Even the explanation is celebrated.

ART AS FORMING

Every discipline seeks to show the structure and function of some specific phase of the totality of the world experienced. But art is not concerned with this kind of exploration of the structures of things, nor with the best formulas or models for explaining them. Art is, rather, a concern with the "pure form" of these events, of shape, or motion, or tone, or color, or sound, in the purity of the moment.

But how does the act of metaphorizing, or analogizing, produce this purity of form? We have argued that we metaphorize one thing, one relationship, by transforming it into the terms of another thing, another relationship. We look for the hard evidence for such metaphors in order to justify the transformation that is made. But how do we metaphorize what is imaginary? How do we transform that into something concrete and expect it to carry aesthetic effects? By giving the credentials of existence to our "inner sense" of things, however individual and transient that "sense" may be. For this reason, Cassirer says, no painter paints the "same" landscape in the same way. It is not the same landscape. It is each painter's transforming some moment of his or her own sensibility into some metaphoric form. The painter is not looking, as the scientist does, for some law, for some explanatory principle, by which every such event could later be explained.

Beyond all the explanations that human beings are capable of producing about the ways that things behave, set into general statements, there remains the "inner" unity of a moment that demands expression, and for which explanations are simply not relevant, however important these may be to the person who seeks to develop laws for an understanding of the world. Living in that world, in this sense of a quest for explanation, does not exhaust either the person or the world. There is this other world to be celebrated, the world of one's own formulation, the world of form within the world of function. The thinking process manifest here is as much a cognitive process as is the explanatory act.

Language in Poetry

IMITATION, SIMULATION, FORMATION

Art could not be mere replication. The leap of the lion, the sound of the cataract, are not presented literally in dance, or as poetry, or in a painting. They are symbolized. We know, of course, that mimicry is a source of delight to both performer and observer. But what makes for delight is our awareness of the limits of the imitation. It is imitation to which has been added qualities and characteristics that the original does not have. A perfect and complete imitation of a bird, when the imitator is not seen, leads us to look for the bird or to dismiss it as a bird that has gotten into the wrong place. What seems to be imitation is really the illusion of the bird. The bee that settles on a flower in order to suck the honey gives us one reaction. The bee that settles on the illusion of a flower, seeking to draw out honey, gives us a pleasure of an entirely different kind. We praise its reality precisely because we know it is not real.

So, too, language in poetry is a simulation of ordinary sounds that humans and nature make. But the simulation is quickly recognized as metaphoric, and it is to this that we respond in delight. Consider Robert Southey's poem:

> How does the water
> Come down at Lodore?
> . . .
> Through moss and through brake
> It runs and it creeps
> For awhile till it sleeps
> In its own little lake
> And thence at departing
> Awakening and starting
> It runs through the reeds . . .
>
> The cataract strong
> Then plunges along
> Striking and raging
> As if a war waging . . .
> Rising and leaping,
> Sinking and creeping,
> Swelling and sweeping,
> Showering and springing,
> Flying and flinging,
> Writhing and wringing,
> Eddying and whisking,
> Spouting and frisking,
> Turning and twisting . . .
> Collecting, projecting,
> Receding and speeding,
> And shocking and rocking,
> And darting and parting,
> And threading and spreading,
> And whizzing and hissing,
> And dripping and skipping . . .

And this way the water comes down at Lodore.

Has not the poet produced an imagery that the natural event does not contain? Has not Southey, in deliberate analogy, given form to his own sensibilities, his own perceptions? And form to our own experiences?

In our more mundane terms we must recognize that the language of poetry is not, nor could it be, denotative. For, to say that art is not imitation, however it may at times appear so, is also to say that art does not denote the thing that it is about. It may, as Nelson Goodman says, "resemble" something in the world, but it does not, insofar as it is art, *represent* that thing. It is a depicting, perhaps, of some event "seen into" at a particular time and place, by an eye, observed by a mind, already full of memories or longings or wondering that makes it possible for us, now, to see in that thing the attributes laid bare by the poet, who thus "takes and makes" the event into an image which reflects as much this penetration of the observer as of the event observed, and penetrated.[5]

SUBJECT MATTER IN POETRY

Denotation.   If art does not simply imitate, then what would be its *subject matter*? Clearly, a portrait has, as its subject, the person who is being depicted. Clearly, Frost's poem "Birches" is about birch trees. However, it is more apparent in poetry than in painting that it is not precise enough to say that the subject matter is some event or thing in nature. In painting it is the intensified combination of features of a specific person, or landscape, whose qualities the painter "takes and makes" into some portrayed form.

In the poem, however, there is not even that much beginning specificity about the subject matter. If it is about birch trees, it is about their perceived shapes, or the forms that allow small boys to do certain delightful, perhaps dangerous, things. The poet himself may have done them, yet it is not even about what he did when he was a boy. It is at once more clearly about feelings when one swings away from the earth, reaches great heights, and comes gently back to earth again; and about the metaphoric vision this action makes available for appreciations of other, equally ordinary, experiences. It is about a sense of self in a world of sweeping motion and not a simple denotative statement about trees.

The connotative and illusion.   The subject matter of all art, then, is some illusion, a vision of a real world disintegrated into some strange form. We acknowledge that there must be enough faithfulness, somehow, for the illusion to be communicated. But the formed illusion and not the way the thing actually is, is its subject matter. Thus, in poetry especially, the subject matter is both a conceptual and a per-

5. N. Goodman, *The Languages of Art* (Indianapolis: Bobbs-Merrill, 1968), chap. 1.

ceptual illusion; an illusion of form impossible of being presented in a declarative sentence [6] and still carrying the same import. See in Thouless's charming illustration the difference between connoting and denoting. Here is a line from Keats' *The Eve of St. Agnes:*

> Full on this casement shone the wintry moon,
> And threw warm gules on Madeline's fair breast.

Transforming it into a simple declaration (keeping the first line intact to show the contrast), Thouless makes it read:

> Full on this casement shown the wintry moon
> Making red marks on (Madeline's) uncolored (white) chest.[7]

Connotation, says Webster, signifies more than the explicit event or exact meaning. It is more than simply the sum of the parts of something. It symbolizes a pervading quality shared by all members of a class of things. Thus, whatever else we may say about the language of poetry, we must say that it is more than a matter of the precise, discursive statement that describes a particular event. It goes not only to essential attributes, but also to a responsiveness to those attributes that the writer seeks to bring to consciousness in the reader.

At this point the whole matter becomes more and more curious. Putting these two points together, we must conclude that art connotes the illusory. This appears to move it farther from the hard realities of the world. And of course, it does just that, although it also makes possible an understanding of why we may, in art, become persuaded to the most astonishing impossibilities. More than that, it makes understandable the deepest realm to which art addresses itself, that realm that is our "inner" world of thought and feeling, of feeling about thought, and thought about feeling, in which the stimuli of feelings and thoughts are of less concern than the thoughts and the feelings themselves. Whatever else we may say about poetry sharing fundamental cognitive characteristics and qualities with other studies, this illusory connotation marks the hard edge of the distinction between thinking poetically or in any of the arts and thinking in any other mode of inquiry.

Symbols.   But what poetry does share with all the other processes of thinking, without which thinking must remain forever markedly prim-

6. E. H. Gombrich, *Art as Illusion* (New York: Pantheon Books, Bollingen, 1965), esp. chap. 7.
7. R. H. Thouless, *Straight and Crooked Thinking* (New York: Simon & Schuster, 1932), chap. 1.

itive, is the significant symbol, the ordinary as well as the special linguistic forms by means of which thought is given form and made
communicable. This makes both for the special power of poetry and
its special dilemmas. For, the same language that enters into descriptions and denotations of the things of the world enters also into the
connotations of illusion. And it has produced much dispute.[8] More
than any other art, poetry seems a cognitive effort, and the presence
of words compels us to look for meanings of a kind that seem to lie
on the surface of the words. But if we seek only the objects referred
to, we destroy the poetic force of the work.

Poetry does not have the fortunate character of painting, where
colors have no possible denotative characteristics in and of themselves. Red, as color, does not *denote* bravery or martyrdom or ruth-
lessness. We must construct a special vocabulary in the arts to suggest
the intention of the colors or the textures of the materials in a given
work. *We* give them symbolic meaning, which already indicates social
determinations. But words in their common-sense use already have
their dictionary notations. Social conventions have given them objective significance, and we are never far from the act of reading a
word or a phrase in a sense that associates it with one of the other
disciplines where it has denotative function.

Taken literally (or denotatively), words in a poem produce the
absurdity of anthropomorphism, or fallacies that are not pathetic but
simply erroneous, for there is always the mingling of the real with
the metaphoric. Great care must be taken to allow the mind to enjoy
a kind of play that is alien in the laboratory. Thus Swinburne:

> Push hard across the sand
> For the salt wind gathers breath
> Shoulder and wrist and hand
> Push hard as the push of death.
>
> The wind is as iron that rings,
> The foam-heads loosen and flee;
> It swells and welters and swings,
> The pulse of the tide of the sea.

The realities of the sand, the salt wind, death; each are events about
which the metaphor is deliberately constructed. But these events are
not the contents of poetry. They are only the vehicles through which
the illusion of the restraints against the freedom of spirit is pictured.

---

8. S. Langer, *Problems of Art* (New York: Scribner's, 1957), esp. chaps. 2, 4, 7, 10.

Or William Watson:

April, April
Laugh thy girlish laughter
And the moment after
Weep thy girlish tears.

Clearly, the language of poetry is the ordinary language we use,
and sometimes embellish, but for purposes other than denotative meaning. And except where the referents in a poem are very special—to
some other literary work, to a moment of history, or to a legend that
may require a bit of esoteric knowledge—it is not the unequivocal
meaning of the words that describes poetic thinking. It is the metaphor of ordinary language given symbolic, living form that is the heart
of the poetic creation.

This cognitive familiarity is, in its way, essential to its writing and
to its being understood. We cannot shake out the literal meanings of
our words and thus hope to treat them as we treat color or sound,
simply as so many textured things, whose texture, given shape, produces its aesthetic effects. Poetry is always on the verge of being read
discursively. Therein lies its awkwardness, yet its remarkable intellectual force. For, in the tension created between its literal and metaphoric senses, it becomes alive, possessing the power of evocation. In
that tension we are drawn to language as symbols of envisioned forms
and imagery.

Metaphor in Poetry

FORM AS METAPHORIC CONCERN

Transformation.   What does it mean to say that in poetry the metaphor
finds its most complete and its freest employment? It means, simply,
that although there is a tendency to observe the literal meanings of
terms and phrases, the use of the metaphor depends not so much
upon what one can first derive from the literal, but what one can
transform that literal meaning into. Goodman says the term "blue"
used about a picture is both metaphoric and literal, and that its
literal side, or referent, must be there. It cannot be a red picture.
But metaphorically, though the color denoted lies validly in the object,
the "blue" does not actually refer to the color in its literal sense. The

significance of calling it "blue" runs much more deeply and more subtly, referring to the transfer of those external qualities to private intentions or responses, as, for example, when it is intended as a synonym for other familiar expressions, such as "needy," "depressed," or simply "sad."

Forms of metaphor, repeated.   Simply stated, we have said that metaphor is the deliberate application of a name, a trait, or a quality to something that, in its literal sense, belongs to something else.[9] Such deliberate distortion, or misapplication, takes place in several ways. We may apply to a single event the qualities that belong rather to the class of events of which it is only a member. Or we may apply to the whole class what properly is literally true of only one member of that class. In the first case, we metaphorize the whole of the law by talking about the *court*. In the second case we metaphorize a single court by speaking of the *law*. The first is what we have identified as synechdoche, and the second metonymy.

In simpler forms we metaphorize by talking of the qualities of one event as if they belonged to another, giving human powers to inanimate things, or giving to animate things powers associated with non-human events. So, Watson's poem gives to April the qualities of "girlishness." When we speak of China, or America, or France, each in turn as "a paper tiger," we are ascribing for purposes of derision the diminished qualities of a jungle creature to the behavior of a nation. (The same could, with a small change, be ascribed to a man with more laudatory intention, as it was when Georges Clemenceau, during World War I, was called "the tiger of France.") If these particular illustrations do not show themselves as poetry, they nevertheless show the metaphoric function of transference.

What is also suggested is the fact that sometimes the play of language is limitedly tonal, or syntactical, and not verbally metaphoric at all. When this happens, we are obviously more tricky than poetic. Onomatopaeia falls into this classification. By itself it presents a kind of wordplay that may even arrest poetic vision. The oxymoron (where within a phrase the terms contradict each other, e.g., "the thoughtful fool"), which has some possibilities for metaphoric use, quickly dissolves into a deliberate construction of clichés, and ends by numbing the poetic vision.

But here we have an opportunity for making still clearer the difference between the metaphoric models used in science and history

9. See chapter 4.

and those used in the arts, especially in poetry. We shall see later how wide is the use of metaphor in the sciences. For example, we sometimes encounter a discussion of human motivations in the terms of electronic forces, of human frustration in the terms of hydraulic machines with their force and counterforce straining against each other.

On the face of it, in terms of metaphor alone, there is little here to distinguish science from poetry. What, then, does distinguish them? Clearly, not the matter being metaphorized, but the intention for which the metaphor is constructed. In the sciences, as in history, the intention is to construct some handleable model of the condition or the operation of something, so that it may be more clearly described, and most especially, so that its behavior can be explained and, where possible, predicted at some later stage. But in art we are concerned with texture, the sensuousness given an enduring form, with the quality of experience given *stasis*. That is, its concern is to present a vision, an image, of some kind, timeless and complete, for contemplation, absorption, and enjoyment.

IMAGINATION

We come now to the role of imagination in poetry, and to the ways in which it differs from its employment in the development of explanatory systems.

Wheelwright offers four ways in which the imagination functions: (1) *confrontative imagination,* which acts upon some object by particularizing and intensifying it; (2) *stylistic imagination,* which gives distance or perspective to an event, thereby providing it with a distinctiveness (or objectivity) of form; (3) *composite imagination,* which brings together separate elements of different events and fashions them into unity; and (4) *archetypal imagination,* which sees a particular event either in a larger context of ideas or visions, or addresses it at a higher or broader level of concern. The metaphors of poetry either display one of these ways of imagining or show a subtle interweaving of two, three, or all four of them.[10]

These four ways operate whether we are addressing ourselves to the things of the world for scholarly or research purposes, where explanation is the goal, or whether we are concerned with the purity of an imaginary world where the metaphoric qualities, interwoven to

10. P. Wheelwright, *The Burning Fountain* (Bloomington: Indiana University Press, 1968), chap. 3.

give structure to the vision, are designed to express our feelings about the forms of inner and outer experiences.

Confrontative.   In confrontative imagining, we are concerned with something that is being explored or contemplated. By transforming a general concept into a particular existence, we concretize the generality into something definable in the physical world. In this particularizing we intensify specific events, or specific qualities of events, and endow them with an emphasis to which we can pay attention concentratedly. In poetry, especially, this way of imagining prevents "mere vaporizing," mere drift about generalities, which make definition of reality or form impossible. The working out of these details makes the imagery, the illusion-world, appreciable. It is the act of paying attention to some specific region of a landscape and making it, in its details, the basis of some metaphor yet to be developed; then, by means of the metaphor, we intensify further the isolated detail. In poetry we often find it as some detailed moment of a larger complex of events, and of intensifying its quality. Thus Coleridge's

> Day after day, day after day
> We stuck, nor breath nor motion
> As idle as a painted ship
> Upon a painted ocean.

The stillness of the image and the intensity created is irresistible.

Stylistic.   Imaginative distancing has at least this in common with the more familiar concept of *psychical distance*. It permits the attainment of an objectivity about expression, as in psychological terms we consider an event in such a way that our own involvement with it is part of the event and not part of ourselves. There is always the danger that in achieving this distance our involvement in the perception of events also disappears, so that the living quality of the event is displaced by some idealization. Despite this danger, in this imaginative distance the quality of play, the play of words, and the uniquely poetic import and imagery are possible. It remains the means by which the style, the living form, the juxtaposition of images, the tensions of that imagery, the sound of words, the cadence by means of which vision is realized are all matters of direct invention. It makes it possible, Yeats writes,

> to prolong the moment of contemplation, the moment when we are both asleep and awake, which is the one moment of creation,

by hushing us with an alluring monotony, while it holds us waking by its variety, to keep us in that state of perhaps real trance in which the mind, liberated from the pressure of the will, is unfolded in its symbols.[11]

But this "play" in poetry is serious in intent, not mere whimsy. It gives a shape to the world that the world does not in its own nature possess. The more deliberate the attention given to style, the more this distance becomes possible. Shelley's "To a Skylark" is a splendid example of this invitation to contemplation, where even monotony becomes enchanting:

> Teach me half the gladness
> That thy brain must know,
> Such harmonious madness
> From my lips would flow,
> The world should listen then, as I
>   am listening now.

Composite.   In the fullness of poetic vision the above two ways of imagining are made coherent with one another by the composite imagination. In the composite imagination we find fashioned the quality of that distortion that makes the metaphor so arresting a force.

This idea of art as deliberate distortion should not put us off. Immanuel Kant held that all knowledge is produced by the act of the mind shaping a variety of sense impressions into unified and intelligible structures. New knowledge is created not only by discovering what lies more deeply hidden, yet is always there in nature, but by the deliberate act of unexpected juxtapositions. And this, after all, is how we have defined metaphor. In this bringing together, new visions within the familiar suddenly appear, new meanings are developed. The familiar takes on qualities in the composite that it does not have in isolation. Without this, science would produce no new knowledge, and poetic imagery would be impossible. We moved closer to a dependable explanation of genetic transfer when someone brought together the form of motion known as a helix with the concept of genes as the carriers of human physical traits. In poetry, Shakespeare's sonnets abound with remarkable "composites," and the imagery they create is inescapable.

11. Ibid., p. 44.

. . . the morning sun of heaven
Better becomes the grey cheeks of the east.

If my dear love were but the child of state,
It might for Fortune's bastard be unfather'd,
As subject to Time's love or to Time's hate,
Weeds among weeds, or flowers with flowers gather'd.

Why is my verse so barren of new pride,
So far from variation or quick change?

So are you to my thoughts as food to life,
Or as sweet-season'd showers are to the ground;
And for the peace of you I hold such strife
As 'twixt a miser and his wealth is found.

Be wise as thou art cruel; do not press
My tongue-tied patience with too much disdain;
Lest sorrow lend me words, and words express
The manner of my pity-wanting pain.

From each such unexpected bringing-together, the separate events or concepts, now joined, create an image that the separate segments could not have. But, of course, there are cautions that must be observed. There must be poetic time and distance within which to play with such compositions so that they do not produce haphazard consequences to the reader or hearer. Nor can they show a ruthless insistence on our part for bringing together ideas that wash each other out in dissonant disbalance and thus obstruct creation of the imagery being sought. There must be, in such composition, suggestions for sudden images that provoke an idealism that makes sense, enchants, intensifies with wonder and worth the qualities already possessed. There is still a great openness, to be sure, and the warnings do not pretend that the worthy is already fixed. Nevertheless, it might be reasonably argued that the gruesome, the composite that offends by its unrelieved cruelty, closes down the world that the poet seeks to open.

Archetypal.   As great as are the demands made by these first three modes of imaging, by far the greatest, because of the wit and subtlety demanded, is found in what has been called the *archetypal imagination*. Poetry is not produced in the mere quest for rhyming words at the end of a line or the deliberate construction of some observable rhythm. Bad poetry comes out of the mistaken notion that poetry, to be lofty, must deal with so-called lofty matters in a lofty way, free from the trammels of small events. The tendency to become very abstract in order to produce "fine" writing generally produces blather, while pretending to be sensitive to the grander aspects of life and thought and feeling.

Yet, we have shown that as formative thinking poetry speaks to universal qualities at the very moment that it addresses itself to the particulars of experience. This person is better understood as a specific human being when we come to understand the more abstract form that defines humankind. For, by a person's membership in that larger class, the archetype called *humanity*, we are enabled to read into particular acts and thoughts a depth and significance revealed, not from direct examination of the individual, but by discerning in that individual hints and traces of that larger quality of the form that belongs to the whole class, which lies hidden to us until we have envisioned those transcendent qualities. (This is the opposite of confrontative imagination, where humankind is distilled into this human being.)

Those metaphors that express about individuals qualities that belong to the species as a whole are evidence of what is called the archetypal imagination. It provides poetry with the surest evidence of cognitive dimensions. It is evidence of the act of generalizing, then returning to particulars to imagine each particular as an element in the larger turbulence of living. Now, bad poetry, Wheelwright would imply, is poetry in which the abstract and the universal, by losing connection with some particular, become didactic, even moralistic. When the particulars are presented, they become only illustrations of the universal discourse, as, for example, in allegories. Think, for example, of what would have been the quality of Arthur Miller's *Death of a Salesman* had it been primarily an effort to exploit the universal quality of self-deception, of which Willy Loman was simply an illustration. We would have had only a moralizing thesis. The human quality, the power to move and enthrall by means of tragedy and compassion, would have dissolved into some curious, merely sentimental discussion of whether this moral thesis was or was not creditable. But as we are presented the daily anxieties and oppressions, the wheeling and dealing of Willy in his efforts to cope with keeping his job in a failing market, where age is an implacable enemy, and his pride in maintaining his sense of dignity is eroded by grinding little events, the forms of living are not separate from the particular events. They arise with our understanding of each smaller form of his struggles.

Archetypes are created by contemplation of individual experiences; but just as often they are learned from the literature of philosophers, from science, religion, mythology, and all such mental efforts past and present. Their treatment as illumination of the worlds that are intensified in quality, along with the aesthetic distance that allows for contemplation, is created in subtle compositions in which one element of the composition is some universal concept. This last is the rich contribution of the archetypal imagination. (Read Matthew Arnold's "Dover Beach" for a fine example of this.)

Poetic thinking is not mere airiness. Nor is it achieved by waiting for some sudden bolt of inspiration to hit us and drive us to write. (It is incredible to see how many generations of students grow up with this foolish conviction.) It is a formulating affair, deliberately created by addressing oneself to the concrete details of the world. It is generated in the attention we give to the detailed elements of what we already know. We begin always with the manifest world, or with symbols of such manifest worlds, and by attending to forms find ourselves free to move about by the deliberate choices of bringing together matters that we normally do not see or think about together. If this be imagination, and indeed strong cases have been made for it, then to speak of a lack of imagination in people is to speak of (1) a lack of knowledge of events; (2) a lack of awareness of what can be known, or of the elements of what we know; and above all, (3) either an unawareness of how to compose new forms from among the old forms we know or have available to us, or the fear to do so, for whatever reasons. (It is not at all unfamiliar for a teacher to hear a student say, "I don't dare think in this way, my family [friends, preachers] would be furious if I did.")

Expression in Poetry

METAPHORIC FORMULATION

To be acquainted with how metaphors are formed is to be ready both to read and to write poetry. For the poem, as it directly appears to us, is a matter of words, of language treated in a specific way in order to produce a specific effect.

Poetry offers an expression, creates an illusory perception of human experience. To this extent poetry reveals that private world in the special form of which all thinking partakes, whatever the intention or the arena of concern. It is the deliberate, special use of ordinary language, that symbol system available to us for making our private worlds public. For one who has developed such powers of expression, everything seen and contemplated, either in the external world or in the world within, is formulated into expressive imagery. The great Belgian poet Maurice Carême shows this power not only in his published poetry, but even in his most ordinary conversation. With him, all things take on the quality of his expressive formulating powers. Activities of shopping, dressing, and dining are transformed from their ordinariness until they have a quality teeming with vibrant color and movement, of private perceptions suddenly made public.

However, such expressions, we note again, are not to be evaluated for their truths in terms of their assertions about the facts of the world. They are not even the representations of the inner life of the poet; not, that is, *merely self*-expressions. They are, rather, symptoms of it, as Langer says. They are evidence of imagination at work on the matters of experience, but revealing not a truth about the matters experienced so much as forming the words so that they become the experience. It shows, in its expressive forms, the feelings that are had about a world of such varied aspects.

But can we provide formulas for such expression? Can we set them forth in any classification, to be used by those who want to write poetry, or better understand poetry? The effort to do so, it must be obvious, runs the grave danger of reducing creativity to a mechanism. Nevertheless, some general ideas might be borne in mind relating to expressive linguistic forms that might provide an understanding of the structures and features of metaphor without assuming that metaphor construction can be produced by formula. To put it paradoxically, we cannot form by formula.

TYPES OF METAPHORIC IMAGERY

The context of a poem is its metaphor, as the context of scientific inquiry is the model developed and put to use in the investigation of something's changes and behavior. Thus, the building of the metaphor becomes the first requirement; the choice of words and juxtaposition is its fulfillment.

The types of imagery carried within the variety of metaphors that make up the literature of poetry are vast, and it would not be possible to suggest more than a few of them. But some illustrations would be of assistance. A deeper study, ranging through a larger repertoire, could be as delightful an undertaking as wandering through the galleries of the Louvre.

Paradox.   Metaphoric imagery can be formed in paradox. Read Swinburne's

> Time, with a gift of tears
> Grief, with a glass that ran
> Pleasure, with pain for leaven
> Summer, with flowers that fell.

The second line is not paradox, but a variation of pathetic fallacy. The other lines, however, are clearly paradoxical, though not as harsh as an oxymoron would be.

Congruity.   They may be *congruities* among the otherwise particular forms of things or concepts. Listen to Matthew Arnold:

> Let the long contention cease!
> Geese are swans and swans are geese.
> Let them have it how they will!
> Thou art tired; best be still.

The congruence between swans, geese, and disputation ("contention"), unusual as it must be, is apparent in the quatrain.

Deliberate ambiguities.   In the use of that plurisignation discussed in chapter 4, this is often come upon. This, if you remember, is the deliberate use of two different definitions of a term within the same context. Carl Sandburg, in "Killers," has this line:

> And a red juice runs on the green grass
> And a red juice soaks the dark soil.

We do not usually talk of blood as a juice. Its use here is unexpected, yet it gives an image of cruel levity to the poem.
Wheelwright's illustration comes from Goethe's *Faustus:*

> See, see where Christ's blood streams in the firmament.

Here the ambiguity derives from using one phrase in two different contexts.

Secondary definition.   Sometimes metaphoric imagery is derived from the deliberate use of secondary definitions where the primary use was expected. More often this occurs in the adjectival position, and gives intensity to ordinary visions. Read Elizabeth Browning's

> A heavy heart, Beloved, have I borne
> From year to year until I saw thy face
> And sorrow after sorrow took the place
> Of all those natural joys as lightly worn
> As the stringed pearls . . . each lifted in its turn
> By a beating heart at dance-time. . . .

The equivocal intent of terms, in these lines, of *heavy, borne, joys,* as lightly worn as the stringed pearls, and in the last twelve words should make clear the form she fashioned.

Concretizing.   Concretizing an abstraction, that is, a generalized concept. Matthew Arnold, again:

> The Sea of Faith
> Was once, too, at the full, and round earth's shore
> Lay like the folds of a bright girdle furled.
> But now I only hear
> Its melancholy, long, withdrawing roar. . . .

Logic of the imaginary.   At times imagery is constructed by ascribing the logic of reality to a domain of the imaginary, where we consciously or intuitively know that it does not apply. Yet its unexpected intrusion is evocative. As Stevenson's

> I will make you brooches and toys for your delight
> Of birds' song at morning and star-shine at night.
> I will make you a palace fit for you and me
> Of green days in forests and blue days at sea.

The logic of the construction of jewelry and real palaces employed to explain or to describe how he would build this other sanctuary gives vivid form to the illusion.

Sound imagery.   Nor can we deny that imagery is created by using words whose sounds are evocative, not only of the things referred to, but also of qualities within those things that are suddenly revealed to us. The *Cataract* excerpt quoted earlier is a fine example of this, as is the line

Like cataracts that crash from a crumbling crag.

Pathetic fallacy. Finally, although we could go on to much greater lengths, the familiar pathetic fallacy, where powers, traits, or functions normally ascribed to one level of reality are given to another, to which they really do not belong.

> The wind, as it strikes the sand,
> Clutches with rigid hands
> And tears from them
> Thin ribbons of pallid sleet.

or

> I lean against the bitter wind
> My body plunges like a ship.

Examples are endless. Nor are these the only techniques that can be found of modes of imagery created by different metaphoric types. But they are examples, and they need to be recognized for the ways in which they formulate, and in that formulation, create the visions that we call poetic. The deliberateness that is demanded must surely be apparent.

METAPHORIC ECONOMY

An interesting comparison can be made between compression and intensification in poetry and in science. The clear assertions in the sciences, or in history, become the assertions that are tested in further thinking and experiment. Clarity in poetry, however, has a different quality. In science precision of the expression of the logic of nature or of recorded events obliges us to avoid ambiguities. In poetry, force in imagery derives from deliberate ambiguity and equivocation. For, where any metaphor is designed to weave two totally different referents together until they become a singular new referent, we must be careful that the poem does not contain such verbs and articles as would directly suggest some reference against which we can measure the truth of what has been said. Words whose literal meanings cannot be avoided may well have to be eliminated, and in the elimination the suggestivity becomes greater precisely because the referents become more diffuse. Wheelwright offers as an example this little phrase:

An ideal
like a canary
Singing in the dark
for appleseed and barley.

If the word "is" had been inserted after "ideal," the poem could
easily have been lost for its claim to a senseless identity. Without the
verb the metaphor enchants by allowing the mind to make its own
transformations without the need to test its hard validity. This is
what is meant by compression, that judicious economy of words that
frees the mind for evocations. For it is not the objects talked about
that are the center of interest, but the verbal imagery evoked, and
the feelings expressed in those images. We need some references, to
be sure, if the poem is to have force, a power to stir, to absorb or be
absorbed. But it is not a matter of being absorbed in things. We are,
rather, compelled by the vaguer, more ambiguous qualities that reside in forms, as illusions that are yet intensely real. In such contexts
we come upon ourselves in new ways, and find in ourselves dimensions of sensitivity and understanding vastly different from that
achieved in the understanding of the ways and the whys of things
scientifically treated. It gives credence to the world "within," to the
person beyond the psychologist's capacity to account for him, into
which the outer world may enter and be re-formed, given new
shape, new quality, new intensity.

Symbolism and Imagery in Poetry

There is another aspect of the metaphor in poetry that we need to
consider. If every metaphor is described as the deliberate mixing of
concepts not normally brought together, how does it appear, particularly in poetry, where the imagery created is not necessarily visual, but
rather verbal? The imagery created is one of sound—the sounds of
words, rhythms, tonal tensions. Consider the verbal, tonal imagery that
the following express:

Walls whose shuttered eyes hide shattered hopes.

The trellissed trees that shackle this earth's yearnings.

The lisp of leaves, the ripple of rain.

We cannot look for visual images here. Nor are we expected to, when we remember that with poetry, especially, the illusions created are illusions that sound alone can evoke: illusions in rhythm, tone, verbal pulsation, flowing sound.

But as with all art, the question of good rather than poor metaphors is important. The good metaphor arouses excitement. It has the vitality of living forms, which move and pulsate. It intensifies the images it creates. It is self-contained, drawing the mind into its own formed image more and more deeply, independent of "the facts" of life that its words may sometimes be read to denote. It is experienced unto itself and not necessarily as an analogue of the physical world beyond. By contrast, a poor metaphor is one whose imagery is already either too familiar, too easily anticipated, or simply not intense enough to arouse images. But this does not say much, and certainly it does not say anything that can be objectively evaluated. For what is familiar to one comes as a surprise and even a delight to another who has not encountered it before. What is obscure to one may well be clear, even luminous, to another. What does not arouse an image in me may do so in you.

Moreover, unexpectedness alone would hardly be a strong criterion for the good metaphor. It may, indeed, be novel, and we may be surprised by it, yet it still may be poor. What really makes for good metaphors are images that are made possible, images in which the familiar, perhaps even the ordinary, are suddenly shown in a new light, in which the ordinary is given in new form, new value; where dullness is stripped away and new excitement grows. We are brought to pause, to wonder, and to contemplate them as if we had not observed them before. And of course, we have not. That is the point of the poetic metaphor. It has created a new and vibrant form in its symbolism.

In this pursuit the development of symbolic forms becomes fundamental. For in the symbol, unlike the sign, we distill ranges of meanings of events not present, and give them the tangibility that beguiles in its possibilities. But because the events symbolized are not present, the symbol itself becomes the subject of our contemplation. Signs are announcements. They tell us that there is a railroad crossing ahead, or that smoking is prohibited. But a symbol transforms the quality and promise of an event past, or future, into a presence before us. The word RESTAURANT on a map is a sign. It denotes a specific event. The depicting of a fork and spoon is a symbol of that restaurant, although a weak symbol, to be sure. The cross worn around the neck is a symbol, yet a better one for most of us, even in its simplest, most primitive form, because what it symbolizes has a cultural and historical depth that has an expanding range of meanings.

But even here there is a weakness on several counts. We carry over from science the idea that the symbol has to be a symbol *for* someone, as well as *of* something. We may be provoked to discover what the symbol symbolizes if we have no previous knowledge of it. However, that would depend on the quality of the symbol itself. Suppose we were in a strange land and observed that everyone wore a certain symbolic form around his neck, or on his arm. The very frequency of its appearance can stir us to inquire, to seek out its meaning, and thus its history. Yet its history remains extraneous to its aesthetic effect. For even if worn by only one person, it has or has not such quality, either of beauty, provocation, or unexpectedness, that the one alone is enough to excite the interest.

Of course, the meaning attached to the symbol, *what* is being symbolized, gives force to the symbol too. The discovery that what is being symbolized is trivial may well weaken the power of the symbol. Symbols of surface, transient events that are not likely to affect our lives all too often produce little or no response in us. Somehow they must refer to or create for us qualities of experience, visions and longings that are, in definable or undefinable ways, unable to be shared. Any metaphor, serious or witty, will contain that weight of meaning, so notable in good symbols, which are expressions of fundamental human experiences, of joy and grief, of pity, wonder, terror, passion, and the like. Potentially, then, every such symbol is as fully powerful as any other.

There is one further point to note here. Sometimes a symbol that has been widely used, whose meanings are full, extended, and of great significance, declines in its powers to attract us because it has become too familiar, too frequently used. Elizabeth Browning writes of love:

> With a love I seemed to lose
> With my lost saints.

New qualities are added in the symbol itself. The cross is reworked into more carefully wrought gold, into new lights and shades of different precious metals, into new spacing among its jewels, into newer shapes. New meanings come to be invested upon the whole event, which is the Crucifixion being symbolized.

In poetry the symbolist movement of the nineteenth and twentieth centuries shows this awakening. Coming at a time when commitment to the uniqueness of the individual, to the "private" world each inhabited, was replacing the standard of objectification developed in the concepts of natural laws and natural rights, the person of the poet was suddenly made the primary matter of the poetry. In seeking to express his identity, his private world, the poet begins to create a special language to express his person, his visions, his desires. With increasing attention given to the inner world, this absorption with the intrinsic quality of symbols seems a natural development. For, by creating these symbols, the private world is kept private and yet made public in the means of externalizing the deepest and most intimate reflections. Yet, most profoundly, there is no effort in the symbolist poetry of Yeats, say, or Eliot, to *impose* these visions, only to *expose* them.

In this, however, as in other symbols whose subjects seem no longer to be of moving importance, the symbol comes to be detached from its subject matter and is treated in its own terms. Here we can better recognize clues to the good metaphor.

First, it is one that does not impose itself upon the unwilling as some kind of new doctrine or dogma, a new rational explanation of the world and humanity, to be accepted and followed. It is good by its persuasiveness.

Second, it is good by its intrinsic power to give life to what has become ordinary and inert. In this it brings the sense of the present in vivacious form to all things, past or distant. The vivacity is embedded in the metaphor; to contemplate it, to take it in, is to turn light inward upon the imagery and make the dark places gleam with vivid sensuosity.

Finally, the good metaphor, in its remarkable way, makes privacy not only continuously worthy, but enhances the privacy of thought even more by expressions of such power that what is private becomes public and gives the illusion of profound reality.

In any art, the capacity of the artist to quicken in the reader this sense of his own identity marks the ultimate value of the symbols he has used, the metaphors he has created. For the artist enriches us within ourselves by this indirect revelation of his own inner world. It is not so much that we share his world, but that in the reading we are given new ways to create our own new inner worlds.

The bad metaphor is made bad by being passed from "hand to hand" in the public domain so frequently that its value is rubbed away to literalness in the passage. Consider the metaphor of the fish in Christianity. In its earliest times, it was the symbol of Christian identity. Christ called Peter and his brothers from their tasks as fishermen to become "fishers of men." The fish became, then, the symbol that identified them, and those whom they "fished" for. The fish has long since lost that metaphoric force in the modern world, and now appears only as a sign of membership in an institution that often seems far removed from its original intention. We find the fish symbol on key chains, amulets, and lapel pins. Yet, in the hands of a Jean Cocteau, this symbol comes alive in so rich and joyful a form that its history cannot diminish its wonder.

See how this good metaphoric creation appears in the quotation from T. S. Eliot's "Ash-Wednesday," and consider the imagery it evokes, if you can manage to suppress the need to look for a psychological interpretation:

> Because I do not hope to turn again
> Because I do not hope
> Because I do not hope to turn
> Desiring this man's gift and that man's scope
> I no longer strive to strive toward such things
> (Why should the aged eagle stretch its wings?)
> Why should I mourn
> The vanished power of the usual reign?

The sense of sadness, the coming to terms within oneself amid the striving for gain and power, is remarkably compelling, even though there might not be a single specifically determinable point in the poem at which you could say: Here, at this point and in this word, he has said precisely this. Yet there is no question about the clarity or the power of the metaphor of the turning, of the "aged eagle" no longer striving to "stretch its wings."

The World Made Manifest
in Poetic Thought

My purpose in this chapter has been to show the forming function of poetry. I have tried also to show, however indirectly at times, the role that thinking must play in the writing of poetry, and that poetic thinking is as possible of being fostered as is historical thinking, or psychological thinking, or scientific thinking.

No man is born a physicist, a psychologist, or a historian. Each becomes a member of the community (of physicists, psychologists, or historians) when he has learned to use the concepts, models, analogues, and metaphors employed by the scholars and researchers in each field. Nor is any man born a poet, a painter, or a musician, whatever we may want to say about "tendencies," "dispositions," or "special talents." Whatever these dreadfully vague words may mean, in actuality they can be discovered only after the fact, after the evidence of thinking has been made available in some specific expression. We become poets when we have come to understand the nature of a poetic metaphor. We are not born with the imagery or the visions that identify poetry, and simply develop the skills little by little. We learn to create verbal and visual illusions.

The labors we perform in the construction of these metaphors work back upon us and transform the accidents of our inner development into those forms and qualities that are our poetry. Our worlds within come to be full of the poetry we have learned to write, or the pictures we have learned to paint. We are not born lovers. We learn to love in the vivacity that love infuses into all experiences. We are not born lovers of words. We learn to love the play of words when wordplay has absorbed us into newer visions of our inner worlds. We must resist the easy mystification of this learned play as an excuse for our failure to give ourselves to it. In a genuine sense, writing poetry is intrinsically a rebellion against a dying world of fixed institutions and mechanistic procedures. In its unique way, poetic thinking shares this appeal to rebellion with every discipline that teaches, beyond the uses of the prevailing models, how to construct such new models as will make new visions and new actualities possible. Every new paradigm in science, or in history, Kuhn has argued, is a revolution against the standard ways of doing things and seeing things. Every new poem is a rebellion against seeing oneself and the world in the habituated ways. In every poem the poet creates himself anew, and holds in his imagery the same promise for those who read.

There appears something ineffably romantic about such a view of the world and of oneself, but to reject it because of this label would be a serious error. For it is romantic only in a context of a world that has come increasingly to be treated by the mechanical models upon which we have become dependent. The potentials for living reduce to just those needs that the mechanistic world has imposed on us and can satisfy. But when we come to suspect that nothing is as fixed as our technology would have us believe, not even the mechanical instruments themselves, then we may recognize that what is called romantic may be only an indication of the individual seeking a richer understanding of the potential of all things. Intelligence, in this sense, is defined by the imaginative powers of inventing the process of reasoning itself. What has been heretofore considered unrational or irrational may yet appear as a newer rationality, derived from newer metaphoric insights. It is we who see the orders of nature, its laws and principles of behavior. If we learn to construct other models, other metaphors, and by that creation see in nature what others have not seen, we may learn, too, how responsive all things in nature are to those new powers of ordering. If sometimes we are offended by other suggestions of such orders, it is only a matter of time before we see what others have enabled us to see; before we learn to use the metaphors they have created, and thus see what they have seen. The poetry of Blake and Wordsworth, the paintings of Monet and Van Gogh, are familiar examples of this. Each invented a new "language," a new symbol system; formed from it a new metaphor and showed us the world and ourselves as they could be seen within these newer forms. If we persist in learning them, their worlds become ours and we take on new forms, new identities, new qualities of persons, new powers with which to live. For the world is never simply out there, to be looked at, to fit ourselves into. That world and our feelings and cognitive powers are intertwined, and the distinction between the objective and the subjective dissolves into a new structure where there is never a mind that is empty of the world's appearance; nor a world that is a disengaged reality, demanding that we attend to it in disregard of ourselves. Whatever is in the world we know is already qualified with human thought and human explanation. When we look at that world, who knows what ordering minds and sensitive creations we are also looking at, or looking through? It could be Van Gogh's world as easily as it is Newton's, or Einstein's. It could be Mozart's world as readily as Darwin's. It could be Picasso's world as well as Marx's. Who shall say which is the real world? And as real, whose reality? The economist's, or the musician's? The physicist's, or the poet's? Surely each of theirs, perhaps all of theirs.

But it must be clear that such attainments are not to be had in sentimental vacuity. If new laws are to be created, they must be created by hard attention being paid to the matter about which the new laws are being written. If new poetic imagery is to be created, it must be created by close attention to the character of language, to the import the words bear on their surfaces and beneath their surfaces, in their connotative possibilities. If a new scale is written in music, it is written to be employed in the writing of new music. New worlds and new persons are not the work of random coursing of vague impressions, or of total and exclusive absorption with the self. They arise from diligent attention paid to the elements of the thinking process, going from phase to phase, culminating in that new person and that new world.

There is a demand made in this act of formulating poetic imagery that is as difficult of achievement as anything anyone ever commits his or her energies to. Most people even will argue that it is harder. For Hard models are so much easier to deal with than Soft. But it can be learned, and that is the point. If some would argue that not all people can learn to write poetry, we might just as readily argue that some people will never be able to repair a car, or perform surgery. That may well be, but it may also be because not everyone either is needed, or finds fulfillment in, writing poetry, repairing an automobile, or cutting out an appendix. Yet the fact is, it can be done. If not every poem is as fine a work as every other, neither is every automobile repair job as competent as every other. What is important is the awareness that every poem we write is an experiment in formulative thinking, in imagining, in metaphorizing. Each one shows a growing mental power that the next poem would show.

The world we live in is a world full of things and of relationships between things, and among human beings. We give shape and meaning to that world; we explain and interpret it, control and predict it, use it and enjoy it as the forms we give it allow. When we direct all our attention, all our growing powers, to the act of forming models from which we derive direction and organization, we are creating the means upon which every future development of the world depends. The qualities of grace, balance, rhythm, tone, time, tension, the playfulness and wonder that the world comes to have, we have first formed into our metaphors and our models, in music, painting, dancing, drama, sculpture—and in our poetry.

Historical Thinking

The past as analogue for the present. The present as analogue for the past.

The most immediately recognizable characteristic of the models and metaphors of history are their time determinations, by means of which change is discerned and interpreted. In no other discipline is this fundamental. In the sciences and the arts, metaphors and models are treated analytically or, when empirical, occupy space as essential traits. This, indeed, distinguishes the historical from the ahistorical. Later in this chapter I give a more extended illustration of this most distinctive fact of historical thinking (see pages 149–54). But one thing I must point out here, in advance of a later examination. Every history ever written becomes quaint, archaic, and not a little naive without necessarily becoming foolish. We know this happens as we know histories come to be "out of date" and new ones need to be written about the same matters. What we are saying in such cases is that the metaphors employed in the past are simply inadequate to the problems of the present, but that they retain attractive possibilities, nevertheless.

Any discipline, I have said, will be receptive to the models that other disciplines have employed and in that employment shown to be fruitful. In history, however, the models we borrow are those that must have added to them the time and change dimensions of some career (and all that is entailed there) as intrinsic to the model itself. The model is completed with phases of growth and decline in specifiable duration. Ideas, relationships, organization, intention, and recorded attitudes or behaviors then are given narrative form, and we expect they will include the phases of their existence.

More directly. If we borrow a Jeffersonian doctrine, say, of human rights as a model for explanation of some present problem, we are clearly in the realm of the social sciences. But if we turn to the *career* of Jefferson, or the career of the doctrine, the model for inquiry begins to show historical thinking.

It is often remarked that the surest indication of maturity in an individual is the ability to make use of the ideas and instruments of the world in which he or she lives, and to do so in such a way that ends and means are brought into that harmony where each is formulated in awareness of the other. But such maturity is, above all, manifest not only in the way that present things and ideas are employed, but in the ways in which instruments and ideas of change in some past career are brought to bear on the given present and the looked-for future. Psychologists will point to the various stages of development in children, moving first from graduated awareness of the objective state of things to the ability to grasp them, physically and conceptually, then to recognition of the relationship between words and things, and so, slowly, to an awareness of space, of time, and of simple relationships.

But when the child begins to recognize the force of ideas and comes to understand that the career of past events that he has never seen and will never see has had bearing on his existence, and that, in some remarkable way it forms a part of his identity as a living, growing human being, he is developing a historical sense.

Nothing so completely identifies the conceptual domain of human existence as the role of history in it. For this is the reservoir of the ideals and beliefs, and the modes of social behaviors, the monuments of value, the rules of life and of work, of language and thought, of modes of dress and proprieties of relationship between human beings in every kind of recorded relationship at all levels of human experience. Thus the study of history becomes the study of humankind in its fullest range of development and potential. For it is human history that reveals our growing ability to choose and to act in the world with an increasing awareness of the continuities that have come to furnish and decorate our world. The fullest understanding of one's self is never complete unless there is included an understanding of the manifestation of the past in the present, and its portents for the future. Without it, we are prone to living through our moments of time on little rafts of isolated activities.

If this means anything at all, it means that the past cannot be understood as mere chronology, nor is the study of the past the study of that chronology. The static time notations of past events, the time-isolated sequences of the lives of others, the arbitrarily determined important and unimportant events, all are simply the data from which historians weave tapestries in which lives and acts in episodes are given such dimensions and perspectives, such wholenesses, as make the totality of their lives understandable.

In such weaving, the perceptions and the craft of the historian appear as intrinsic to what is woven. The patterns we observe are not to be found intrinsically in the events presented, but in the mind of the historian.

Within this chapter we will see why it has been argued that historical thinking occurs only with quite Soft models. For, as evidence becomes less complete, less likely to be tested empirically, it becomes softer. The more the spaces within the model must be filled with purely theoretical and logical connectives, the softer the model becomes.

By its very nature the evidence we deal with in history is separated from us in time to such an extent that all we have available to us is some constructed analogy or metaphor by means of which we examine and give meaning to that time-distant matter. The two-symbol system that any model of explanation requires has this peculiarity in history: the completions added to the explanandum can never finally be verified. This means that the explanans explains not demonstrable data, but such data woven together by hypotheses that cannot be proven true or false.

A history of Martin Luther, for instance, begins with the evidence available in some symbolic form. But it is not enough. We need to fill in the spaces left between evidence in order to develop a clear and complete narrative of the man and his works. There is evidence that Luther was an Augustinian monk, that he suffered extreme physical pain, that he was outraged by papal and hierarchical decisions and behaviors. We have records of what he wrote, and of what others wrote, of conflicts that occurred and resolutions reached. But those records and conflicts and resolutions bespeak others for which there may not be evidence. And those implied meanings, and the evidence available to us, are what constitute a more complete picture of change over time, which becomes a history of Martin Luther.

No historian just tells us what happened. He also offers an account of why the world was what it was, and by so doing justifies his account of why things happened as they did. He tells us, indirectly, what he sees as the structures, movements, potentials, and bindings of reality itself. If he argues for laws of history, he is telling you one thing about human nature and nature. If he argues by means of probabilistic explanations, he is telling you something quite different. If he argues for Intention as the clue to history, this vision of the world is different from the other two. Thus, even while we read history, we read a theory of nature, and of humankind, society, change, and development, along with the narrative presented to us.

Distinguishing History
from Other Disciplines

What makes "history" such a difficult field of study? The fact that in its most familiar meaning it includes everything that has happened at a given time in given places. Gallie writes that "historical results are ultimately the world we wake up to every morning." [1] If this is so, then the field is ambiguous because it is so inclusive, so extended. If ambiguity is to be avoided, if history is to become possible, limitations must be of first concern.

For one thing, of people or events for which we have no record at all, no history can be written. In this sense, there can be no "primitive" history, for no organized record was ever found of the lives and changes of the primitives of this world. And for another, we might argue that, however sly or evasive it might sound, "history" is what men have written from the record or the evidence of those events in time and place. "History" is what historians write.

From this follows a constant effort on the part of analysts to narrow the domain by agreeing upon fairly specific rules for describing and explaining a past for which we *only* have evidence in the form of records of one kind or another, not the events themselves. Moreover, those records lend themselves to interpretation in a variety of languages, which historians have available to them. The languages of metaphysics, psychology, geography, biology, and others in the range of language which together comprise a culture. The employment of these languages in the analogues used produces disputes among historians. Yet they also produce originality of insights.

All this adds another curious dilemma. If we take the concept of history in this still broad sense, then everything that has a career would have a history, and history would be the most basic of all disciplines. All other disciplines must be acknowledged as depending on the findings of the historian, and the knowledge that has been made available. For here historical thinking would be identified as that which is concerned to develop an account of the origins and nature of the development of the events that other disciplines also study, in their specific ways. But we need to distinguish between history and genetic tracing, between history and psychological de-

1. W. B. Gallie, *Philosophy and the Historical Understanding* (London: Chatto & Windus, 1964), p. 51.

velopment, between history and biological growth, and so on. If we do not, we are led back to history as chronological report, the chronology of any conceivable event in nature. Moreover, it would also be possible to establish a chronology of ideas as readily as one develops a chronology of tangible events. However, such a chronology leaves the basic question of the subject matter of history untouched. Consider Darwin. Surely his work prepared the way for refinements in biological and entymological tracking of changes. His influence on the social sciences is considered more fully in the next chapter. But Darwinian influence on Freudian psychology is apparent. Yet to accept this as the subject matter of history obliges us also to accept the primacy of chronological causal sequence on every occurrence to which the historian addresses himself. The real cause of anything, then, lies in its genesis. And the more precise we can be in our descriptions of its genetic state, the more true our history becomes. In the long run, then, history disappears into one or more of the social sciences, and individual choice and preference, individual minds at work against what appears to be determined for them, is dissolved into social or biological destiny.

However, the question remains: Does such an approach exhaust what can be known about the human experience? Gardiner [2] explores the profound difference between the geologist and the historian respectively, exploring the eruption of Vesuvius in A.D. 79; or the historian and the psychologist each analyzing the mental condition of Alexander I of Russia.

It must be evident that what the historian looks at, and what he looks for, is different enough to make his discipline sufficiently distinctive to be worthy of a specific preparation, and it will call for the development of an explanatory system unique to this discipline. His purpose for examining a particular event is not as a step toward the construction of laws for the understanding of other events (which are discussed later in this chapter). Rather, he is concerned to use whatever laws are available to him, in whatever other discipline, to produce a better understanding of a particular event, in and of itself, with all its connections to others, and all the trails and traces it has left, leading on to other events to be explained in the same way. Thus, though it might appear that history is a parasitic discipline, it would be more accurate to say that it is a discipline that borrows lawlike concepts that appear to be relevant to its concerns and purposes, transforms these into tools for its own concerns and objec-

2. P. Gardiner, *The Nature of Historical Explanation* (London: Oxford University Press, 1952), p. 59.

tives, in order to produce an understanding of the events of change in the past, in and of themselves. But in doing this the discipline of history does nothing more than any other discipline. All practitioners of any discipline, indeed all of us, are borrowers of the instruments, ideas, and models that exist about us. It is not *that* it borrows that makes history different, but *what* it borrows, and what it does with the borrowing, that gives historical thinking its distinctive identity. When we borrow the languages of other disciplines, it is to better grasp the data we will be talking about.

Gardiner sums it up in this way:

> The crux of the distinction between the historian and the scientist is as follows: The scientist frames hypotheses of precision and wide generality by a continual refining away of irrelevant factors. Things are otherwise with the historian. His aim is to talk about what happened on particular occasions in all its variety, in all its richness, and his terminology is adapted to this object.[3]

To concentrate, then, on the point of "particular occasions" is to allow us to suggest the distinctiveness in historical thinking. For particular occasions in which people are involved must also include the plannings that are part of those events, the purposes for which those plans were made, the specific circumstances that surrounded the occasions, the changing currents of belief that prevailed, and the unique forms those beliefs were given by individuals or by groups. We need to consider the modes of reasoning employed for which we can find some evidence. In such thinking, the models of inquiry that the sciences make available to us hold great promise for what we will be enabled to say. But the fact that the historical events we examine cannot be reproduced under laboratory conditions prevents us from deriving the kinds of scientific laws that the physicist or the biologist, or even the sociologist, might derive.

The Forms and Components of Historical Models

THE FUNCTION OF LAW

What forms or "pictures," then, do historical models present? What qualities are found in those "pictures"?

3. Ibid., p. 60.

Historical models, at the outset, often look much like the models of psychology, physiology, or some ideal social structure. But this is only the beginning of historical thinking. If we go no further, the results are not history, but further outcomes of inquiry in physics, psychology, chemistry, or sociology. And indeed, so much of history does appear to take that form. Moreover, if we remember the intrinsic relationship between a model and the language it makes available, the very character of historical talk, though it may begin with the language of physicists, psychologists, or anthropologists, must move to its own language or be lost in those other disciplines.

When we address ourselves to the specific events of the past for historical purposes, for the advancement of the understanding of some segment of that past, then the law components, the idealizations, the classification systems that are borrowed must be recast. The data examined, the day-to-day experiments lived through, show the limitations of those idealizations. The pictures offered as historical models are *wholes* in which the idealizations are submerged in particular events, as parts of those particulars, as intentions, plans, aspirations. The idealization, for instance, of the soldier-lawgiver is illuminated in a history of Napoleon, and the distance between the ideal and the realities described, to the extent that they can be described, makes possible an understanding of the humanity, of change in determinate time in the career of the man. A history that does nothing but make the idealization central is not a history at all. It is an act of proving further the range of applicability of the ideal concept, as, for example, in theology. What have been refined away are the human factors irrelevant to the ideal. In such an event we would not have just bad history. We would have no history. Bad history would at least be concerned with the particularities of human experience, however incompetent its treatment of these were. What we have in its place are moral analyses of supposed human inadequacies.

As to the substance that is developed into the picture itself, the differences between history and the sciences become even more apparent. There is argument as to whether the singularity of events, or the uniqueness of occurrences, alone, is what distinguishes the subject matter of history from that of science. Generally, it is held, this is not enough of a distinction. It is not so much the fact of the uniqueness, it is said, but the ways in which the uniqueness is treated, is thought about. In scientific thinking we look into the behaviors of singular events for that kind of evidence that would make it possible to identify regularities, and from these, general laws. In history, the law already accepted, on whatever ground, is the "filter" for seeing not only regularity but also the unique in events. In the metaphor of photography, such laws show the positive and the negative of particular occasions. We note the irregular, the anomalous, the negations of the law's regularity. In history these are our focal concern. But this leads to another aspect that it is important to consider.

HISTORICAL EVIDENCE

In the sciences direct evidence of things is a primary requirement, for science begins with problems observed in existential phenomena. But in history, we recognize, it is rarely ever the case that the evidence itself is directly present before us. What we have are some records, signs, or symbols of events that occurred, but that cannot be brought back again for direct scrutiny. Now this will add a type of complexity that we do not find in the sciences, where the concern is to propound a general law and a theory of explanation for the evidence directly at hand. On the contrary, the very data of history, the so-called *facts* that are to be built into some model of explanation, appear to us already cast into some symbol system. The first requirement, then, is a reasoning process, a logic of history, which is a logic of symbol systems requiring decoding in order to establish a complete narrative, rather than the logic of relationships among physical phenomena. This fact makes it likely that the logic of history will more nearly resemble the logic of literature than of science. Historical "facts" are very different from scientific "facts." For when all we have are the signs and symbols of the past, the translation of those symbols into completer pictures necessarily obliges us to go to imaginative sources, and to conjecture that we will use analogies and metaphors from which such descriptions will be developed. The tests for the warrant of these analogies and metaphors lie in the symbolic notations with which we have begun, and in the total narrative produced.

In no discipline, therefore, is there likely to be so much tentativeness of "picture" and of interpretation and explanation as there is in history.

What is even more disconcerting and curious in this tentativeness of historical thinking is the fact that we use the present in order to construct an analogue for understanding the past. But before we can do that, we must first address ourselves to what the past has left with us, from which we have already begun to shape an analogue. The past, then, is an analogue against which we construct another analogue from the present, in order to compare the two, for the insights that the comparison will make possible between actual events of past and future.

Consider the Declaration of Independence. The language of the document, that symbolic record left to us by the revolutionaries of the late eighteenth century, tells us in lofty terms all that they have done to make themselves congenial to the rulers of England. But they precede this litany with the restatement of the well-known and glorious metaphor of the equality of all men created in common by a just God. From this primary model we have the record of the justification of the acts that they have already undertaken, and will continue to undertake. ("Whenever any form of government becomes destructive of these ends—life, liberty and the pursuit of happiness—it is the right of people to alter or to abolish it. . . .")

Now, if this document is to be treated as evidence, it must first be connected to something of significance in the present.

The Vietnam war is certainly an event that compels the attention of historians today, especially that aspect of it in which a government committed a nation to actions that one could easily suspect were "destructive of the ends of life, liberty and the pursuit of happiness."

So, with clues from the metaphor that served as the basis for the Declaration, and from other sources (but I limit myself here to the Declaration, since that is my point), we shape a metaphor of the present in order to explain and interpret the Vietnamese war. From sources readily available to everyone, we discover the defense most frequently offered for the government's action was the conviction that America must accept its responsibility for holding back the dread forces of rampant communism, wherever it is encountered. So men were drafted, against their will, into the army.

Now we have a historical problem, at least partially clarified, and we might proceed with it. What we do now is match symbol systems with symbol systems, which is the evidence we have, decoding each within the context of its time, placing clues of meaning against clues of meaning, for all the world like Sherlock Holmes, connecting his clues from a variety of sources until he unravels the meanings of the symbols in all the analogical systems he is dealing with.

MODELS OF STORYTELLING AS METAPHORS OF HISTORY

But history has not only to be concerned to establish its distinctiveness from the sciences. Just as clearly it needs to be distinguished from fictional narration. Good history often has the quality of good fiction. Many are even convinced that the best way to learn history is to read historical *novels*. Here the threads of sequential episodes, when well done and carefully presented, are so coherent that we can understand the "truth" of the past by being absorbed into the human passions made present to us through aesthetic suasion.

The distinctions between fiction and history are too apparent to worry about. Rather, it is the similarity of many aspects between them that sheds special light on what we come to understand as historical thinking.

The clearest illustration of the concept of thinking with which this book began is a well-written story. For, to write a story, or to read one, requires us to follow out a sequence of actions and ideas that describe the lives of people and events. In doing so we find ourselves absorbed into their actions, tensions, conflicts, as if they were as real as we ourselves are. We begin by accepting them in their symbolic identity, concretize them in imagination, and end by identifying with them. In imagination we experience what they experience. (If history is to be concerned with the lives of people in human predicaments, what better way to understand them than to identify ourselves mentally with the figures of history, experiencing their mental lives. This is R. G. Collingwood's basic thesis in his *A Study of History*.)

But three special traits need to be considered in this matter of similarities and distinctions between the narratives of histories and those of fiction: (1) the completeness of the narrative, (2) the logic of each, and (3) evidence as a requirement for justifying the narrative.

Gallie has analyzed this problem engrossingly.[4] Whatever the sources of fiction may be (and we may well assume that writers often, though not exclusively, derive the basis of their fiction from experiences they have themselves undergone), the essential quality of the story lies not in merely recording events as they have taken place, but in the way in which the narrative has been deliberately developed. A basic theme is formed, part of which is disclosed at the outset, the remainder allowed to develop through the tensions deliberately created by the author. By its form the reader is led, episode by episode, through the events to the climax and the aftermath. Within the story we can discern the logic of the tale itself. Was enough of a basis given, somewhere before the end of the story, to justify the way in which the story concluded? Were arbitrary and illogical sets of events suddenly intruded so that the tale becomes logically unac-

4. Gallie, *Philosophy and the Historical Understanding*, chaps. 2 and 3.

ceptable to us? Was it all carefully prepared for, so that although the conclusion was sudden and surprising, we might, on reflection, be able to go back to the data and say: "Yes, that is logical. That is just what should have happened"? Must we characterize it as a *deus ex machina*, that Greek tactic of suddenly introducing saving powers from some external, irrelevant source to resolve a conflict that defies the logic of the story?

The story is altogether a human construction in which the whole moves toward its completion, and in which the evidence itself, that is, the terms of the story, may be formed from whatever is familiar, now given the shape that bears the author's intentions. We acquiesce in full knowledge that it is "literary license," and to that extent, quite conventional. We need not ask that the author take account of evidence that we might summon up, but rather that the work be "true to" the spirit of human possibilities, even though we might have no precise way of validating them. "It could have happened, of course," we need only say. The important aspect of the story, its aesthetic dimension, lies not so much in the content of the story, but in the way in which the author has built the imagery, tensions, conflicts, climaxes, and resolutions. We really do not demand proof that they did happen this way. On the contrary, we collaborate in the happenings, so to speak, when we are able to associate ourselves with whatever the author has developed in the way in which it was developed.

But history makes more of a claim on us than this. Evidence cannot be relegated to so insignificant a role.

This matter of evidence, then, marks a significant and sharp difference between stories and histories. To write the history of Napoleon, or Charles de Gaulle, or Franklin Roosevelt, the evidence that is available to us in symbolic form must serve as the justification for whatever interpretations are finally offered. And these interpretations, with their accompanying explanations, must encompass that evidence. To the degree that evidence is unavailable, unvalidatable, or not attended to, the likelihood that we are doing stories rather than histories becomes more apparent. Consider, for example, Abelard, the medieval philosopher, and his relationship with Heloise, who was his student and the niece of the canon of the cathedral of Notre Dame. Historical evidence remains available. That both actually lived is not disputed. That he was badly mangled, physically, is also a matter of evidence from his own brief diary. That he was a brilliant scholar and that he replaced his own master as a teacher of philosophy in Paris, was denounced by the church and forced into a monastery after some success among the young students of Paris is also attested to by the records of the time—his own and those of others. But all this evidence is still insufficient to do a detailed or extensive history of Abelard's life, works, and influence. The rest is story, and not history. And the fact is that Abelard and Heloise are better known through the romances of Helen Waddell, Henry Adams, and other novelists and playwrights than through any historical work.

The most absurd empirical thesis can produce great fiction. The form of such narration can become so absorbing that the mind of the reader is protected against the demands of critical inquiry. The Aristotelian notion of catharsis is fulfilled by the very structure of the story, which allows us to relive the events related for us yet keeps us clear of the necessity of taking it so seriously as a description of an actual world that we, too, are caught in its determinations and powers.

But history, clearly, is a different matter. Here we begin with the fact that evidence, in the final analysis, is the check on the writer's choices for development of the telling. The logic to be followed here is, indeed, partially the logic of the arts, but primarily we are compelled to examine the logic of the possibilities and probabilities of human experience. And it is this, as Stuart Hughes has argued,[5] that makes history fall between art and science, yet it is not to be reduced to either.

Now the record of the past does not of itself dictate the ways in which the empty spaces between fragments of evidence are to be filled in. But however they are filled in, in history the filling must follow, not the logic of persuasion and aesthetic absorption, but the logic of the probability of human behaviors in the light of what we know has occurred. This is the fundamental point. Events in history do not have the carefully wrought character of the well-shaped novel or play. They are not planned in the mind of a creator as sequential steps leading to the completion of a deliberately created story. They follow the line—if, indeed, there is a line—of the sometimes deliberate, sometimes compulsive behavior of the individuals involved. We no longer accept the idea (if we ever seriously did) that history is a matter of characters playing out roles carefully written for them by some divine playwright. Their responses, their judgments and choices, as well as the reactions they show to their own acts and to what they have observed, derive from the specific situations in which they found themselves. If historians, afterward, impose a determinate form on such choices of action and of thought, it is they

5. H. S. Hughes, *History as Art and as Science* (New York: Harper & Row, 1964).

who have done so, after the fact, in order to sustain an explanation and an interpretation. It is the historian, afterward, who has proposed rules of the behavior of events and people in order to ascribe certain meanings to their acts. The acts themselves are not responses to those laws. They are expected only to illustrate them.

Nevertheless, storytelling does serve very well as a model for history-telling. The force of the story lies in the telling of those events in some sequence or continuity, in order to show how character alters in the cauldron of events, how lives are changed through this unexpected yet acceptable series of actions. What it requires of both writer and reader is the developing ability to *follow* events, to follow the story as it is unfolded, and to evaluate each event as it occurs against the understanding of the conclusion for which the story has somehow prepared us. Writing history takes the same form.

To learn to follow a story, then, is to learn to follow history, becoming sensitive to the sudden events that reveal and change the lives and characteristics of the individuals involved. But in history, the end of the story brings with it, not the sense of victory or defeat, as it does in a game, a carefully wrought drama, or a contest, but understanding, primarily of the lives of the individuals who are the subjects of the narrations. If we are able to generalize from this understanding to the possible understanding of others whom we see caught up in similar situations, then the purposes for writing the story, or the history, are achieved.

We run into serious difficulty, both in the story told and the history written, when the narrative is fashioned to illustrate a moral injunction. In that case, the ending, the victory or defeat, is more important than the narrative of change as it is told. The character development, fulfillment, or tragic destruction ceases to be of primary interest. It is more important that some moral doctrine is vindicated. What we have here is a kind of bad history, as in fiction it is a kind of bad storytelling. History idealized to the point that it simply iterates a moral is not history but a dramatic catechism.

There is a negative side to the analogy between stories and histories, which is illuminating. The closer we come to transforming history simply into telling a story, as is done in the so-called historical novel, the less important the historical evidence becomes; and the more important its aesthetic quality. As we are more and more moved by the passionate quality of the story, become more and more emotionally identified with its people and experiences, historical understanding is less and less likely to develop. In the novel, character development is shaped, not with respect for the symbolic events that are evidence, but from the events that have been deliberately constructed in order to fill out the picture planned by the writer from the outset.

So histories and stories share the formal traits of narratives, and some of the logical strictures that are part of narration. But the differences seen in the contrasts make it possible to understand history as being something other than art, however much it may share some of its qualitative force. For in history, evidence is primary and cannot be ignored or loosely manipulated. In history there are no completions as there are in stories; no fixed endings, no finalities that set the whole of the work into final form. In history the logic of the narration must respond to recorded human actions and thoughts, with all their waywardness, unpredictability, and undefinability. Events in one phase of history do not prepare the way for the next phase, as the storyteller constructs them to do. Episodes in history may come to an end, but not in the sense that a story does.

The Historian's Task

What can we say, then, is the historian's task? To begin with, it is primarily determined by publicly available evidence; that is, by records of the past as they have come to him, and as he makes them available to us. If the historian is required to be a researcher into previously discovered or undiscovered archives, these are nevertheless still a matter of public records, even if they have not yet been made widely available. This obliges the historian, as it does not oblige the storyteller, to hew to what is possibly true and to avoid what is possibly false, as the available evidence will attest. If both historian and novelist are concerned to develop and to make available a "picture" of some segment of experience, historians' pictures must have the smell of truth about them. Their pictures must show the possibilities of being *truths of* the past, whereas fictional writers need only be *true to* the *quality* of some set of events and of persons who figure in their "picture." The latter, it must be observed, finally comes to have the "stasis," say, of a painting or a sculpture. In history they do not.

Further, the matter of evidence required gives to history a necessary location in time and in place, qualities that are only contingent in the novel. To this extent there is, indeed, an objectivity in the writing of history that cannot be dissolved altogether into the historian's preferences or private interpretations. For the records of events demand intellectual allegiance. This is one test of the historian's interpretations. In fiction it is quite the reverse. The events described, their acceptability in the flow of the story, are tested by the interpretation and the intention with which the work has begun, and which appear increasingly as the events are permitted to unfold.

We are led to suggest, then, that whatever will finally appear to us as the historian's task begins with the experiences that human beings undergo and have recorded as moments of careers that occurred at some earlier time. But this, of course, would not limit history to a particular individual. It means that the historian must, at some point, take account of the earlier experiences of men and women, in important ways just like ourselves, who lived at some earlier time, whose exploits and whose reactions to these exploits have come to us in some form of tangible evidence: in monuments, artifacts, legends, the memories of our elders, or some symbolic system. Now, individuals undergoing certain experiences may have had purposes or goals to direct them. But those purposes do not enter into history as teleologies, that is, as fixed ends toward which history itself is moving. That history is, and remains, open-ended as the events in human experience are open-ended. For always there are other events that follow, even from what might be seen as the most consummatory experiences.

History, we have said, arises out of the reports or records of just such ongoing experiences. What historians have before them are the evidence of the lives and strivings, the attainments and failures of others. What they do with these is what history finally comes to be. Some seek in that evidence clues to general laws that would be held to explain the dynamics of the lives of individuals and of groups in unfolding time. For these, history is the reservoir of the evidence that will reveal the existence of those determining and regulating laws that it would be better for all of us to understand.

Others, however, look into history for the lessons of the logic of human affairs, without the insistence that such a logic is derived from anything that might be called "laws of history." It is, rather, the logic of pragmatic consequences, where people attempt to respond to immediate problems created by particular, immediate dilemmas that they confront, in the terms of hoped-for beneficial consequences. In this sense, history seems always to be the effort of some historian to fill in the gaps in the evidence. Were it not for the fact that there are such gaps, there would, in this view, be no need to do history at all, for the record would be complete and could be read by all for the directions clearly lying within those records. But from either of these approaches, the function of the model and of analogy is apparent, their particular differences notwithstanding.

There are other approaches to the doing of history, which we will examine in time, that are no less model-born and model-bound. But for the moment, let us turn to an aspect that falls directly within the domain of our fundamental concern in this work. What of the role of description in history?

DESCRIPTION IN HISTORY

Inevitably, histories are full of descriptions that bring the past vividly before us. But if we require that a description be a series of statements that can be checked for faithfulness against what is being described, can we logically say that history contains descriptions? To the degree that actual evidence is available to the historian, we might anticipate that accuracy of description is obligatory. But it is rarely the case that the *evidence* of the event is the event itself. The remaining monument, artifact, parchment on which the character is written, is only the symbol of some event, not the event itself. The Magna Carta is the record of the decisions reached, and does not replicate within itself all the events that led up to the document. If this be so, then a description of such evidence is not the description of the events memorialized in documents and monuments. Thus we could not have a description that could be verified in direct or first-hand evidence. Indeed, in history, description is invariably of just this kind. Are we concerned with the physical traits and features of Caesar, Napoleon, or the Magna Carta, or the beheading of Charles I? To some degree, of course we are. The major concern, however, is with the relationships among individuals and groups, with ideas that direct behaviors, with beliefs and purposes, with plans and the record of the execution of plans.

Often what appears as a description in history may not be a description at all, but rather an interpretation of partial evidence made more complete by conjecture. When we treat this as description, we reveal the well-known fallacy of assuming that every word reflects something in the world, which is clearly not the case. The failure to recognize this leads us into treating the "picture" created by the historian as the events themselves. How important is it to recognize this? As important as clarity and distinctiveness are to thinking. As important as is the distinction between the explanandum and the explanans set forth in chapter 2.

This condition has much to say about the scientific status of history. For however extensive and important the conceptual realm may be in the sciences, and we cannot doubt either its extent or its importance, science is, after all, concerned with things in the world now present to us, susceptible to inquiry and to further testing. Even the most abstract terms in the natural and the social sciences, terms like "atom" and "Social Darwinism," refer to the qualities of force or of relationships amid observable events. In history, however, even when we treat it in the familiar notion that all history is contemporary, we are only partially referring to the events that lie before us. More extensively, we are concerned with the recorded careers of other events that are believed likely to have occurred, and in terms of which we offer an account of the traits and features of the events that are present to us.

So this matter of description in history does make for problems. Especially it prevents any historian from ever claiming an historical statement as being an absolutely true description of the past. It can only be hypothetical, imaginary, or possible—but nothing more. The requirement deriving from this is a liberalism in the writing of history. This promotes, quite logically, the right of each historian to address himself to whatever matters he chooses, and to deal with them in ways that most suit his own inclinations and purposes. Historians need only agree, at the outset, on an interconnectedness among events, and on other such axioms as will make their narratives understandable. It is to these interconnections as they see them, and to axioms about human purpose, sequence, contextual influence, and others that they devote all their analytical skills and their scholarship. As they are able to persuade to the connections between events, they are able to provide an understanding of portions of the larger whole they are describing, or "painting into the picture." In this sense the objective public records of the past and the inevitable selectivity that is made manifest in any given historical work are so woven together, become so thoroughly integrated, that they cannot be taken apart without destroying the historical texture presented. Yet, however complete any historian's picture may be, it is never, nor could it be, the whole of what happened in history. This is a limitation that historians and students of history must learn to live with. If science is not absolute, imagine how much further from absoluteness history must be.

At any rate, as with descriptive passages in fiction, whatever descriptive elements there are in history, are—as we will show—descriptions of some metaphor of the present in which some record of the past, some symbol at hand, is the primary domain. What we are left to look for in these analogies is what only analogies will allow. Not the empirical truth of assertions made, but the logical truth; the internal consistency among the records of past events being considered is primary. What is of concern are the logically possible consequences of those records, and we evaluate and validate them within the analogies of events of the present world. Always, however, other analogies are possible; thus, so are other descriptions, as we shift analogies.

The aim of the historian is not, we may conclude, simply to reveal the face of past events in all their precise details. This cannot be his aim, since it cannot be achieved. Rather, he must aim at providing an intellectually acceptable version of change in time as the forebear of the present world that his interests have driven him to seek to explain. This he can do only by means of the frames and instruments of analogies of the present.

EXPLANATION IN HISTORY

The Covering Law Explanation.   Carl Hempel discusses at some length three different views of how historians explain whatever it is they are reporting or describing. Either they insist that they are using *covering laws*, or they look for *genetic continuity*, or they try to find *motivating reasons*. Each employs a different basic model from which historical thinking is determined and directed.[6] Hempel's own conclusion is not hidden. He shows that whatever either of the other two claims, they are ultimately forced to rely on some covering law to explain whatever it is they think they are explaining in some other way. To argue in favor of a genetic explanation, an explanation of a later event, by showing what it is genetically connected to, one must sooner or later invoke some lawful series of sequences and relationships. His illustration of how it was that indulgences became so much a part of the fifteenth- and sixteenth-century Roman church shows the reliance historians have on cause-effect consequences. Islam believed that to die in battle against the heathen meant to go directly to heaven. Christians had to wait in purgatory for eons. Because men will fight on the basis of beliefs about heaven and earth, at some point a change was introduced for Christians. The alteration held that those who died fighting pagans would have their waiting period lessened. From this genesis it is no great difficulty to trace later developments, from fighting to contributing to the sustenance and growth of the church as an institution. Each of these promised a shortening of the waiting time before one is judged worthy of an

6. C. Hempel, "Explanation in Science and History," in *Philosophical Analysis in History*, ed. W. H. Dray (New York: Harper & Row, 1966), pp. 107–23.

eternity in heaven, in the sight of God. So, Hempel argues, even the genetic approach relies on some covering law about man's behavior.

As to explanation by motivating reasons, that view that disengages itself from genetic explanations by allowing for the idiosyncrasies of people in their choices, even this can be reduced to the covering-law thesis. Hempel insists that reason means that when one is in a situation of a given type, one reasons to the appropriate thing to do in that situation. The moment you introduce the idea that in a given situation a reasoning person will do the following, you have again invoked a law, this time a law of reason as the explanation for what people do.

For Hempel, every other model is only a weakened variation, often a self-deceiving variation of the one true model of historical explanation.

Alternatives to the Covering Law.   Let us consider a different model, not because it is better but because it shows the characteristics of any historical model more clearly by contrast.

The function of explanation in history, Gallie says, still within his analogy between stories and histories, is to make it possible to follow human social developments where the story that is told is based on evidence and presented as a logically defensible, and thus a logically persuasive, account of what happened. If this is its function, then by what methods, in what ways, is it achieved? What models and what metaphors may we identify as distinctively historical, which would enable us to achieve this end? Indeed, are there any distinctively historical models? Is there a particular way that historians develop and employ metaphors that mark them immediately as historical, whatever their sources?

But now we are especially faced with the dilemma of a discipline that seems to have no special language of its own. If we are concerned with human developments, the descriptive language is either of common sense, or of the special language of more distinctive disciplines such as religion, the natural sciences, art, psychology, sociology, which are equipped to do just this. The models and metaphors that historians use are those of common-sense events in sequence, in continuity, in interconnectedness; the specifically constructed models of a more defined field. And the modes of explanation will also be drawn from the realms of common sense for the most part, as well as from the special realms that have become common but that may have had their origins in special types of inquiry. This is also clearly evident in Hempel's scientific "covering law" model.

Now if we consider writing history as analogous with telling a story, even though we acknowledge the significant difference between the evidence required to support the one that is not required for the other, then history would need no explanatory statements, as art does not. Here the role of the writer is fundamentally different from that of the scientist. But if we admit to the importance of evidence in history, whatever the character of that evidence, then the need for explanation cannot be denied.

In history, the nature of the evidence being quite different than it is in the sciences, and the character of the descriptive sentences also being different, the explanations must have a different character altogether. They will have the character of almost pure hypothesis, and will always remain in the realm of hypothesis, purely conceptual, to be tested only in a logical, *following* sense. The only evidence that can be adduced is the *logical* evidence. "Does it logically follow that from the symbolic data given, and the interpretations ascribed to the data, the event is best explained in such and such a way?" Every such explanation is at best conjectural and tentative, awaiting only logical support, the support not of overt vindication but of intellectual satisfaction. And every such explanation simply awaits the development either of additional *records* that can be shown to have been relevant and therefore structurally (in that logical sense), though not empirically, necessary. Or it waits the development of a new model of organization of the recorded data, from which other meanings can now be derived of the evidence available and accepted as relevant. (It might be, however, that with a new model, data not considered relevant now can be shown to be relevant, on the basis of logical consistency.)

In this sense, then, Hempel would surely say that a case could be made for saying that historical explanation does, after all, follow the hypothetical-deductive method of explanation claimed, for the most part, for scientific explanation. The difference, however, is to be found in those differences that cannot be eliminated; in the modes of proof that things of the world make possible, as compared to the modes of proof that records of the past will respond to. In the latter case, it would be impossible to reconstruct the whole of any segment of history, develop all the conditions that the evidence seems to imply had existed at that time, and then set the affair going again in order to see if a descriptive explanation indeed qualifies as faithful to what occurred.

We find, then, that explanation in history appears very frequently as interpretation. Explanations that are laden with interpretive features bear heavily the marks of an individual historian, and less the demonstrable lawfulness of the way things and people *will* behave in a given situation, under given conditions, in a given time and place. Thus, differences in explanations in history cannot be so readily adjudicated as they can in the sciences, either natural or social. One may reject someone's claim of what is evidence, and argue in favor of something else as evidence. But in a unique way in history, the evidence cannot be disengaged from the context that the model of inquiry has established. When Galileo peered into the heavens, the motion of the stars could be observed in a determinate, empirical way outside the context of any model of inquiry; and though it might not have been fully understood nor carefully described until some paradigm of measurement and of explanation had been introduced, its presence alone had to be taken into account. In historical explorations, the records that become evidence in a given context or model are not matters to disturb us when the model does not make room for them. Moreover, what certain records meant in one model, they do not mean in another. And the models that are employed in order to transform "raw files" into coherent evidence in order that a story be followed, depend far less on the characteristics of the evidence, and far more on the imaginative character of the model that has been borrowed or developed. Moreover, within each model evidence is treated differently. In a genetic model, for example, we must wait for more and more evidence until the whole of the event is exhausted by data. In the covering-law model, we need to add precision to the universal premises so that more accurate deductions can be made, even with the data already available. In a probable-statistical (stochastic, which we will consider later) model, more evidence will lead us to a general, lawful, predictive explanation about every such experience. In the motivating-reasons model, new evidence could compel a complete change in the explanation, a fact that is not likely to occur in any of the others.

In the physical world the pull of gravity is evident in the erratic behavior of the planets that can be observed, sometimes by the naked eye. Satisfaction achieved by sense data is very different from satisfaction in logical data. And, indeed, where the conceptual occupies as large a role as it does in history, not even the greatest amount of data is likely to prove satisfying, or promising of a fuller explanation. Quite the contrary. For the mind that is undeveloped in this logical sense, more data are likely to prove only more confusing.

Now, in light of the role of the model in historical explanations, what can we say about the objectivity of the evidence of the narrative? Only that it is as objective as the model of analysis and explanation allows it to be. Which means that even the claim to objectivity is very much compromised by individual choice. For however much we may claim that evidence exists somewhere, in some recorded form, it is some mind that chooses to make the claim and to identify it as evidence, and does so from the context of some model already in use. If there is some record, it is a record without intrinsic identity, without meaning; and whether it belongs in the narrative or not depends on the preference of the observer or the historian for this or that explanatory model.[7]

More is said about the character of historical explanation in the next segment, but perhaps it will be better illustrated in its complexity if we consider now more specifically the character and the unique functioning of what might be called distinctively historical models and metaphors.

The Models and Metaphors of History

When models from the specialized world of research in the various sciences enter into historical thinking, they must be translated into ordinary language before they are used. For history, when it is written, is only rarely written for a cognoscenti. It is directed toward the general public; its purpose is to teach something to someone about the relevance of some past of the human race to some present situation, if not directly then assuredly indirectly.

The young of every group are initiated by being confirmed into the basic models that define the group, which contain within themselves not only an account of their origins—the moral codes that the young and the old are expected to live by, the structured relationships among members—but also the vision by means of which the group lives in the world. To this extent each generation is made a historical part of that group, expected to project that group into the future by maintaining the model, with its metaphors and its myths, against all challenges. What the historians of a nation do is tell their national narratives within the context of that broad and basic model while acknowledging the variations that exist within. Of course, when among the subgroups insistence arises on giving primary allegiance to more immediate models and metaphors than to the

7. Read J. Hexter, *A History Primer* (New York: Basic Books, 1971). He demonstrates what would be a logical and thus an acceptable explanation of how a kid's pants get muddy, and what would not. Altogether a worthy and delightful work.

more distant common models that undergird them, civil acrimony in some form results. But this acrimony only underscores the role that primary and immediate models play in the lives and thoughts of people. Such acrimony, when it appears in historical writings, is as likely to be presented in a calm and reasoned way as it is in angry denunciation. But it is evident, not only in the basic disposition of the historian, the vision he is communicating, but also in the choice of the data that he weaves into his narrative, and the meanings he gives to those data. Can we doubt that this is both inevitable and unavoidable? Each historian is, after all, telling *his* story, illustrating *his* vision, presenting *his* model of humankind and things.

Compare, for example, those sections of Samuel Elliot Morison's *Oxford History of the American People* that deal with much the same material as Harvey Wish's *Society and Thought in Early America*.[8] The "Camelot" model of the former stands in remarkably clear contrast to the intention of the latter, which is to circumvent the "mountains of myths" that obstruct a clear view of this nation's history. Note, too, what an ordinary term like "revolution" comes to mean in each. Admiral Morison narrates the exciting details of wars and battles, the victories and defeats of the nation. For Wish, the social historian, revolution means revolution in institutions, attitudes, commerce, culture patterns. Not once does he describe a military battle. This is not to say that Morison is not concerned with the basic American cultural institutions, only that he treats them within the context of his "beautiful" model, always connected with heroic military deeds.

Yet what shall we read into the final short paragraph of Morison's voluminous book?

With the death of John Fitzgerald Kennedy something seemed to die in each one of us. Yet the memory of that bright, vivid personality, that great gentleman whose every act and appearance appealed to our pride and gave us fresh confidence in ourselves and our country, will live in us for a long, long time.[9]

And following this Galahadian peroration, as a coda, a half-page reproduction of eight lines of the song "Camelot." One wonders if later records coming to light would have led him to abandon his metaphor, or alter the interpretation.

8. S. E. Morison, *Oxford History of the American People* (New York: Oxford University Press, 1965).
9. Ibid., p. 1122.

I have indicated what it is that especially distinguishes historical models. This should be evident in Morison's work. Whether the models are simple or complex, the time component is imperative, for it allows us to collocate a present to some concept of the past, and vests it with the qualities we have come to know and accept about that past. If that past, as it is built into a model, is more complex, and by the inclusion of many dimensions of human possibility has become more luminous and more durable, it is nevertheless by its quality of some past that we recognize its historical usefulness. For the root meanings we are propounding or celebrating are meanings that are attached to some period past. The hold it has on intellectual appreciations and on the imagination, too, derives from what we have come to know about that past. Those models have become our traditions. It is for this reason that historians are always in part polemicists, in part story tellers, in part myth makers, in part heretics. Morison revels in a tradition that began long before the American experience but was brought forward in time by and in that experience. In Wish's history there is something inescapably heretical, for there is clear implication that he is critical of certain traditional American models of explanation and interpretation.

I need not spend any more time on the Camelot metaphor, for it has remained, even in the twentieth century, an enduring one. Part of this durable quality arises from the fact that there is a sense of wholeness about it, although the wholeness has retained a simple form. It deals with the clarity of moral ideals, of easily discovered good and just as easily discovered bad, of heroes and villains, of noble and ignoble men and women, of generosity and ungenerosity in war and in peace. It contains within itself propriety of relationships among men and women, of hierarchies of responsibilities, of the obligations that those of different classes owe to one another, of loyalty and honor, modesty and decency.

Of course, the Camelot model of historical thought can be given a different form. In *The Once and Future King,* T. E. White sets other details of that same period, but these details have now been overlaid with concepts that, in time, appeared long after the original was developed by Mallory. By combining two different periods of the past, the specific identity of the model must alter in so rude a way that it distresses those who have accepted the original model. Add Freudian concepts to the model of Camelot and put it to use in organizing and explaining America; and Generals Lee, Washington, and Grant; and President Kennedy. All will appear as different figures from when they are seen through Camelot's metaphor, untouched by the "impurities" of a later time.

What we have here is an illustration of an earlier point, that all historians are on the verge of showing quaintness in their works, for they cannot avoid the use of time-determined models and analogies in their explanations. Even when a historian is especially conscious of time boundaries, and the specific relationships, aspirations, and conceptions used to identify a particular person or society, he does so against the model of some more recent time. When J. Hexter explores the narrative form of history, the analogies he uses all derive from mid- and later-twentieth-century experiences, especially in America. And if he is delightful and wittily trenchant today, he has already prepared for his own quaintness fifty or a hundred years from now.

There is, however, nothing static in this matter of analogizing one period against the knowledge of another. As I have shown earlier in this chapter, of all known disciplines history is the most likely to be a borrower. This makes it appear that history lacks uniqueness as a discipline. For what makes for a model of a time are the selected characteristic relationships that exist at that time. These might be relationships in governance, religious beliefs, industry or agriculture, sex patterns, working conditions, education, scientific and medical developments, or linguistic forms; indeed, in all those dimensions that distinguish cultures from one another. In each of these, some discipline has made advances and has provided its own models as instruments for reaching greater knowledge and understanding. Thus, a later historian who has become versed in theories and theoretical models of psychology, sociology, or physics puts them to use in his examination of the past used as analogies for some present investigation. The historian may have come to accept, say, Konrad Lorenz's model of man as inherently aggressive and destructive, and writes of this "Camelot" of America as "ritualistic aggressiveness and expansion." And his explanation of the Indian and black experiences in this country becomes illustrative of that model. If he prefers Erich Fromm, it is not inherent aggressiveness, but the dreadful insecurity and quest for an identity that explains it. It is not surprising that one historian finds a nation's greatest manifestation of its spirit and its potential in the wars it has fought and the way it fought them, while another finds it is the Democratic Dialogue. Choose Camelot or choose Athens (historians have chosen one of these, or others, for their histories of this nation).

But the borrowing of the models of other disciplines in order to do history, to think historically, does not reduce history to the status of an applied or a parasitic discipline. When a psychologist decides to study and to explain George Washington within the strictures of his own discipline, he does not write history; he does a psychological analysis across the years. If he were to write history, he would have to direct his attention to more than the psychological data identified in his model. Although he uses his psychological models, *what* he explains are all the events that can be discerned as being part of the whole human culture-setting in which Washington lived, strove, and died. Thus, his history, as does any psycho-history, illuminates the influence of time, changing culture, and experience on his psychological facts.

Originality in historical thinking, then, is discovered in the original or the unexpected use of analogy. Military models, that is, military models of particular times, have for the longest time been the most widely used. And they have fostered specifically identifiable appreciations and understandings of the world's nations and individuals. However, it is obvious that there are others.

Robert Nisbet has written a remarkable book built entirely upon the metaphor of organic growth (a specific form of the genetic model), the life cycle of the organic things that surround us in the world, which he shows to have been one of the "taproots" of historical writing. Darwin and later investigators have endowed us with rich possibilities for variations in this model. It is, in fact, as solid an illustration as I could find of the thesis that history, in its own way more completely than any other discipline, is the act of metaphorizing from the common experiences of the present to explain the past, and of the past of one period to explain the past of another. This is the means we have not only for making that past intelligible, but also for making it coherent with our own world; giving the present a continuity with determinable origins in the past.

"No one has ever seen a civilization die," Nisbet writes, "and it is unimaginable, short of cosmic disaster or thermonuclear holocaust, that anyone ever will." [10] Nor have we seen growth and development in societies, or in cultures. Growth, then, is not to be empirically observed on the face of civilization. Yet it is characteristic of living physical things and of the works of human beings that we can see by direct observation.

Yet the whole process contains appropriate events that can be metaphorized by means of which we can think about people and societies as historical events. In its terms we may see in the careers of civilizations stages and traits that are not, in fact, visibly present to us.

10. Robert Nisbet, *Social Change and History* (New York: Oxford University Press, 1969), p. 3.

Historical thinking without metaphor is inconceivable. For it is by metaphor that what could never be seen can be seen in the events about us, in their alterations. By means of warfare models we can surely see social or national beginnings, movements toward enlargement, diminution, declines, endings. But as the military model contains within itself the metaphors of conflict, it directs us to look for "wars" of ideas, beliefs, ethnic preferences, as well as of regions and of nations. And we can see them as applied to worlds that have long ceased to exist. The effectiveness of a historical metaphor depends on the complexity of that metaphor, its scope, the details built into it, the relationships it presents. Historical models, for example, enable us by their elements to identify medieval patterns of belief and behaviors in the twentieth century.

The metaphor of growth has, recognizably, a depth and range of worth that our ordinary experiences will support. The world itself is replete with things that grow, showing beginnings, variations, further generations, additive qualities, states of arrest; all this only underscores the stages of growth, decline, and dissolution. That the metaphor has this pervasive power and force in thinking is attested to by the fact that it is, as Nisbet says, "the oldest, most powerful and encompassing" of our metaphors. Its special traits give to our histories those same traits. From newer forms of this model we look for growth that derives from the intrinsic character of events, for change that is continuous in the structure of events, that moves from stage to stage and shows fulfillment in sequential stages. But growth models of an earlier period were not always so characterized, for not all growth metaphors direct us to ends that can be divined from within their stages, so that mutations and unexpected shifts may also be detected. If the model contains a teleological element in its view of the growth of plants or animals, we have no choice but to look for the telos in the histories of individuals and societies. If there is a basic pattern of growth in the events we come to metaphorize, it becomes understandable to note that often historians, employing this metaphor faithfully, will look for those patterns in our histories. From this is it but one short, logical step to the preferring of a thesis of historical necessity in the same way that there exist stages of biological necessity in the living things about us. Isaiah Berlin writes:

> To offer historical explanation is not merely to describe a succession of events, but to make it intelligible. To make it intelligible is to reveal the basic pattern; not one of several possible patterns, but one unique pattern, which, by being as it is, fulfills only one particular purpose, and consequently is revealed as

fitting into a specifical fashion within the single 'cosmic', over-all schema which is the goal of the universe, the goal in virtue of which alone it is a universe at all, and not a chaos of unre-lated bits and pieces.[11]

That neither Berlin nor Nisbet may be supporting this particular form of the model is not important. But that they are showing how simple it is to make a metaphor and to see in history what the meta-phor permits, in the quality of that metaphor, is important. For what is a necessary characteristic in the metaphor becomes a matter of historical necessity. To refuse to acknowledge this necessary factor is to be on the verge of challenging the metaphor itself; that is, the thinking manifested in it.

By concentrating on sequence and continuity, which are parts of the growth metaphor, historians have been able to develop that con-cept of continuity in human history that might never have been other-wise developed. (I say *might* never, but I am aware of the wide range of metaphors other than that of *growth* that might have done about the same thing, or some similar thing. Even so simple and naive a metaphor as the "human *race*" could do it.) We come to look into any stage of the past for those traits that sequentially grow and become important elements of a later stage of history. From the metaphor we trace the continuities that, at last, enable us to identify and give richer meaning to our own lives, beliefs, and behaviors in the histori-cal sense of their origins in earlier periods. And in this continuity, what is ours today becomes intelligible and meaningful, for they are now clearly seen as later phases, contemporary forms of earlier stages.

More than that, what appears to us often as a puzzle in our world can be better understood when we take the pains to identify the par-ticular forms of continuity that are part of our own version of the growth metaphor, if we are using it. Cyclical growth, evolutionary growth, and emergent and irreversible growth are all possible forms of growth employed by different historians who at different times ad-dress themselves to different events to be explained.

What of other metaphors, then? The two already mentioned do not even hint at the range of models that have been developed for his-torical explanation. It is impossible to anticipate what the next fruit-ful metaphor might be. Indeed, nothing in the evidence will indicate to us how best to organize and explain that evidence. There is no a

---

11. I. Berlin, *Historical Inevitability*, quoted in Nisbet, *Social Change and History*, pp. 76–77.

priori condition that determines the metaphor. There is as much freedom in metaphoric development as there is in imagination among historians, as there are periods or moments of experiences in time that
might be metaphorized for explaining others. Toynbee's metaphor,
Challenge and Response, readily lends itself to explaining whole careers of humankind. Others have chosen machinery as the basis of a
historical metaphor; still others, a given social trait (the family structure and interrelationships); or economic theories or psychological
models transformed into metaphors for historical explanation. There
is literally no end to the possibilities, and each, potentially, has the
power to create intelligible pictures of the world we live in and the
worlds from which we have emerged.

Are all metaphors feasible? Insofar as they can give a coherent account of the evidence available, they are. Insofar as they are fruitful
enough to allow wide ranges of data to become evidence, and thus
to be given meaning in the expanding historical explanations that
illuminate our appreciations of ourselves in our world, they are feasible. But this does not also mean that any given metaphor is equal in
conceptual and empirical value to any other metaphor. The pragmatic dimension, both logically in what it includes, and empirically
in what it makes possible to us, becomes the final criterion of the
worth of one or another metaphor. And even this is not final in any
sense, at any stage. New probings and new research produce new
matters to be considered, and drive us back to look for counter-
parts in the past. But whatever historical explanations we develop
and come to employ, they are necessarily derived from the metaphors
given or created. The historian who does nothing more than put to
use the already known clichés is only concerned not to appear pre-
sumptuous.

Anatole France, in his Preface to *Penguin Island*, writes:

Why compose history when all you need do is to copy out the
best known . . . ? If you have a new outlook [in our terms, a
new metaphor], an original idea; if you present men and things
under an unexpected aspect, you will surprise the reader. . . .
Don't try to be original. . . .[12]

Unless, of course, you want to learn to think historically.

---

12. Anatole France, *Penguin Island*, trans. A. W. Lane (New York: John Lane, 1909).

7 Thinking in the Social Sciences

The softer models of the social sciences include symbol notations of realities such as motivations, aspirations, intentions, and purpose, none of which can be denotatively measured.

Between the world of things that we must come to understand and the role that the past has in nurturing maturity in human beings there is the wide and deep realm of present individual, institutional living that shapes us and is itself shaped by us. If we become competent as human beings to the degree that we learn the behaviors of the physical forces into which we are born, and if we become more mature as we learn to take into account the influences of time and change that have shaped our cultures but that we can never directly see, we become increasingly aware of ourselves as living, growing creatures able to discern in the world about us those present societal laws, rules, and institutional organizations that foster, limit, and strengthen our individual and social human potential.

But how should we treat the "laws" of society, the "laws" of economics, the "laws" of urban and rural life, the "laws" of cultural change, the "laws" of territorial imperatives (to name only some "laws")? That we identify and resolve social problems, problems arising from the fact of social transactions by means of constructed "laws" deliberately or tacitly learned, is conventional knowledge. That such laws derive from models for living has been one of our basic theses. As they are "laws" to which we address ourselves, they must surely share something in common with the "laws" of nature, which we consider at length in the final chapter. But that the term "law" can be treated in precisely the same way in these two domains is a matter that we must first consider with great care. For if it is so treated, would it not imply that the traits of the matters about which those laws are written are much the same? And would it not also imply that if they are not the same kind of "stuff," that only one application of the term might be valid and the other either metaphoric or clearly invalid?

It is of humans only that we may ask: What kinds of models determine thinking about that social domain? What are the analogies that are built into those models? What truth values do they have? We need to go even further. Why call the social sciences *sciences*? This chapter explores more fully the distinctions (and the curious and unexpected traits) between those Hard and Soft models introduced in chapter 3.

In modern views there are obvious similarities between the natural and the social sciences. In both we are clearly involved with at least three fundamental questions. One is the obvious question of what we know, or can know, within each domain. Not quite so obvious is a second question, how what is known enters into the direction of our conduct. The third asks, what is the form of verification of our beliefs? If we find agreement on these, still another problem awaits us, which is even more fundamental. The social sciences address themselves, as the natural sciences do not, to our most ordinary life relationships, of human beings with one another, individually and in social groupings. The beliefs that we hold, then, whether on the basis of demonstrable knowledge (what we can know) or on the basis of standing conventions (how knowledge directs behavior) create that fundamental question to which we must attend. So we have the questions *How shall I think about these beliefs that direct my actions? How shall I use what is known in order to think about obligations imposed upon me for action, for choice, for obedience, for making judgments of my own?* In the natural sciences such questions occur only after the "facts" have been established. Here our questions often arise before facts have been determined, but where behaviors derive from prior convictions of any kind.

When I find myself confronted by various persuasions as to what is real in the social context of my life, by a Marxist on one side, by an Erich Fromm on a second, by a McLuhan on a third, by a Galbraith on a fourth, by a Peter Winch on a fifth, by a Skinner on a sixth, by a Harré on a seventh, by a Sartre on an eighth—how shall I respond within this at-least-octahedron of persuasions? What processes shall I set to working in lieu of simply accepting what is closest to what I already believe? Shall I make all my determinations on the basis of a strictly logical analysis, where each event is assigned a symbol in a closed, neatly determined system? Shall I demand empirical verification for the claims each one makes upon me? Will such verification make choice indisputable? To be sure, both logic and experiment serve vital functions, but unhappily, each has assumptions that often

obscure the question to be answered. In the social domain every claim
made upon me compels the development of a logic of its own. Further,
each claim will direct me to some form of experimentation on matters that it will have marked out for me, and that surely will prove
out as its advocates proclaim. The more fundamental question is one
that addresses the context within which the logic and the empirical
claims have both coherence and consistency. Does either logic or empirical verification make possible a total resolution of problems of
social choice? There must be basic analogies and models that each
member of the octahedron has accepted in order to argue the validity
of his claim. How do these enter into their advocacy and my judgments? In other words, is there a way of choosing from among
these "correct" arguments?

Is there a more mature and formalized discipline that we can employ as the paradigm (in terms of methods, models and analogies,
its conceptions of nature, reality, determinancy, explanatory modes)
for inquiry into such problems?

The most obvious course in the modern world is to employ whatever we can of the models of the natural sciences. Not only do we find
here a technology for dealing with the things in nature for purposes
of developing knowledge of their behaviors, but we have both theoretical bases for such technologies, and procedural rules or agree-
ments for how one goes about developing needed theories where
none exist.

Not so obvious, yet no less persuasive, is a modern philosophical approach. Modern philosophy, having turned so resolutely to a concern
with language, with symbols for things and concepts, has developed
important and effective models for the analyses of meanings, intentions, concept relationships, and tests for truth and for falsity
about statements made and espoused.

It would seem that I am implying that neither of these provides
a proper way to develop those social scientific ways of thinking about
which we are concerned in this chapter. Such an inference, if drawn,
may be premature. For is it possible to make such hard and fast
distinctions between the various disciplines?

Ordinarily, this problem ought to be approached by trying to distinguish what each of the social sciences is trying to contribute to the
fund of knowledge we need to have in order to comprehend ourselves
and our world. So, we might ask, what knowledge can we expect from
economists, what from anthropologists, what from sociologists, what
from political scientists, what from psychologists, and what from any
others who fall within the general classification of the social sciences?
I have said enough in the previous chapters to suggest that the pre-

suppositions undergirding such questions reduce the quest for knowledge to a static affair and no longer make much sense. The question of what realities we are addressing ourselves to must also arise. Is there only one reality, the physical, which has many phases? Is the social best understood by first being reduced to the physical and then explored by the models that explain and describe the behaviors of those physical elements, because these have been so successful in their own domains?

Would this give a full account of the analogizing, the model-*making* processes we have defined as the act of thinking? Make no mistake about it, much of modern psychology argues for just this. Behaviorists have conducted innumerable experiments to prove that thinking is entirely a matter of association, and that human beings are so many physical bodies whose passive responses to external associative influences can be explained in terms of electrochemical mechanisms. If that *is* the case, then social and individual private behaviors of every kind—including model making, analogizing, and metaphorizing—are as adequately explained in mechanistic or mechanical models as are the mechanisms of things in the world.

But are there no anomalies in such explanations of human social experiences that show the limitations of the employment of mechanical models of science? Are the physical the only realities for which we must construct models and analogies? What types of models and analogies will provide us with understanding of other realities that mechanical models bring to light but do not explain?

Hard and Soft Models
in the Various Sciences

Have Hard, strictly mechanical models been used in the development of sciences of society? To be sure. Can we learn to think about those individual and social problems that readily fall within the classifications of the social sciences by means of such models? Most assuredly. It is the characteristic of thinking seen as model making and model using that we can learn to think in the ways that any model demands of us.

However, our concern is to analyze thinking about the thinking process. This obliges us to examine with greater care the assumptions of the models themselves. Hard models teach us that only that which can be verified in experiment will enter as subject matter to be considered. In this way, we are assured, we are forever freed from myth, superstition, and metaphysics. (It would be interesting, and no great task, to outline the metaphysical assumptions of those very Hard mechanistic models we have considered here.)

In this age, urging the use of Soft models (whose symbol systems include connotational references as often as they do denotative) rather than Hard seems to be proof of inadequacy, a throwback to some romantic age. Imagine, for example, someone arguing that in the sciences experiment can be dispensed with, that it need not be conceived as the centerpiece of scientific inquiry.[1] Yet the primacy given to experiment has an undeniable metaphysical basis, as well as an epistemological commitment, however many scientists stoutly deny it. For to claim that physical, empirical experiment is absolute to any possible inquiry is to claim:

1. That nature's truths can be revealed only by some empirical, experimental "pushing around" of the things in the world until they stand revealed in all their variable behaviors.

2. That the only way we can know is to experience something directly, and that the more we experience, the more we can know.

3. That *what* we know is what is empirically revealed to us, and we know it in the forms and functions that things themselves intrinsically have.

On all three grounds, experiment is the heart of the scientific method.

This classical model has so entered into the mainstream of Western thought that even to raise the question is, for most, either foolish or a pretentious challenge of simple and enduring truth (as the challenge to the existence of God was, at an earlier stage, also a brazen and perverse challenge to an obvious and enduring truth).

Yet if there has been any wit in this work, it has been shown that most of us did not arrive at this model by reflecting on what nature itself contains. Rather, we have come to see what nature contains by means of this very model that we learned, not from nature, but from our teachers. To hold to such a model exclusively is finally to replace the events of nature by this model, and to see only what the model allows us to see, *as if it were the world itself*. To deny the absoluteness of the model, then, or of any part of it (in this case, the centrality of physical experiment), sounds like denying that the world itself exists.

In recommending the use of softer models for the explanations and

---

1. M. Oakeshott, *Experience and its Modes* (London: Cambridge University Press, 1933), chaps. 2 and 4.

descriptions of the events that fall within the domain of the social sciences, let me suggest (after Kuhn [2]) how shifts are made in whatever models we use in thinking within any domain.

1. We begin by acknowledging that there is a world of events (not all of which are *things* in the physical sense) that constantly makes demands on us.

2. Human beings are characterized by actions that require the employment of conceptual contexts. These must be constructed so that impinging events come to have sequence, order, continuity, direction, and organization. But these events may or may not have such characteristics as intrinsic traits. Further, we shall never be able to get ourselves out of the way of those events long enough to know whether those orders and continuities are truly intrinsic or whether they are social facts, since we can never remove human perception from that which is humanly perceived.

3. By means of these intrusive activities, the events we perceive are given meaning, facticity, variation, value, and use.

4. These activities are themselves the acts of modeling, or analogizing, uniquely human operations to which we give such general names as "thinking" or "conceptualizing."

5. But there are always more things in our surroundings, in our encounters, than any one model could ever allow us to organize completely and without residue. These *more events* continue to impinge upon us, upon our senses, or upon the concept systems we are employing, and oblige us to reconsider whatever contextual systems we are using. We find ourselves altering them or constructing newer ones in order to give a better account of what expands before us. In such alterations we are obliged to loosen the hard demands for strict denotation, to recognize the indefinable as indefinable, and the ambiguous as ambiguous, and to allow more and more symbols of connotation to enter into newly developing models.

Science is not necessarily weakened when it does this. If this is so, then we might also see that the social sciences will not be any less scientific if it does the same. It is generally recognized that the natural sciences have not been abandoned when the strictly denotative mechanical model was abandoned. What does come to be of more primary concern, however, is the question of what events we

---

2. T. S. Kuhn, *Structure of Scientific Revolutions* (Chicago: University of Chicago Press, 1942), chap. 1.

will be concerned to symbolize into our models in order to account for them.

Characteristics of the Natural and the Social Sciences

Harré and Secord [3] have argued that what has hampered the social sciences in their efforts to become increasingly scientific is not so much that their domain resists "scientification" but that too many of the workers in these fields have too limited a conception of what science is. They have been totally absorbed by the mechanistic model. As a result, they have been treating social and individual human affairs in terms that can only oblige them to reject as significant what surely ought not be rejected. The mechanical model requires reducing the number of variables to handleable proportions, thus adhering to the Positivist's dictum of verifiability and measurability. The best way to do that is to treat all events as having the same traits of passivity as things of the world have. Thus, the variable which we call "individual perception" (by whatever name), the variable of "independent judgment" for which no determinable cause can be assigned, and all other totally independent variables, are eliminated.

But would a science of individual and social behavior derived from such a model be of much worth in the pursuit of human understanding of human beings, as individuals and as societal members? Are we, in short, explaining the same things when we employ a mechanical model as when we employ a human-perception (vision) model?

It seems clear that one thing that distinguishes the social from the natural sciences is the fact that natural science has for its specific subject matter all substances that respond determinately and predictably to stimuli. The methods developed to describe and explain those events, and the assumptions on which they rest, all derive from, or are constructed for, purposes of treating with direct, immediate examination of the already determined, passive things in the world. But in social affairs no such precise and clear determinations are to be found. So, for example, Tom Burns writes:

3. Cf. especially R. Harré and P. F. Secord, *Explanation of Social Behavior* (Oxford: B. Blackwell, 1972). One does not need to accept their Realistic metaphysics in order to appreciate the brilliant analysis they offer of the role of models as instruments for explaining matters in the social sciences.

The substantive areas of sociological studies are composed out of the way in which sociology operates upon previously organized bodies of knowledge not . . . merely upon bodies of scientific and academic knowledge, but also upon systems of belief, and codes of accepted practice . . . by questioning the assumptions which seem to be made by people . . . in authority in education, law, politics, and so forth. . . .[4]

Where models in the natural sciences are expected to make possible exploration and explanation of the structure and behavior of things in the natural world, the social sciences must sooner or later, in some way, be concerned to construct models for explaining the assumptions that undergird the activities of practitioners in the "territorial boundaries of each system of organized knowledge and practice." Thus, we find such undertakings as "the sociology of science," "the sociology of the law," "the sociology of politics," "the sociology of education." [5] In his view the substantive area of study is defined by some discipline (law, politics, education), while sociology is the way of thinking, the methodology for mapping that substance in terms of its assumptions about humankind, society, values, and the role of nature in the lives of individuals and members of groups.

What the social sciences share with the natural sciences, and with every other discipline, Burns holds, is what we have been at great pains to argue.

All branches of knowledge, scientific and other, are concerned with descriptions as well as with explanation, have their substantive content as well as their methodology, are fact-finding (*we have called it fact-making*), diagnostic or taxonomic activities as well as theoretical and model-building activities.[6]

But what kinds of explorations and what types of models, what forms of description and explanation, are indigenous to the social sciences?

DESCRIPTION IN SOCIAL SCIENCE

Let us consider what appear to be surface differences and surface similarities between descriptions and explanations in these two modes

4. Tom Burns, *Sociological Theory and Philosophical Analysis,* ed. Emmet and A. MacIntyre (London: Macmillan, 1970), pp. 59 ff.
5. Ibid.
6. Ibid.

of science. Dealing first with descriptions, there is a sense in which both can be claimed to be narrative. That is, in both cases, descriptions may be seen as a narration of changes in the events examined. A description of changes in the spectrum of color as the frequency of light increases or decreases can indeed be seen as a narrative of the event. In the same general sense a description of changes in the voting patterns of a group bound together by religious convictions is also narrative. But the differences become quickly apparent when we consider what each narrative is about. In the one, the narrative focuses exclusively on what appear to be objective, publicly determinable behaviors of events that operate in accord with the structures and conditions that actually define the event. They do not include powers of private, self-determining capacities. Even when the experimenter's intrusion alters the frequency of light, we are not measuring him as a social creature. We are measuring the physical, quantifiable fact of physical, electrical intrusion. The experimenter can be successfully replaced by some event with the equal amount of electrical energy.

In the social sciences, however, such intrusions include beliefs, aspirations, perceptions, motivations, judgment making, the powers of reflection manifest in the making of comparisons and of choices among alternatives, the act of seeking out, or of constructing alternatives not immediately present in a given situation. All these will enter into the descriptions, which must be considered to be significant elements, affecting the conclusions reached, the knowledge produced. Now, such descriptions are efforts to capture to a fuller degree all that enters into a given process, say, in the political arenas, in social and in cultural transactions, in law, in education. And because they do, the descriptions offered are more connotative and complex.

The kinds of descriptions that are likely to be adequate in the natural sciences, then, are only the first stages of social inquiry. For when they have been presented, great pains must be taken to test not only the faithfulness of that description to what can be observed, but to test also the *logical* and the *psychological* adequacy of those descriptions to the intention, perception, and motivation in those individuals or groups being described or offering the description. Thus, if it is true that what belongs to the reality we are examining is given to us in the model we use, the social model is much more complex than a physical model of reality.

In political consideration, for example, the perceptions of individuals are an intrinsic part of the narrative produced and thus become part of the subject matter to be explained by the political inquirer. He cannot long avoid the requirements of a clearer narration of the perceptions that have entered into the choices made. The statement "I voted for Jones because he has shown by his record that he is sensitive to my religious feelings" is indeed inclusive of the matters to which the social scientist addresses himself, and no part of the statement falls outside that domain. A scientific narration of an automobile accident will, in a sense, be socially neutral. But a description by the social scientist is inevitably a *version* determined, in part by where each observer (or participant) was, by the perceptions of each individual, by relationships of individuals to each other, even, perhaps, by personal histories. So a narrative here is the starting place for the quest of a more precise, and if possible, more objective description, which may or may not be possible. (One burning question that had to be answered in the Watergate hearings was what a given individual claims to have known, and beyond that, what he *should* have known, given the description of where he was at such and such a time; who he was, meaning, what position did he occupy, not only in place and in time, but in authority or in function; what evidence did he say he had and what evidence can we *assume* he had by virtue of his position of *authority*, but which he has not admitted or even mentioned?) So a beginning narrative description in the social sciences moves us in the direction of inference making, from private domains and private decisions toward normative realms. In the natural sciences both inference making and normative thinking play a part, to be sure, but not in the same way or for the same purposes as they do in the social sciences.

The kinds of instruments that are constructed to make such descriptions increasingly precise are not the kinds of instruments the scientists use. We need no questionnaires, for example (nor could we develop any), to determine why molecules behave in the random way they do. Yet, some form of a questionnaire seems to be a fundamental requirement if we are properly to describe and then explain the patterns of behavior of voters. The paradigms of inquiry that are constructed by social scientists show evidence of a concern with assumptions of preference that do not appear in standard scientific paradigms.

A problem appears in the attempt to develop such descriptions in the social sciences that never appears in the natural. For in the former, descriptions, whenever they are presented, inevitably refer to data for which there is, or could be, no empirical evidence that could ultimately be expected to serve as the test of that description. All we can expect is a justification for criteria selected, not proof of their validity. In the natural sciences, imaginary descriptions are sometimes offered of purely theoretical or conceptual events. Since the theoretical or conceptual status is acknowledged, there is no need to ascertain that the event is being faithfully presented. From such a description we turn to behavioral evidence from which the presence of other supposed empirical events can be inferred. So a description is, in part, a description of *evidence* with inferences made about the *possible* empirical states that have produced these evidences.

Yet the social sciences are much more completely empirical. There are two different kinds of data here, but both are empirical. One referential form can be readily observed and used as a check on what has been asserted. Did the accident happen? Were there two cars? What was the speed limit? The other, however, is also empirical, though it is not directly susceptible to observation. It is actual, and thus the description must extend to include that actuality. It is empirical to say that one driver was restless, the other was lost in thought. Each assumed the other was law-abiding. It is this second kind of empirical data of purpose, belief, drive, etc., that is the problem. In what sense are these empirical? Could we not argue, rather, that they are concepts, by means of which we see empirical events?

To get to this evidence we invent questionnaires whose design it is to develop connections between direct evidence (the vote) and that other domain (motives, aspirations, values, comparisons.) In the social sciences, then, there will always be these two dimensions, each demanding a place in its model of inquiry. The natural sciences do not require these inclusions. In a social science model it is not a matter only of direct and indirect evidence, and the developing of means for detecting consistencies and inconsistencies in human behavior and human judgments. It is also a matter of seeking to determine the relationships between prevailing beliefs and action produced by such beliefs. In the natural sciences we do not look for the private grounds on which the molecule will have decided to leap about at random.

In brief, models in the social sciences will have to be constructed in such forms that they will provide conditions for descriptions that will include the concepts of understanding, of deliberation, of value. Now some, like Durkheim, have argued that to do this is to prevent the development of a *science* of sociology. This we shall examine with care later in the chapter.

EXPLANATION IN SOCIAL SCIENCE

I have said that the social sciences are much more extensively empirical, direct, and indirect than the natural sciences, with their clearly theoretical procedures for dealing with sharply denoted empirical data.

In the social sciences we are concerned to explain the behaviors and conditions of different orders of events, events characterized by a far greater complexity. Of course, human beings are as much physical as the physical events that are earth, water, air, and fire. But a person is a physical thing who can produce consequences that are perhaps themselves not altogether physical. The laughter we hear is, of course, a physical fact, but it bespeaks matters that are not fully explained by its physical traits. The eye is, of course, a physical event, but perception, "seeing" events in meaningful relationship and having purpose, cannot be completely exhausted by a description of the eye. The brain is a physical event, and the ways in which traces that we call memory are left in the brain can be given a fairly complete description. But the most complete description of the brain will not give a truly adequate account of the treatment to be given to memory, or the mode of its functioning in human affairs. Nor, it has been argued, can we explain in such physical terms how human perception occurs.

Now this is not being offered in an attempt to reintroduce the existence of mystical or mysterious powers that reside within the human organism. It is not in the least bit mysterious to any of us that laughter occurs, that memory is a means of transforming the past into a power in the present, that we see a physical gesture and understand it as having a meaning beyond its physicalness. It could not possibly be mysterious, happening as it does constantly and being understood by each of us. It marks, rather, the extraordinary complexity of the physical condition of the human being, as compared to any other physical event in nature. If these are physical in origin, they are not all exhaustively explained in the language of genetics or physiology. Indeed, it is made mysterious only when the type of explanation offered for its existence and its mode of appearance declares it such, and thereafter makes any other explanation unacceptable.

This is so obvious that it must appear trivial. But as obvious as it is, it is hardly trivial when one considers that the whole effort at explanation in the social sciences is designed to deepen the understanding of just these matters, in the hope of shaping more satisfactory and more fulfilling modes of living for and among human beings.

There is, clearly, a difference in the social sciences and in the natural sciences; between asking the questions "why?" or "how is it that?" about the evaporation process of water, and asking the same questions of the "evaporation" of democracy in a given country. To recognize the metaphoric use of the term "evaporate" in the second is to prevent us from reducing the realms of the social sciences to those of the natural.

Consider, in view of the above, the question of the writing of laws in each of the two sciences. In what sense is it possible to write laws of individual and societal *human* behavior as we write laws for individual and "societal" behavior of ostriches, molecules, or stars?

We cannot answer this question simply by looking at the two different types of data identified (human and astral). If that were the approach, then we would be assuming the very answer we were seeking. We would be beginning by assuming that things have such regularity that we need only observe them in order to write laws about them. Which means that we begin with the view that things themselves behave in lawlike ways; therefore, we can write laws about them. ("Things" now meaning human beings, molecules, stars, and ostriches.) But the data of the social sciences help to prevent this question-begging process because here there are so many variables that the very assumption of regularities is cast into doubt. If, therefore, we are to write social laws here, the ability to go beyond the data denotatively given is a basic requirement.

Traits of the Analogical Content of the Social Sciences

The apparent differences between the models of the natural sciences and the models of the social sciences lie in the types of analogies that each selects to develop in some coherent, confrontable form. The differences between the laws of nature and the laws of individuals or of societies are not trivial. If we decide to employ "natural" laws (the laws of the nature of things) to explain societal and individual behavior, we will find ourselves employing concepts such as the behavior of molecules and of atoms to organize the data of social experience. It must be remembered that the terms "atom" and "molecule" are not specifically created to name existential events that will be seen under given conditions or will one day be seen under certain conditions of mechanical advancement. They are, frankly, theoretical terms that do *not* seek to identify substances in time and place. They refer, if they refer to anything, to deliberately constructed elements of a theoretical picture, not so much of the world, but of a world that subserves the world of experience. From such an analogy, then, we would be creating a like conceptual realm for the social realm requiring explanation. Terms like "social-political," "institution," or "territory," though actually dissimilar, would have analogical similarity to "atoms," "molecules," "nucleus," and the like, and, indeed, sociologists do talk of "molecular families," "nuclear institutions," and so forth.

Science creates models of this theoretical world quite often by using objects as analogues for the nonempirical world they are seeking to establish. So, the wave behavior of water was used to suggest the behavior of the elements theorized as the substructure, or inner structure, of light. What science actually develops is a metaphor of the *process* of some observable event to be used as a basic analogue of which the model of the explanation is to be created.

Methodologically at least, in the social sciences it is not different. We are concerned to construct analogies of processes of substantive relationships. Such relationships are what they are in time and in space. A model in the social sciences turns out to be one segment of direct empirical experience being used as an analogue for another directly experienced event. The purpose of the analogy is clearly the same in both fields. What makes for the difference, however, are the detailed particulars in the analogies created.

We have shown how the mechanical model carries with it the obligation to devote all exploration to what can be directly observed and thus to what can be denotatively described. It is important to note that one result of this is what is known as scientific neutralism, the treatment of events in the context of cause-effect relationships. This is the view that human beings behave in described ways because behavior is determined by external causes. Even moral choices are explained by means of mechanical analogies.

Questions of the *why* of beliefs are not the concern of these social scientists, except if they can be answered from within the substantive model employed by yet another description. "I believe X because I live in a society that believes X."

But, of course, not all social scientists have limited their efforts to such a purely descriptive approach. Talcott Parsons, for example, is openly concerned to develop *theories of society*. In doing so he argues against the view of the social sciences as being simply a description of particulars that can be made into generalizations, as is often claimed for the natural sciences. Nor can the problem be solved, he argues, simply by arbitrarily borrowing theories of other disciplines and applying them to the data of the social sciences. "Neither the theory of mechanics in the older sense, nor that of nineteenth century physiology would be adequate if simply 'applied' to the behavior field." [7]

The social-structure models that Parsons looks for will not be limited to precise descriptions of behavior, though they will, of course, be constructed with relevance to them. And the theories of another day must be translated into a new language that adequately symbolizes the data now awaiting explanation. But the model itself, if it is applicable to described data, has more in it than that. Some theory, and a derivable law from that theory, will also be present, providing the context for the inquiry, so that from some law and a conclusion reached in respect of that law, we are able to explain how a particular case fits within the model being employed, and a resolution to a problem can be adduced.

For example, we want to explain why busing children from schools in a rural setting to an urban center is justified. The model we use contains a theoretical law of democracy; say, that democracy entails two basic freedoms, the freedom of intercourse among people within groups, and freedom of intercourse among the groups themselves. From this context, it is reasonable to conclude that democratic education is achieved by preparing for such freedom of intercourse among all children. Busing, then, is one such case of behavior that promotes freedom of intercourse, and fits into the whole model consistently and coherently.

Both empirical description and other theories become the sources for the analogies Parsons will develop, though the analogical character is not being offered as a faithful description of some other dimension of experience. It remains just that, an analogue of relationships of some set of substantive events. It is only from such analogies that explanation and interpretation are brought back into the social sciences, from which the Positivist approach had "freed" them. [8]

Laws of Nature and Laws of Individuals and of Society

Every science, as it goes about the business of describing and explaining the structure and function of things in the world, ends with the writing of laws about those traits and behaviors. In the natural

7. T. Parsons, ed., *Theories of Society* (Glencoe, Ill.: Free Press, 1961), p. 32.
8. See esp. T. Parsons, *The Social System* (Glencoe, Ill.: Free Press, 1951), chaps. 1 and 2.

sciences they would be laws about motion, change, mass and energy, of time and of space. But what would they be about in the social sciences? Perhaps one of the bases for the constant disputes among social scientists lies precisely here. The subject matter of those descriptions, the explanatory and predictive laws is in dispute. What one should consider to be societal facts, about which laws are to be written, are matters of profound disagreement. Indeed, are "social facts" the kinds that can have laws written about them? If we are to have a "pure" science here, and if the natural sciences are our paradigms, then laws must be written. Else how is social inquiry to continue to mature? But the ambiguities that cluster about the potential data are obviously a primary cause for the continuing absence of clarity in even delimiting the field. Disputes over what can be or what ought to be studied issue forth into an even more crucial kind of a dispute, a dispute over what the purpose of social science study is, or should be.

PURPOSES

If we accept narrowly the natural sciences as our primary paradigm for establishing laws of human and social behavior, we will, of course, look for the same kind of data about which those laws can be written. We will look for *movement*, and *change*, for natural *generation* and equally natural *degeneration* of elemental structures. But we must assume with such a paradigm that the elements of human and social behavior are, if not identical, at least similar enough to the elements of matter for the writing of such laws. We would have to be able to identify material conditions, sequences, and interactions in the human body, or in the "body politic," for the laws to be about. We would also have to have evidence for, or at least assume, a passivity in these events, that we could include in our primary models of their behavior, similar to the passivity of things in the natural world. In this way, laws of society and of human, individual behavior could take the form of causal laws, laws that describe, explain, predict, and interpret the regularities of that behavior. Examples abound of such laws among the writings of Behaviorists and of those who see the world as an entirely determined event, even unto its human components. The Marxian view is a form of this, although it admits to difficulty when it conjectures on later phases of development in human evolution.

The broad alternative to this model of man and society is, as Harré and Secord indicate, one that replaces the elemental characteristic of *movement* with that of *action*. Basically, the argument is this: The individual is not moved by external influences alone; he or she *chooses* to act upon personal perceptions, beliefs, knowledge, expectations, aspirations. As these alter or differ among individuals and in different societies, the actions taken or the actions deliberately repressed must necessarily differ. Though such a model would be softer than the models of the natural sciences, it is argued, they would be taking into account characteristics of human potential that mechanistic models just ignore.

In this shift the redirection of the purposes of laws of social and individual behavior between the two can be also distinguished. In the mechanistic model, the purpose is to find with increasing exactitude those causal stimuli which move individuals and groups to behave in what discernable ways? In the other, the laws would have to make room for symbols of deliberate judgment as a fundamental element in human behavior.

The first would, of course, be easier to write; the second, more difficult because it would have to be so full of variables that they could not be firmly anchored into lawfulness.

WHAT ARE SOCIAL LAWS EXPLANATIONS OF?

In this seemingly simple distinction, we find one of the most familiar arguments about the social sciences. Is the study of the social sciences to be limited in its concern to the *forms* and movements of social organization, seen as so many units of movement, whose basic powers derive from some coherent, passively responsive nucleus? Or must we struggle with it, even as we know that it cannot be defined or demonstrated to be regular in physical experiment? The argument shows no signs of being settled. Some have argued that the human being, as an individual, as a behaving, choice-making creature, is the achievement of a social group. Others, with equal vigor, have argued that societies come into existence as contracts or compacts are agreed upon, even if these are made only tacitly, reflecting cognitive responses to external demands. Still others have argued that the debate is a meaningless one since what is described as "social" is the behavior of individuals seen collectively. When we talk about organizations or institutions, we are talking about *individuals* in group situations (that is, either as passive responders or as self-determiners of action, depending on the status and choices of members of the group). Whatever view is accepted leads to a decision, for example, on whether or not there is such a field as *social psychology*. Pragmatists have chosen this third alternative, and in the social sciences they are represented by such investigators, in addition to John Dewey, as George Mead, Gordon Allport, and Hadley Cantril. Opposed to these are Freud and Adler, on the side of the individual, and Watson and Skinner on the side of social determinism.

Let me illustrate just what is involved in this struggle among the different model-adherents, by showing a pattern for recommendations for writing laws of behavior, first in the context of the physical model, and then what happens when there is a shift into the context of the second, the activity model, say, of a Deweyan.[9]

Maurice Mandelbaum presents an example of a common-sense problem. He talks about going into a bank and drawing out money by following the rules for such withdrawals that the bank has established. Now, suppose you had been with a Trobriand Islander who knows nothing about banks. He asks you to explain what went on. You describe each phase of the transaction, and with it the role of each phase in sequence, and the rule followed at each step. What we have here is a "rule-established" situation from which we present a description of the behaviors of each of the people involved, the influence or direction exercised upon them, the conditions of passivity required of each law-abider, and the causal sequence of events.

If more than a cursory description is called for, if you wanted to assure yourself of being understood, you might add more specific details in the context of the model. You might move to a more complete description of the banking system, both in this particular bank and in the state or nation as a whole. You might further include a description of the status and role of each member of the transaction; of the part played by the building; the function and the features of the money exchanged; the relationship between deposit and withdrawal; and the limitations each aspect of the activity places on all others.

However more detailed you become in a situation so defined, it would appear that you are not really concerned with the *development* of laws (for these already exist), but rather with a description of the rules in effect in a given situation, which you are following. The description implies that these described rules and behavior patterns prevail in every bank in the country, and that every aspect of the money transaction is a phase of following those rules. The descrip-

9. In A. Ryan, ed., *Philosophy of Social Explanation* (London: Oxford University Press, 1973), chap. 6.

tion of this law is an explanation of the transaction, and this description sets out the social facts.

CONTENTS OF LAWS OF SOCIETY

Now let us shift to the Activity model, that third form mentioned. We respect the orderliness of the sequence of rules that are established, and followed, and appreciate the added fact that such rules are followed, with unimportant variations, in every bank in the state or nation. But the broader model, which contains symbols of the relationship between this banking act and a range of other human transactions, of which this particular act is an analogue, obliges us to explain what we have seen in the wider context. We then develop descriptions in which saving money by depositing it and following the rules of withdrawing that money can be better understood as we come to understand a whole range of "putting out and getting back" activities. The rewards derived from contributions to religious associations, in family living, moving from one social status to another within a structured society, getting married, or preparing for one's burial are all analogues of the rule-following banking activities, and the explanation of these includes not only the rules followed, but also the human purposes on which such social transactions rest. Here are included the deliberative, cognitive activities that mark the shift from accepting a description as an explanation to offering an explanation of what has been described. The assumption of passivity in those who follow rules, as if all action is both described and explained as direct response to immediate stimulus, is replaced by an assumption that purpose in the individual must also be accounted for, and makes the writing of new laws an important phase of continuing human transactions.

It is, thus, not only the subject matter that the social scientist ought to address himself to that is central to the thinking in the social sciences, but what level of generalizations, and what kinds of generalizations; above all, what analogies shall be developed in order to serve as the subject of inquiry. What laws, about what behaviors, shall we be concerned to construct? Such laws as can be written would be expected to apply with equal relevance to economic institutions, or to the human being as an economic individual, societal institutions (family, clan, in various horizontal and vertical relationships), anthropological patterns of relationships, political institutions, as well as individual political behaviors. From this approach we would identify the social sciences as a concern with a diversity of specific human (individual and social) concerns within a unity of thinking which is defined by some explanatory model and with the law-full statements that can be derived from those models.

The Language in the Models
of the Social Sciences

It is indicative of at least one form of the movement toward making a more fully developed science of the social sciences that its analyses are increasingly cast into mathematical terms. To be sure, this does not always sit well with many sociologists, and even less so with non-professional people who read sociological studies for advancement of their own knowledge or for guidance in respect to their own affairs. For such a linguistic system seems to sterilize the problem for which answers are being sought. Uniquely human and humane variables are reduced to the unitary character of this most abstract of symbol systems. Insurance companies, for example, and college registrar's offices reduce the whole, lovely, appealing (or appalling) complexity of problems of each individual member of each individual social group or subgroup to a quantitative system where these lovely (or deplorable) traits and personal identities are eliminated in the interests of whatever efficiencies a particular institution is seeking. Life insurance companies increasingly offer policies to all people, not after the specific examinations by means of which risks are sorted out, but without physical examination. They do so by quantitative groupings in which those individual promises and problems do not enter into the calculations, except as unitized notations of response in a range of possible causal conditions. Yet we cannot deny that as a result more people are insured than ever before, more people are registered in more efficiently controlled school spaces and times, and insurance companies and colleges grow larger than ever. (Of course, the very fact of size, of continued growth, then becomes a new problem for the social scientist to explore, explain, and interpret.)

Nevertheless, rapid registration and the attainment of a seat in a course do not answer the fundamental questions that appear inevitably to arise. There is always the question of the worth of the work, and the quality sought. There is always the question of specific consideration of the individual insured making a claim. Will the employment of mathematical language make possible decisions at this level? Can the perception of value, which derives its force from an ever widening context of concepts as well as of operation, be taken into account by a language whose effectiveness is achieved by the reduction of events into quantified units? More important, what is gained and what is lost when such efforts succeed? Is the study of society and of the individual as a social component, in such a language, and in the analogues limited to its calculus, able to account for all behaviors as that same language can of the behaviors of the subject matter of the natural sciences?

In *Hard Times* Dickens allows Mr. Gradgrind to give an exclusively quantitative description of a horse, from which very little of the appearance, or the behavior, or the quality of the horse could ever be recognized. What is offered is precise and clear, but unfortunately the *sense* of the horse does not appear at all.

Molecules, atoms, protons, electrons, and structure are all part of the vocabulary of the science of physics. But when the term "structure," for example, appears in both vocabularies, shall we take it to mean that both things and human families are analogues of one another? The activist model holds that the "structure" of a society embraces reason, purpose, disposition, motive, belief, choice; none of these traits are present in an acceptable description of the structure of the atom. When these traits are ascribed to the atom, we are in the presence of an imaginative metaphor that has been developed for purposes of increasing human comprehension. But clearly, it is an example of the pathetic fallacy, perhaps even of catechresis.

What is referred to by terms that may be used in common by both vocabularies is frequently different, not in degree but in kind. This difference in kind between the substance of the physical and social sciences points to the differences between the denotative language of science and the connotative; or, as Harré and Secord say, the *ordinary* language by means of which social matters are usually talked about. When the symbols of the natural sciences are imposed upon social matters, all social and individual movements ought to be comprehended in them. The very language renders the events passive and determinate. In the social *arena,* however, we quickly recognize that the symbols themselves become the instruments that the members of the society use to maintain certain behaviors, foster them, or change them. And this, too, marks a profound difference in kind between the models of the two approaches to social inquiry. For, in the one, the substance does not alter when symbolized or named; in the other, the symbols are not only used, they produce effects as symbols, and are analyzed in the terms of the consequences that their use produces. In the one, language denotes; in the other, language is action.

Things of the world share energies with one another. Individuals and societies share not only energies but *ideas* about energies, and along with these, statuses, aspirations, motives, intentions—all concepts that are as much a part of that world as quantifiable energies are elements of the world of things. Yet, if we cannot be as precise in our language in the social sciences, we can, in terms of models of explanation, be as successful in the pursuit of that understanding that is the aim of any science. The adherents of this action model will argue that if we do not impose upon ourselves the demand for an unnecessarily narrow denotative precision, we will undoubtedly achieve a greater understanding in this far more complex arena of investigation than strict adherence to paradigms of the natural sciences will allow. The scientific process will still be fulfilled. But it demands that we do not simply import the language of the natural sciences. For then it becomes a jargon that obscures, rather than a language that fosters understanding.

Hypotheses, Hypothetical Descriptions, and Explanations in the Social Sciences

In some of the social sciences, notably in economics and in political science, the concern for prediction appears central. In others, prediction, as well as retrodiction, while not a primary concern, is certainly one among a number of objectives. Where this is the case, laws are sought that will contain descriptions of the regularity of behavior in societies. From such laws prediction and retrodiction would indeed become possible. We had earlier concluded that the focus on prediction has been shown to be insufficient and at times impossible, and thus perhaps not as central to science as it was once held to be. In the social sciences it may even be less so. If this is the case, then hypotheses and explanations are constructed for very different purposes and will take very different forms.

Laws of nature that describe regularity in the behaviors of things in the world do indeed make prediction possible. For, having discerned such regularity and its conditions, laws are actually statements of later states of an event, and of the stages through which it will pass until that state appears. But where it is not possible to demonstrate that the laws indeed describe the regularity of processes as well as a regularity in the conditions of events that show these processes, the laws, we have shown, are at best only accidental regularities (which we discuss in the next chapter).

The moment that the cognitive and the emotional domains enter as part of the empirical data to be explained, the likelihood of the conditions of regularity diminishes to such a point that their appearance can be attributed only to deliberate institution on the part of the inquirers. For, once the subject of inquiry becomes cognizant of events about him, including the inquirer's own involvements, it becomes increasingly difficult to determine that lawlike regularity is being manifest.

A simple distinction can be made here. There are events in nature whose behaviors are clearly lawlike. There are other events (human beings as individuals and as societal members) that *learn* to behave lawfully. In the first case law is descriptive, explanatory, sometimes predictive. In the second, law is recognized as normative, and contains within it, sometimes explicitly, sometimes implicitly, notations of approval and disapproval, reward and punishment. In the social sciences law can contain both traits. In the natural sciences only the first form is present. We learn the ways in which questionnaires (or tests) are given, and we respond, sometimes to the questions, sometimes to the questioner, sometimes to our own needs of the moment, sometimes in order to manifest independence or submissiveness, or any number of other *reasons*. (For, in this domain *reasons* replace *causes* in an explanation.) This directs the questionnaire makers working from the mechanical model to attempt to construct "foolproof" instruments. That is, they seek to have the questions answered "intuitively." Responses ought to be to the questions themselves, as absolute and isolated, in some autonomic form. To answer on the grounds of some private cognitive choice lessens the validity of the answers because independent variables have been intruded. But there is no possible way that this can be achieved as it could be achieved, for example, when Newton "put the questions to nature," and nature responded according to what he had marked out as nature's intrinsic laws. It has been wisely said that once human beings begin to think, it is never possible to predict where they will come out. Once a society begins to act with increasing consciousness, the future of that society becomes less and less predictable.

If this be so, then hypotheses and explanations do indeed come to serve different functions than they do in the natural sciences. In fact, they become not so much the instruments for prediction as the instruments for instruction; means for attaining to the *ends* for which norms have been established. So we may posit the idea that both hypotheses and explanations in the social sciences are persuasive instruments as much as they are the means of expanding the understanding of the present or of predicting the future. Every hypothesis appears as a preference of the hypothesizer, and every explanation turns out to be a justification of the hypothesis and the laws that have been constructed to guide behavior. Thus "scientific neutrality," so cherished in mechanical models, disappears in human involvement. Social science inquiry comes to be inescapably polemical in its character, rather than exclusively analytical. It is bound to concern itself as much with moral rules as it is with behavior determined by the natural biophysical structures of individuals or of societies. Thus, the hypotheses of the social sciences are rarely, if ever, verified as true, or proven false in an empirical sense. Aspects of a hypothetical proposition, of course, will be shown to be vindicated by evidence here and there, but the proposition as a whole is more than just the sum of its parts. If I say you ought to stop smoking because smoking *causes* disease, you may well agree that evidence vindicates me, but that that statement alone is not sufficient *reason* for not smoking any longer. You have better reasons for continuing (relaxation, keeping weight down, the lovely taste of inhaling, how well you look with a pipe or an elegant cigarette holder).

In the social sciences hypotheses come close to the status they have in the modern, nonmechanistic view of the natural sciences. They are held to be axioms that cannot be tested, and thus cannot be demonstrated to be either true or false. Here, hypotheses set ground rules for mutual inquiry and make possible a common undertaking. In fact, they are best seen as recommendations for ways of talking together, exploring together, working together.

Consider this hypothesis:

> If social order is to be developed and maintained, then it is necessary to develop social ceremonies in the form of social dramas within which the traits and features of the desired social order are illustrated and communicated.[10]

The axiomatic part of the propositions suggests a relationship between ceremony and social order. Now this may look just right, but since the primary terms are undefined (social order, ceremonies, social dramas), it is not an assertion so much as it is an invitation or a

10. Hugh Dalziel Duncan, *Symbols in Society* (London: Oxford University Press, 1968), p. 183.

recommendation for a way of looking at some as yet undefined empirical set of events. Thus, it becomes a means for giving names to events and for developing descriptions, but it is not itself a description of any events whatever.

From such a statement, however, we are now required as much to move backward into an explanatory activity as to move forward into a further exploration of events, which will be made to fit the hypothesis. The hypothesis needs to be explained. And with it there needs to be introduced a justification of the grounds of that hypothesis. From the justification and the explanation will appear a moral choice, too, for it will not be enough simply to offer a metaphysical statement supposedly reporting on the human-social condition of individuals and society. Thus, the value judgment arises logically from some mutual consideration of the hypothesis. Duncan's term "drama" already is a clear hint of this, and the argument that ceremonies should be dramatic requires justification as well as an explanation of its role in societal human affairs.

Is Duncan implying that "social ceremonies in the form of social dramas" are intrinsic elements to social life in the same way that hydrogen and oxygen are intrinsic elements of water? If he is, then his explanatory system is identified with the explanation of molecular behavior, or the behavior of elements of nature. If not, if he is being consciously metaphoric, implying no identity of relationships between social acts and physical components, then his explanation will not only have a different character, but it will also perform a different specific function. It will perform the function of connecting acts into a totality, a continuity, in which each phase is connected to an ensuing phase by conscious reasoning and purposive action.

Moreover, if causal explanations are adequate in the natural sciences (and doubt has grown about even this, as the ranges of the behavior of increasingly numerous data makes applicability questionable), it is going to be even more difficult to demonstrate that it is meaningfully applicable to the complexities and varieties of data of the social sciences. The Positivist behaviorist's attempt to establish causal explanations for human and societal choices and actions must of necessity eliminate all connotative aspects of language. We can deduce, in a very tentative way, some conclusions from some observed behaviors, or available empirical evidence. But are we dealing with a domain from which necessary deductions could be made? Even with the addition of more and more evidence to justify such a deduction, it is still only that, a justification and not a necessary, empirically true conclusion.

Even descriptions in the social sciences partake of this reasoned and purposive characteristic. No description in the social sciences could possibly be complete. It is always partial, for there is always more in the event than is being reported at the moment. As we get closer to one part of some event, we become aware of other parts that are either in some empirical or in some conceptual way entailed in what we are bent on describing. To describe an act leads us further to discovering the need to describe some perception of that act, and then some aspect of the motivation for the act, the expectations sought in the performance of the act, the beliefs that undergirded the act, and so on, endlessly expanding or narrowing in precision, fully aware of further elements present.

Nor can the explanation of what has been described be any more complete than the description. From a model of reasoning and purposiveness we cannot expect to exhaust the meanings of social experiences. We settle for fitness rather than for exactitude. No one has ever given a complete explanation of any war ever fought, or is it possible to do so. Every new discipline arising within the social sciences only adds another panel to the whole mural of social-human events to be described and explained. Only probability explanations will serve, and in terms not of the elemental structure and movement of events, but of ranges of the possible in human action that come into view as the inquiry deepens. Thus, even the precision of the insurance rate system is not as precise as it would seek to make itself, neither in terms of describing the possibilities of accident or disease nor in terms of the payments to be demanded and paid. And not all of the explanations for the improvement of the precision in the registration of students will account for all that enters into the problem of accepting students into a school and sorting them out, administratively, so that each will have the education he or she desires.

Models and Metaphors
of the Social Sciences

In his analysis of societal needs and behaviors, Duncan frankly develops the concept of the drama (that is, the presentation of a play on a stage) as a metaphor by means of which he explores social relations in all their variety. The metaphor presents every societal fact as some aspect of a drama being played out. In its terms we look for beginnings, middles, and ends. We find ourselves looking for the various *acts* in a coherent development, including certain portions that are introductory to conflicts that can be expected to arise, to expect its development, to identify the "plot," to be prepared for the rising tensions that make for the plot, to await the dénouement and the final resolution. (To say that you see nothing like this in any segment of social data being examined is only to say that you have not accepted, and therefore have not used or do not understand the "dramatic" metaphor.) But even more interesting, the metaphor comes to take on the meanings of the data to which the metaphor had been applied, and social problems are not only understood as dramas, but when dramas are presented on the stage, we look into them for presentations of individual and social struggles.

Thus the thinking process in the realm of social and individual actions and transactions. The metaphor gives specific quality of traits to human events. And the metaphor itself is enriched by the data to which it is applied, to the point where it comes to be institutionalized. The metaphor itself becomes an institution of intelligence.

If this be so, and apparently it is, then we derive some direction as to what metaphors we might choose for our explanations and descriptions in this vast domain, and what we ought to avoid.

I earlier suggested that the sources for these metaphors lie all about us in our present world, in our past, in our perceptions in the present, in our imaginations. Some metaphors will mislead, and move us in a direction farther from the deeper and fuller understanding of this complex domain of experience. But to argue that the data themselves suggest the metaphor *and* that some are intrinsically wrong is a curious argument, for this implies that those data are already, in a sense, comprised of their own conditions or traits to be taken into account in the analogies we construct. It is far more defensible, in the light of the arguments we have pursued, to accept the view earlier presented, that the similarities that exist between events are created, not by those actual events, but by the metaphor chosen. And when we note the responsiveness of events to an ever widening range of metaphoric development, we can also observe that any known matter can be used as the basis of the metaphor for anything we are attempting to explain. The machine is just as much available as grounds for metaphor as is the drama, or the mystery story. It may take time for an unexpected metaphor to take hold as an explanatory model, and indeed, some may never offer the illuminations that will satisfy minds in quest of understanding. The tests of the merits of any metaphor lie in an evaluation of the data that have been included, the narrative they make possible, and the comprehensions that result.

Using the machine as the content to be metaphorized in order to

explain human behavior requires only that there be observable behavior. We begin with that. If there were no behavior, there would be
no need to explain it. To select the machine as the metaphor, therefore, and to examine that in order to understand all that comprises
human behavior in the world is now to have a means for describing
that behavior. It may not be as effective as another metaphor, sourced
elsewhere. However, in itself it does serve its metaphoric function to
a highly effective extent. The worst we can say, and it is surely bad
enough, is that it excludes everything but the logic of mechanics. It
becomes, as Edgar Johnson once wrote about autobiography written
from such models, "too orderly, too severely patterned, to convey all
the richness and variety of episode needed to suggest the events . . .
of [life]. [It must not be] crushed into a sort of intellectual geometry."

Within its own logical structure, any metaphor in which that logic
is properly developed can be expected to be irrefutable. If such a
metaphor is abandoned, it must be abandoned only after its application, on the empirical grounds that there are social data or individual
behaviors that this particular metaphor has not given meaning to,
has not absorbed into the coherent picture being presented about the
ordinary social world.

The metaphor of divine authorship of the social-anthropological-
economic-political world in which we live has run into constant difficulties when the impulsive behavior of individuals and of societies
contradicts the logic of the implicit planning of a divine author. And
the use of individual behavior as a metaphor for the explanation of
social behavior, as when we talk, for example, of the "mind of the
crowd," the "goals of the state," or the "deliberations of the courts,"
has both the power to illuminate and the conditions to mislead us into
thinking about the state, or society, *as* an individual.

Nevertheless, some metaphor must be used here. For "metaphor,"
writes Nisbet, "allies itself well with proposals for social action . . .
visions of revolution that we find in the Western tradition spring from
diagnoses that are at bottom metaphoric." [11]

Consider the metaphoric uses that have been made of Darwin's
theory of the evolution of the human species, and the accompanying
"descent" of man. Not too long after it was presented to the world,
and its contents studied, the provocative character of its possibilities
as explanations of matters far beyond the flora and fauna about which
it was first developed became evident. Its most interesting transformation appears in the form of a model for explaining the character

11. R. A. Nisbet, *Social Change and History* (London: Oxford University Press, 1969),
    p. 6.

and the rate of change in human societies. It became the metaphor which we know as Social Darwinism, widely used for explaining change, development, and mutations of almost every aspect of the matters that comprise the social sciences. From the "filters" of biological change and the conditions and structures of that change, Spencer, Sumner, Dewey, and a great many other social inquirers developed explanations of the change in the economic, the familial, the political structures that comprise society. If the problem of determinism, which was one of the elements of the theory of biological evolution, produced similar dilemmas in the explanations of social change, it nonetheless became the most formidable and widely accepted model of explanation of social change and development of the twentieth century.[12]

The career of this metaphor has an interesting added dimension. When a new metaphor is introduced, it is rarely, if ever, a matter of introducing a metaphor where none existed. We become aware of the fact that people are always about the business of developing some explanatory model of their world. Indeed, the understanding of any culture is reached in an understanding of the root metaphors on which the culture rests.

Before the Darwinian metaphor was developed, among the most widely used was the Augustinian Christian metaphor of divine creation, and the continued divine concern with what was created. The Darwinian metaphor, therefore, was greeted with a variety of intellectual and emotional reluctances from among those who had accepted and had long since ceased to question this Augustinian metaphor.

But Augustine's metaphor has, itself, a historical source, and a consequent history. Nisbet explores the way that Augustine developed this particular metaphor, and the grounds on which he did so. Born pagan, converted in middle life to Christianity, and educated in Greek concepts of physics and metaphysics, which included the Aristotelian concept of causality, Augustine shaped a model of growth and change in the world in which he included then-current concepts of the nature of matter, of cause, and of the Uncaused Cause. To these he added the Christian thesis that all these things were bound together in the overarching concept of the uncaused birth of Christ, God, the Son of God, and finally, the Holy Ghost. Within this model, generation, dependency, responsibility, moral law, and even the concept of time were given definition. Thus, the City of Man became an

---

12. Read especially Darwin's introduction and chap. 5.

imperfect image of the City of God, seeking constantly to reach its own idealization in that transcendent city, but unable to do so by the very nature of its reality. These derived from his model. Other models developed, of course, to make man and society understandable after Augustine; yet his has lingered.

The distress caused by the transformation of the Darwinian theory into a new metaphor and an extended model for explaining the same societal and individual data is understandably sharp. The thundering denunciation, the polemic, the derision heaped on it only underscore the fact that the model of explanation now being offered was more than an academic matter. As with all such social metaphors that serve as the justification for perception, for choices and for beliefs, the alternative shattered a metaphor that had offered a complete structuring of the world and its inhabitants. This is the career of every metaphor of explanation in the social arena. Its shattering effects come primarily to those who, in time, have accepted some metaphor as a literal account of the world now, the world before, and the world that must necessarily come.

Those who seek to explain social behaviors against the metaphor of the "drama of living" are not considered to be very serious about life by those who are bound by the metaphors of the "ledger," with its debit side and its credit side, and the accompanying view that government, and indeed all social relationships, including the handling of the arts, are best seen as a matter of business.

What are we called upon to explain and describe within the arenas of the social sciences? Clearly, the behaviors of human beings as individuals with mental activity, as members of social groupings of a great many kinds, in which judgment making must be given an accounting. We are confronted with the problems of human origins, not simply as physiological events in nature, but as creatures possessed of human quality, of language, of a capacity for symbolic means of communication; creatures enculturated into beliefs but who challenge them, who behave, who strive for goals, and who relate to persons and things as human beings do. We seek to explain the relationship between individual choices and the social milieu in which such choices are made. We need to explain the modes of behavior among groups, and the effects of these on individual members. We look for explanations of the ways humans endure, establish their economies for living as individuals and as groups. We need an explanation of human perception, and the role that this plays in all the relationships identified as social. In his own ways, every social scientist, with whatever models he chooses, includes these data, ascribing to them meanings consistent with his metaphors.

This last dynamic of human coherence will probably mark the difference in the metaphors used in the social sciences from those in the natural. Let me give a variation of an example I have already used. In the natural sciences, the familiar metaphor is found in the treatment of light as moving in waves. For purposes of physical understanding, it would be a totally inadequate metaphor to suggest that we consider light as moving with the stealth of a leopard. Indeed, such a metaphor would already reduce a scientific problem to a mythology, for it would be a metaphor that would be so inappropriate that it would die at the moment of its recommendation. But it would not be at all foolish to suggest this as a metaphor for *human* behavior. Indeed, much of the work of an experimenter like Lorenz begins with the provocative question as to whether a human being is best analogized to a wolf, or a rat, or a bird. But to suggest that these qualities are also the qualities found in the structure and motion of light and light molecules is clearly to invest light with anthropomorphic qualities.

We are left to make this final observation. When living substances, or events, are used as metaphors to explain the inanimate things of the world, science becomes literature encrusted with the pathetic fallacy—usually in the genre of science fiction. But when living things are used as metaphors for living things, our models will indeed be softer than in physics, but the social sciences will have a chance to become increasingly understandable, and in their own ways, scientific in their quests, and free of the danger of either dissolving into the arts or pretending to a precision not worth attaining.

8 Scientific Thinking

The Hard models of science are comprised of symbols for data and for concepts that transform those data into subject matter of coherent continuities.

What science is and what scientists do has been distilled into a conclusion of simple clarity through the centuries, and it has contributed to belief in the unchanging within the dynamics of existence. "Science," this conclusion holds, "is a *body* of knowledge, verified in observation and experimentation, and scientists are the seekers of that knowledge." But the clarity only points up the assumptions that become insurmountable deterrents to learning to think. For, whenever we assume finalities, fixities, a predetermined order, absolutes, a state of things impervious to human intervention, all we can possibly do is become technologists in pursuit of the knowledge of those permanent "bodies."

The development of scientific thinking in the last century and a half shows continuing effort to reach beyond these restrictions by offering alternative assumptions. In place of a "self-evident" fixed order in nature, which waits only to be disclosed, there is an assumption that order is dependent on the human power to construct, and that the behaviors of nature are, in part at least, evidence of our human capacities and inventiveness. We inquire into the world of the actions of things by means of tools that we have constructed, models that we have invented, a language that we have fashioned. Whatever order we discern in nature, therefore, must surely bear the marks of our own ordering mental activities. Rom Harré, accepting the idea of permanence but not hedged in by it, offers a useful version of this. Science, he has written, when it is viewed as an active undertaking that is nevertheless theoretical in nature, is comprised of an effort to describe a permanent structure responsible for the phenomena to be explained; a set of conditional statements describing how that structure reacts in particular instances; and a model of the whole, including what is at any given moment unknown, in order to make valid explanations possible.[1]

This chapter, then, analyzes the processes of scientific thinking by considering the following:

1. We need to consider how the models we construct for inquiring into nature make possible, and are themselves made possible by, the "laws" written.

2. We need to consider some of the assumptions on which scientific inquiry has in the past been made possible, and other assumptions that now direct it.

3. In considering whether or not scientific endeavor is determined exclusively by the matter to which it addresses itself, we ought to look at the ways in which data are transformed into the subject matter of inquiry.

4. We need to look at how scientific, or Hard, models are constructed and what elements they must contain. Each of these elements (laws, a dictionary, hypotheses, and analogies) will be examined separately.

5. In doing so we will consider, too, what it is that scientific conclusions assert (and thus, what "to know" means), what types of explanation science can offer, and how scientific analogies are developed. In this pursuit we will also be seeking the distinctiveness of descriptions and explanations in science.

Laws of Nature and the Nature of Things

CLASSIFICATION OF THINGS

Perhaps the most conventional assumption of science is that what goes on in the world follows certain laws, or orders, which show themselves in the behaviors of things. This behavior is determined by inner structures and is sooner or later discernible to the inquiring eye or mind. In that case, what does not show evidence of lawlike

1. Rom Harré, *Principles of Scientific Thinking* (London: Macmillan, 1970), p. 2.

behavior must be one of nature's missteps, and need not be explored, for it is too random to lead to an understanding of the laws of nature.

The circularity here is so obvious one wonders that it is taken so seriously. We cannot begin with the very assumptions about the nature of those things we are examining that we are actually trying to demonstrate to be true.

It is against this view that others have held that we ought to begin with the assumption that the things of the world, in and of themselves, do not come to us already organized into such forms that they are automatically in states that make inquiry possible. This would at least save us from looking for what could never be seen, only inferred. If we begin with the intellectually frugal view that no data that we encounter have so independent an existence that some types must be treated in certain known ways and no other, then we will at least be free to see what conceivable methods on any data will produce what unexpected outcomes. This assumption holds out the promise that human beings will not be reduced to the role of passive observers of the changing world, perhaps knowing what the changes will be, but unable to do anything about nature's ways. In this passive role, science is reduced to a rather stringent, if not bare, operation, that of classifying in terms of categories that already exist in nature and that impose themselves on the observer.

As I have shown in the two previous chapters, inquiry is shot through with perception, with the way things are seen at different times, in different conditions, in a variety of contexts, operations, circumstances. Each of these show human interventions in the observable world. From a recognition of what Nietzsche has called "the impossibility of immaculate perception" the suspicion deepens that nature does not come to us all neatly labeled, sometimes brightly written, sometimes written in some kind of vanishing ink, which reappears when we treat it with appropriate tricks. It is some human being who gives classifying labels to nature, for purposes of identification, tracking, communication, explaining and predicting, even enjoyment. Each of these labels begins as a stipulation, perhaps with a history, certainly with a dictionary of recommendations for its use. The language, that is, the labels themselves, become part of the matter of investigation, even though the data, in and of themselves, are not simply the label attached to it. One fundamental consequence of this is the need to reconsider what could be meant by the "objectivity" of science, which the Hard models present to us. Is objectivity conceivable in the familiar, realistic sense? We shall come back to this question a number of times.

HOW COMMON DATA BECOME THE SUBJECT MATTER OF DIFFERENT DISCIPLINES

At least one aspect of this so-called objectivity is diminished when we recognize that the same raw data can be fashioned into the subject matter of a number of different disciplines, different modes of inquiry, considered in different symbol systems having different foci of concern, susceptible to different purposes, producing different types of knowledge at the conclusion of different kinds of inquiry.

Light, for example, is the datum of inquiry for physics, optics, and botany, among others. The earth's crust is the primary datum for physics, geology, and microbiology, among others. And I have limited myself here to the natural sciences. The social sciences often use the same raw datum—light or the earth's crust—for economic analysis, sociology, archeology, psychological inquiry, and still others.

This is further evidence that each discipline is not determined solely by the data to which it addresses itself, though it cannot be denied that the data do exercise important limitations on what might be sought, and how it might be achieved. Rather, each discipline, beginning as a mental process of constructing and putting to use specific models of inquiry that will respond to perceptual as well as more purely cognitive needs, transforms the common data of experience into the subject matter of the specific inquiry being pursued. (Both Hesse and Harré give careful consideration to this idea. See Bibliography.) What becomes further evident is that such subject matter does not precede the thinking act, the act of inquiry, even though the raw data do. The data are deliberately molded, reshaped, reorganized—in a sense translated (which begins, at least, to hint at the role to be played by scientific descriptions) into conditions or structures that become the subject matter to be probed. The data are transformed by the models we borrow or construct, in the full awareness that, as the inquiry proceeds, not only may the models of analysis alter, but in that altering the subject matter itself may alter.

Now, this act of transformation of the data into the subject matter of inquiry is an intrinsic part of the inquiry. It is the act in which descriptions are begun.

But if it is a misleading, even erroneous notion to equate a discipline with its substance or data, it is no more possible to say that science is purely a methodology. For a methodology that seeks, as scientists do, quantitative measurements and the writing of universal laws (however conditional or tentative they might turn out to be) will have to look at its data to see if they have traits that would vindicate such measurements and the writing of laws. But again, it is not that some data do and others do not have these traits. It is, rather, that any data (or almost any, as far as I can see) can be treated at one time with a view toward measurement, and thus the writing of laws, and at another with only a metaphoric view of lawfulness in mind.

Scientific Models: Their Structuring

Let us go back to the idea that thinking involves the activity of constructing a "picture" of some event in so complete a way that its "mechanisms" or "operations" can be observed, analyzed, experimented upon. Scientific thinking, no less than any other form of this process, begins with the activity of constructing a "picture"—in our terms, a representation or a model for some event in nature, for just those purposes. It is important to recognize that watching a scientist at work gives no promise that the whole of this activity will be observable. In the laboratory he is in all likelihood already embarked upon the *employment* of some model that is available to him or he has previously been at pains to develop, or he is working toward the development of that model and is at some earlier observational or describing stage, as Kuhn has said. Whether this means, considering the almost intuitive or unconscious operation of analogizing, that he has no model at all to work with in his first exploration is seriously to be doubted.[2] For without any organized or organizable analogical concepts, he could not do any kind of sorting of the data before him, nor have any means for translating those data into the subject matter of an inquiry. All this means is that primary analogies are also part of the data to be investigated.

Indeed, it is the epistemological assumption of this work that our memories are reservoirs of models and of analogues, by means of

---

2. Harré writes: "In a creative piece of theory construction the relation between the model of the unknown mechanism and what it is modeled on is [also] a relation of analogy." Ibid., p. 35. The analogy, I am arguing, is the means of connecting the models held in memory to the data of the unknown mechanisms before us, in order to construct a more relevant model for the problem on hand. It is well worth looking into Harré's careful, but by no means simple, analysis of this problem, in chaps. 1 and 2.

which we make our first sortings of encountered events, classify them, name them, give meaning to them. These memories we absorb in the daily experiences we undergo, and they continue to be stored as we continue to experience. Further, we are inference-making creatures, bridging memory to present encounters, from which we perceive positive or negative analogies between the models already held and the matter now being examined. Now, this does not *presuppose* mind in human beings. It rather indicates, as I have been at pains to show, that in the analogizing activity described, the mental act arises and defines itself. Memory alone does not indicate the presence of minds at work. Nor do the data confronted of themselves provide their own classifications. The classification is what the analogizing operation produces.

Thus, the scientific experimentation we observe in the laboratory can either be a display of memory "unrolling" as a series of activities, or it can be a manifestation of an active response to what is present, in terms constructed or altered for the occasion. The former we call technology; the latter, science.

In the analogizing operation scientific thinking has already preceded the laboratory itself. This fact has even raised some questions as to whether the laboratory is necessary for there to be scientific thinking. The apparent Idealism of this view may be made more palatable when we admit that science is, after all, a mental endeavor, "mind-dependent," as Rescher has said.

Let me present here what might be called a paradigm of scientific inquiry, to serve as an example of how one finds a model to begin an investigation, how one tests the analogy used, how it is altered, how a new model is built, and how elements operate within the structure of whatever model is used. It also marks the distinction between social and natural science.

This is derived from an essay called "The Perception of Pain" by Ronald Melzack, which appeared in *Scientific American,* February 1961.

He begins with some observations that derive from prior experience. Pain is private and personally experienced, and for this reason it has not been defined to the satisfaction of all who investigate it. If we were to analogize it to vision or hearing, Melzack says, we would be led to expect that external stimuli, such as an injury, would go through to a receiving agent, unless we are unconscious or anaesthetized. We would "perceive" it as we perceive any external event. But the inadequacy of the analogy is immediately evident in the fact that pain is not always perceived after injury, even when we are fully conscious and alert. This happens with football players, or prizefighters, who are injured but feel no pain at the time. From that first analogy we become aware of the separateness of perception of pain from the existence of a wound.

Melzack proceeds. Perhaps, if we could establish a physiological model of pain reception, we would have a mechanism for discerning how each of us responds to pain, perceiving it in our own unique ways.

There is abundant evidence of this uniqueness of perception in the ways in which a soldier responds to pain, or a woman in childbirth, or an ordinary citizen going into the hospital. The soldier often perceives pain in a lesser degree, perhaps because he is relieved it is not fatal. (This is hypothesis.) The woman responds in terms of her particular anticipation of the child, or the value ascribed to childbearing in the culture. (Congruent with the first hypothesis.) The ordinary citizen perceives it as a possible clue to more serious danger yet to come.

Melzack reorganizes the evidence at this point. In so doing he translates all psychological terms into a strictly physiological language.

He then offers his more defensible analogy and his more adequate language. Assume, he says, that the psychological processes (of memory, experiences remembered, thoughts, emotions, attention) *are functions of the brain*. But in place of the very simple hypothesis of the analogue between vision and pain, he presents a more complex hypothesis: what the psychologist is concerned with may be examined as physiological processes of the brain. In the transformation, memory of previous experiences, emotions, thought, and attention are translated as activities of nerve impulses. All his terms are now derived from the "dictionary" of physiology.

From the work of previous experimenters we know that brain functions modify the nerve impulses that are produced by external stimuli (of which injury would be a case). Messages are modified or suppressed because there are message-modifying fibers in the neural system, which can be identified and investigated.

We now have enough data with which to begin to construct a model for further inquiry, what Melzack calls "a conceptual physical model." What were called psychological events are now seen as physical behaviors that play essential roles in determining the quality and intensity of the perception of pain. But now they are transformed into observables.

The theory constructed contains concepts of physical message transmission, of message modification and suppression, and especially, the physiological conditions for what were, earlier, psychological perceptions in pain. This latter is the analogy that vindicates the development of the theory stated.

We establish in the model as much detail as we can of the structure of the neurological network of various subjects (cats, dogs, humans). We are able to verify that some receptors branch into bushy networks so that damage at any point of the skin can activate networks and activities at other points running to the spinal cord.

Skipping, for brevity's sake, descriptions of brain stem, cortex, cerebellum, and their responses to various shocks, in the details of the model, we come to the finding that responses at one point of the skin can be altered by introducing other stimuli to surrounding areas. We are then led to examine what would happen if interventions were introduced to discernible neural routes—such as cutting some, anaesthetizing some, making lesions, introducing somnolescence by means of hypnosis at some points. Each of these becomes translatable back to the analogical events that serve as the basis of the experiment, the psychological states mentioned. It is not hard to see, however, how emotions, memory, attention, and thought come to be treated as metaphors for lesions, hypnosis, cutting, bypassing, anaesthesia, and so on. But from this conceptual physical model, we can offer a more ostensive account for, and understand the difference between, the perception of pain and the fact of the wound.

But by means of the new model, we become further aware that not all pain can be this readily accounted for. The model does not yet explain certain "bizarre" pain syndromes, especially "phantom limb" pain, for which there is much evidence. The cutting off of a limb does not always lessen or eliminate the perception of pain. It is inadequate to simply refer to these perceptions as neurotic, since that would only return us to a psychological language for which there are no actual referents. What is needed, Melzack says, is a more complete model of the central nervous system, showing even greater details of the possible results of limb amputations on neural clusters surrounding that limb. He concludes by arguing that, although there is as yet no evidence of "pools of neurons," that concept does help us to understand facts that are not otherwise explained.

Now let us consider the elements entailed in this structuring of the scientific model.

Analogue.   A scientific model will contain within it either a verbal or a tangible analogue of the data for whose structure and behaviors explanations are sought. The verbal analogue may be a sentence or a symbol system where each element (either sentence or symbol) is modeled from some event, and is offered as equivalent or similar to it. The tangible model is a scale, or a palpable idealization of the event being examined.

Law. A scientific model will be constructed in such a way that it reveals the operations of some law that has been established, or hypothesized, as "covering" the behavior and character of the data modeled and all such similar data. Thus, the explanation developed is a statement that places the behavior of the data within a framework of what has been described as "lawful" behavior. Against these laws the explanations are both derived and tested.

Dictionary. A model will contain within itself, either implicitly or explicitly, a dictionary of the terms and symbols that comprise the model. These symbols are conventional definitions or icons (analogical replications) or stipulated notations.

Hypothesis. A model will contain within itself some hypothetics (either a hypothetical statement or the existence of some unobservable event hypothesized in some tangible form) that connect conditions and behaviors, and that will enter into the explanation produced as possible or probable events that provide the continuity we need to observe.

Each of these elements can be recognized in the illustration given of Melzack's investigation of the perception of pain.

The Content of the Models of Science

Primarily, the content of a scientific model, whether actual or verbal, contains within it matters that are equivalent or similar to the empirical matters being modeled, either in a spatial if real, or syntactical if verbal, relationship that represents the structural relationships of the event modeled. The model may well include matters that are not to be found, or not yet to be found, in the event itself. But these are introduced in an effort to develop a correspondence to the known structures of the events being modeled. To the extent that actual events are fairly represented, the imagined events may be logically tested for their coherence and consistency. Although the structure and the behavior of the observable explananda are being explained, the imaginary events are also being tested in the explanation offered, and in later operations observed in the "filter" that is the complete model. But this happens in any undertaking, with any data. Beyond Melzack's example, the Freudian model of human behavior fairly includes physical matters, draws from principles of physical energies, and then adds to the content of the model analogical (metaphoric) concepts that refer to processes not known in any discipline. It is, however, interesting to observe that having introduced such metaphoric processes and principles at a time when they were frankly imaginary, they have latterly come to be represented as substantive language in the discipline Freud developed, and made available for later use to later explorers of the bases of human behavior.

What makes this model, or any model, a potentially effective instrument of thinking about the world? Innocently, we might argue that enough of its content is, at the outset at least, faithful to the characteristics of the actual events being examined. But we have already shown that even the "actual" events are shaped into subject matter in some model. All subject matter is model-dependent. No events are so discrete that they can be used as external criteria to test "faithfulness" of the model. Recognizing this, however, does not eliminate all the hardness of Hard models. The range of potential behavior of the data still must be attended to. What we are looking for is a knowledge of the behaviors of certain data when they are embedded in specific inquiry models. And if, as seems clear, we can do this only from the context of some other model, it means that "pure" or "absolute" knowledge is an impossibility. But then, it has always been impossible, in spite of its history. Knowledge is always a coherence of the behavior of data in model contexts that are mental activities, and evaluated in further mental activities without any hope for an absolute culmination.

Some models are offered as exact representations of characteristics of some real event, reduced or expanded in size for greater handleability, but which still have the physical traits of the original event. Some may neglect such physical traits when these are not the center of concern. They will then reflect the known *processes* of the original. A third possibility is that the model may reproduce neither physical traits nor processes, but the known conditions within which events are known or suspected to behave. So, for example, a wind tunnel is constructed as a model of atmospheric conditions; within it, in the presence of a model airplane, it becomes possible through direct observation of the behavior of that model to anticipate the behavior of the atmosphere beyond the model.

In those aspects the builder of any model will borrow whatever he needs from whatever field of inquiry he can, in order to achieve a required faithfulness in this *material* dimension of the model.

In the other area of the content, in the imaginary or purely innovative elements, the scientist may borrow principles from some other discipline, if reason persuades him they are eligible. If they are not, he may proceed to construct principles heretofore never developed. It is particularly here, when he introduces elements into the model that are drawn from sources that have nothing at all to do with the subject he is modeling, that the place of metaphor and analogy in science becomes especially evident. Freud's introduction of "psychic energy" and Bergson's "élan vital" are clearly principles that reveal the metaphoric employment of principles of some other discipline. These have reference to processes that are normally not part of any other scientific mode of inquiry. But if they are to be contributing components in a scientific model, they must contain some mechanism that will help to account for the process we are attempting to observe and understand. Thus, to describe electricity as a "flow" is to take the mechanics of water as a metaphor for purposes of explaining the transfer of energy or of light.

We need to ask not only whether the data shaped into subject matter are indeed the data we want to explore, but whether, when the imaginary or idealized aspects are added, the whole still reflects, in some validly analogical way, what nature itself can or does contain. For the model is evaluated not simply in its parts but in the whole. All too often we find a more or less reasonably valid model introduced, but it is lifted out of the realms of natural possibilities by the imaginary or metaphoric elements introduced.

Models and Laws of Nature

DESCRIPTIONS, EXPLANATIONS, AND DEFINITIONS

Scientific models, we have said, are distinguished by the fact that they are determined, not only in the inquiries pursued in terms of established laws, but by the further fact that a primary objective is to test some law and to write others. This can only reinforce the view that science, as any inquiry, begins with and depends upon some physical as well as theoretical assumptions about order in the universe. One such assumption, for example, is that given events in their natural state not only will behave in certain ways in certain conditions, but also that they *must* so behave. This assumption becomes the premise on which laws are read as descriptions of the structure and behavior of events. When this behavior is observed to be contrary to the description, a more careful reconsideration is required, either of the description of the event being written, or the law being employed, or both. For a law in science, if it is to be a law, must be a generalization that admits of no exception beyond those stated in the law itself.

For this reason it is important to distinguish between lawful generalizations and accidental generalizations. Only the former may lay claim to being scientific. Accidental generalizations, which may be perfectly valid, do not have what we call *nomic* character. That is, an accidental generalization may be valid but limited in its referents. A nomic generalization indicates a necessary condition or function; that is, a condition that *will,* or *must,* obtain even among events we cannot observe, because all like events already observed have shown such functions and traits to be intrinsic.

It is an accidental generalization that every woman in America today owns at least one pants suit. But it is a nomic (lawlike) generalization that every woman in America (and every woman anywhere) is possessed of X chromosomes. It is not necessary to own a pants suit in order to be defined as a woman. But womanness is defined by characteristics and functions of X chromosomes.

In this sense the laws of science also become defining instruments. We define copper, for example, by—among other features and functions—the law that copper conducts electricity. The law becomes a source of the vocabulary, the language for describing events in uniform and discriminable ways.

But the scope of the organizing and explanatory function of laws is not exhausted in the notion that it makes possible definitions and descriptions of the orderliness in nature, of the regularity of events. Laws, we have said, refer to data that are available, asserting the ways they must behave and the structures they must possess. But if they are universal, then they go beyond the facts immediately available. They reach into the realm of the hypothetical by means of which thinking expands into whole new regions. In this sense the firmness of law makes possible innovative encounters into as yet unknown data.

HOW LAWS ARE WRITTEN AND WHAT THEY REPRESENT

How are laws written? From one assumption, at least (that there is regularity in nature), we derive the idea that every law is a description of an already preexisting regularity. Such laws, to put it simply, are *discovered* in nature. Nature, then, is the sole source of these laws. But, if laws describe the structures and behaviors of things, then every law would have to derive from direct observation of some empirical reality. If that were the case, then few, if any, laws of nature could ever be written, for what is observable in untouched nature shows no behavior that it *must* follow, only what it does follow. Thus, whatever we call a law of nature is a logical extension of limited observations. Its purpose is to make possible a classification (definition) of events, and a description of those events, but it does not derive the classification or the description solely from these events. If it did, it would always run the risk of being only an accidental generalization, for its intrinsic characteristics may not be observable, only postulated.

On these grounds laws are not simply discovered. They are constructed by means of rules of inference, or of imputation. This adds another dimension to the character of scientific laws. Though they are employed to define and describe the things and behaviors of the world, greater emphasis must be placed on how they are used. For, in that use to which we are able to put a generalization, it achieves the status of a law.

In this alternative to our old metaphysics, we accept the argument that laws are as much dependent on human powers as they are on these actual events that the laws are said to describe. And since they are manmade, they are not discovered, except in a logical, deductive sense. They are created in the process of a quest for a more precise definition and description and explanation. This would sustain the earlier definition offered, that science is the activity of writing the laws of nature, but in a sense other than the idea that the human being is simply nature's secretary.

One warning must be given. Although writing laws shows the exercise of human imagination, it is not to be construed as either a random, impulsive, or accidental matter, or the judgment of an unrestricted scientist god. It is tested in the behavior of what is being described as the limits of natural events. It is tested, too, in the negative evidence that the model produces, of events not explained in the law. If it is not derived *from* what exists, it must at least address itself *to* what exists. So, while nature imposes no limits on scientific thinking at its points of origin, it does impose limits in its stages of final formulation.

Scientific Thinking and
Its Dictionary

A dictionary is a record of the ways in which terms, words, phrases, and whole sentences are used, and have been conventionally used for some time. A dictionary, in a sense, is a history of forms and parts of forms of verbal communication. It is a history of the career of what G. H. Mead has called "significant symbols," in different times, in different places, in different cultural contexts. Its primary value is as a reference source for the clarification of ambiguities, vagaries, and confusions that often arise in ordinary linguistic communication. And finally, for the moment at least, it is the source book for the *rules* of verbal communication, conventional as well as more recently stipulated rules and usages. Quite often it is used for adjudicating disputes over meanings. So the dictionary derives one of its important roles from the fact that much of what lies within is already known to a great many individuals in society, or to a special community within a larger society.

For, in addition to a general dictionary, advanced societies have special dictionaries; dictionaries of sociology, psychology, physics, mathematics, philosophy, and, in time, of every developed or developing field of inquiry. Such dictionaries are narrower and more immediately functional, applying as they do to very specific, limited, conceptual, and experimental undertakings. But in principle, the narrower dictionary is put to use in precisely the same way that the more general one is. Each provides us with the means of general and special communication by specifying the applicability of languages.

It must be obvious that primitive and early societies do not actually have written dictionaries. Nevertheless, there is value in the metaphoric use of this term. The fact of a common understanding of (unpublished) significant symbols is enough to suggest that some *form* of language is not simply useful *for* the thinking act to occur, but that some form of language in use *is* the thinking act.

Nevertheless, the dictionary concept as such does not begin to suggest what is involved in the development of the symbol system, by means of which observation, description, exploration, and explanations are made possible in science or in any other human endeavor. Its record of historicity usually does not touch on the problem of the relationship between explanandum and explanans. This most complex and fundamental of our problems imposes on us the need to consider the necessity of language, the sources of language, and the character of linguistic transmissions. It is as fundamental as that, and as complex as the whole problem of symbolizing; as the operation of translating the observables of experience, and the unobservables of the private lives of human beings into public forms for mutual, objective, understanding.

In becoming aware of his power to symbolize, Cassirer has said, an individual finds that he lives not simply in a broader reality than any other living organism, but in a new dimension of reality.[3] To the physical universe in which he dwells is added the symbolic universe, the universe of discourse. And the presence of this universe alters the very character of the universe that he experiences directly, physically, through his senses. To see the distinction allows us to recognize that the meanings we find in the physical world are the meanings which we first find in that symbolic universe. For, it is by means of these that we have learned to act in and upon the physical.

The Emphasis on the Denotative
in the Scientific "Dictionary"

It must be recognized that even a denotative language, employed for the purpose of describing what is demonstrably there, is not so simple as it seems. Curiously enough, language precedes the observation of events, although it has sometimes been hypothesized that humankind and nature are so harmoniously balanced that the human mind is comprised of a linguistic power that mirrors the world of things. An even more widely held alternative to this is the hypothesis that the nature and role of perception, as well as the conceptual powers by which humankind itself is defined, are independent of the world experienced. From this latter hypothesis is derived the view that the world, as described, is shot through with human projections onto nature.

But the fact is that we cannot distinguish our modes of communication in so simple a way as saying that on the one hand, objects alone

3. Ernst Cassirer, *An Essay on Man* (New Haven: Yale University Press, 1944), chap. 2.

determine terms, or on the other, conceptualization alone determines terms. What distinguishes those modes, we discover, is the character of the transaction between object world and the "world of discourse."

Observational terms are developed for purposes of making matters amenable to further observation, exploration, and test. Theoretical terms appear in the development of a logic, or a syntax among symbols, whose purpose it then is to classify the events in nature, to connote empirical connectives between events, and to allow predictions, further hypotheses, and conjectures to be formed. Such symbols, inevitably, have reference to objective realities, but that may not be their primary function. The primary function, more reasonably, is the development of a network of relationships that are not available to the senses, from which procedures of further explorations and analysis become possible. If it is the world of things, or objects, to which science addresses itself, it is *in* the world of symbols that this address becomes possible.

Though we can continue to distinguish logically between observational language and theoretical language, it must be recognized that functionally they are so bound together that the distinctive character of that integration becomes the condition for the empirical tests to be made. Indeed, the most notable distinction to be made between, say, a Newtonian and an Einstein model of the universe is to be found in their distinctive integrations of theoretical and observational languages. Even more to the point, we distinguish the models of the natural sciences from those of the social sciences in this same way. Note, for example, how this appears in the illustration on "The Perception of Pain." Melzack finds that prevailing psychological models generally employ observational language that is not clearly referential enough to promote critical experiment, so he transforms it into referential terms that will do just that. In this sense, then, the example becomes a paradigm for the shift from a Soft to a Hard science.

The last point to be made in this section deals with the features of the world to which science addresses itself. The dictionary tells us that the centrality of things that can be directly or indirectly described and explained by one inquirer and observed by another is what an object term denotes. In this sense, then, a psychology of mind in which introspection is a central concern could never be scientific, for claims about it cannot be denoted and observed by a later inquirer. It is curious, however, that in the modern world mathematics has increasingly become the language of all sciences. But the unguarded belief that such terms as "cause," "covering law," "force," or "motion" can all be cast into mathematical terms and be assumed to refer to matters in their empirical behaviors, features, and relation-

202 THE PROCESS OF THINKING

ships only complicates the problem of learning scientific thinking at the moment that it produces its new, advanced knowledge of the world's behaviors.

Hypotheses in Models

The previous discussion could readily lead to the conclusion that to build a model that is completely faithful to something in the world is not to build a hypothetical model at all, but rather a nontheoretical replica of that event. But we cannot escape the realization that no model can be a mere replication of the event. Some theorizing or conceptualizing would have had to enter. In part 1 we saw that to miniaturize or to maximize something, to take it from one context and present it in some selective form in another, in order that it can be observed, is to deal with such nonempirical events as analogies. In every such case, more than the mere replication of the event has been involved. Even the simple fact of miniaturizing has added a dimension that removes it from the replica stage and transforms it into our sense of a model. In this act, hypothesis had to be at work.

Charles Singer makes a distinction that is well worth considering. The word *hypothesis* derives from the Greek, where it meant "a postulated scheme or plan which must be accepted if discussion is to take place." [4] Hypotheses come to serve, he says, as useful fictions, as the grounds on which the data before us come to be organized and judged. But such hypotheses (in the law, for example, or in physics) are none of them "deduced from phenomena. None are verifiable. All are parts of a working scheme into which certain phenomena can be conveniently and tidily fitted." [5]

These hypotheses give to the model the heuristic force it comes to have, as well as the potentiality it contains for making possible a more critical examination whose outcome will be an explanation of the event being modeled. This is the simplest form of the hypothetical dimension of the model, but it already contains within itself enough elements to deepen our understanding of how to construct and how to use a model.

The problem of how a hypothesis is created, or initiated, has always

4. C. Singer, *A Short History of Scientific Ideas* (London: Oxford University Press, 1960), p. 295.
5. Ibid.

been a thorny one. In strictly denotative terms, nothing in the statement of what does in fact exist suggests what might otherwise have existed, or what ought to have existed. Such judgments can only derive from some other source, however much the data before us remain central to our inquiry.

But before we can consider how hypotheses are developed, perhaps we ought to be sure we know what we are talking about. Can we say anything more about hypothesis? It will be surprising to see how a little clarification makes the problem of its development a good deal simpler. First, Singer's view just mentioned. Second, we have recently come to consider a hypothesis to be an inductive generalization made about future events on the basis of a series of current observations in the hope that this generalization will be confirmed in later observations. A third, somewhat surprising view is Nicholas Rescher's idea that a hypothesis is a statement or a proposition that is known to be false or believed to be false.[6] This is a narrower but stronger view of hypothesis than the second mentioned, which takes the familiar *if-then* form. Its special strength lies in the fact that here the ordinary *if-then* proposition, instead of being treated as if it were possibly true, is introduced as a procedural act for close continuing inquiry. For, it is precisely the recognition of the falsity of an assertion, or of an inference drawn, that leads to the construction of alternatives that could be true. In general, Popper and others have argued, we know what is true because we know what conditions, which make a statement false, would have to be changed. More to the point, in an inductive approach, no amount of particular observations could prove that a hypothesis about the next one would also be true. If we are ever to get away from mystery, error, or myth, we need to know limits. And the acknowledgement of falsity at the outset provides us with this limitation.

The outcome derived from a hypothesis is an inference, for the hypothesis itself exists in the premises of some inquiry as a supposition of some kind. Thus, the outcome is properly called a hypothetical inference. So, in a well-formed model there would be a number of assertions about symbolized events that are true to the thing being modeled, and some (one or more) suppositions that we know not to be the case but that we are willing to assume for the time being, for the sake of further inquiry.

Now, how do we go about developing hypotheses such that, although we either know or believe them to be false, they are still

6. N. Rescher, *Hypothetical Reasoning* (Amsterdam: North Holland Publishing, 1964).

justifiable to be included in our model? This, of course, will oblige us to address ourselves diligently to what is already known, or could be known. In this way, we would begin with some assurance that the hypothesis we are constructing will be relevant to the problem to which we have addressed ourselves. For what we are assured about are things we know. So, for example, if we were to be engaged in seeking an explanation of human perception, and we placed into our premises the assumption that the human senses have all the characteristics of a highly sensitive tape recorder, we would be making a false assertion, or at least one not likely to be true. It might be quite absurd, yet it would not be sheer fantasy. We can make a somewhat defensible analogy between a known instrument with a capacity for recording and replaying what it has recorded, and these sense capacities that we are trying to explore more closely.

It is because the false, or suspectedly false, hypothesis nevertheless bears upon the matters before us that it serves a fundamentally valuable function in science. Science, you see, has in modern times been described as the activity of stretching rules and knowledge to the point beyond which they no longer hold, or are no longer true. It is at the point of being able to falsify something that we can draw up a rule about the behavior of that thing. We can establish the tensile strength of a length of copper only by such tests as enable us to determine with precision the weighting point at which the wire will break. Or we can establish a defensible claim about the behavior of some event when we can show that, even if a given supposition is entertained, the event itself would continue to behave in the same way. So medical knowledge moves to a greater precision when, assuming that a given illness is caused by a given virus (which is not to be believed, on the face of it), the virus is treated in such a way that it would have been destroyed had it been present in the body. When or if the specific illness continues to exist, proof has been achieved.

From the illustrations given here, the most important role of hypothesis can be discovered. A theory of the larger career and context of an event is shaped into a model. From this, the hypothesis is derived, in the form of an assertion about those events in the model that do not have actual references. By means of the hypothesis we are able to establish that theory as more firmly grounded, and from which that particular mode of scientific reasoning which we call the hypothetico-deductive becomes possible. By means of some organizing and explanatory theory made manifest in a model, developed analogically from some known data, facts are established, hypotheses are constructed, and experiments can proceed. Moreover, unless we have deduced some possible outcome from the theory now made operable in

some hypotheses in the model, we will not even recognize the outcomes as outcomes.

Content and Function
of Scientific Models

We need to consider a little further the special traits of scientific
symbols (or the language of science) and the role that such symbols
play in aiding in the recognition of what it is that a scientist is talking
about.

We need to consider what a scientific conclusion does in fact assert,
and what kinds of claims are being made in a scientific assertion.

We need to consider further what scientific explanations are, and
what types of such explanations there are.

We need to say something further about the nature of the analogies
and metaphors that are unique to science.

THE SPECIAL TRAITS OF THE SYMBOLS OF SCIENCE

I have suggested that in scientific inquiry the symbols are analogical
notations of certain empirical, or suspected empirical events, and
their behaviors treated in coherent and correspondent ways. Further,
it has been implied that they are treated in quantitative rather than
qualitative terms. Mountains and molecules are quantified so they can
be considered as singular totalities.

Now, this would appear to be simple enough. But it becomes less
than simple when we recognize that not all the symbols in a scientific
assertion perform this role. Some symbols do, of course, enter into
what are called *ostensive* definitions, or descriptions. That is, we state
the symbol and in one way or another we point to or indicate the dimensions of the event symbolized. But some symbols assert unob-
served functions or relationships, which do not, in fact, have empirical
traits. Symbols of number, of modes of relationship (*above, under,
to the right of, to the left of*), and of direction (*toward, away from,
into, out of*) have no empirical reference. They are, rather, symbols of
how certain aspects of the conditions or behaviors of those events are
to be viewed. It is evidence of the crudest kind of materialism, then, to
look for empirical evidence for every symbol that is used in a scientific
report. So, some symbols in science must be considered not so much

as pointing to some specific thing, but as recommendations of how to construe the ostensible events pointed out, how to classify them, how to envision relationships between them, or how to predict other aspects of their structures or behaviors.

Nevertheless, it is the very nature of the scientific endeavor that public involvement must in some way appear in the assertions made, lest we drift away from the world that science has committed itself to describing and explaining. This necessary communal condition undergirds the development of a dictionary of symbols, for without it, scientific thinking would be unavailable to other inquirers.

Now, we learn conventional symbols (the by-now traditional symbols of the various elements in nature that chemists and biologists use are excellent cases in point) as the language of science. But no set of symbols could possibly exhaust the events of nature, and thus new symbols are always being created, either to point to events in nature not heretofore considered or to new ways of organizing and developing meanings of already familiar matters.

In their function of pointing to events, there is a dimension of profound importance and delicacy. For the symbol system both points to aspects of an event, or to specific conditions of events, and contains the rules for continuing exploratory activities of them. In this specificity symbols eliminate other aspects, conditions (or states), and procedural rules. This limitation in the function of the symbol within a system also imposes limitations on any particular scientific experimentation and explanation. A law of nature is not universal in the absolute sense that it applies to all the things in the world. Rather, it applies to all members of a given class of events, seen from a specific vantage point. The law of gravity, for example, is a universal law in that it applies to every event in nature having mass. It does not apply, for example, to any element in the conceptual realm. If you insist upon arguing that there is no reality to the conceptual realm, the important but limited use of such ostentive symbols will not be understood. For then the role of symbols of operations to be performed, or perceptions to be applied, would disappear, either to turn up as concepts reified into empirical facts, or as metaphors whose metaphoric status only hides a physical reality.

We are still left with a final note about the relationship between symbols and the recognitions that they make possible. One of our primary concerns in this work has been to overcome the problems raised by the view that thinking is a private affair. A simple, ostensive approach cannot be said to give public evidence of molecules, positrons, or quarks. Yet without symbols for such events, physics in the modern world would hardly be possible. Nor would the science of genetics exist if we were not permitted to believe in the existence of genes unless we could put our fingers into them.

It must be clear that the uses of theoretical terms are fundamental to all the sciences. Indeed, as has been pointed out, if all we ever had was an observation language, no explanation of the things in the world would be possible or necessary, nor would prediction of future states.

The most prevalently held alternative to this limiting of symbols to matters of direct observation has been an approach that does not do away with observation but relegates it to the outcomes of processes in nature, or to physical experiments, both of which *can* be seen. Sometimes, unhappily, this has led to complete abandonment of any belief that there are events that produce observable outcomes. The observed event is all that is acknowledged; that is, the observed structure or the observed process. This has led to the view that thinking is observable only in the evidence of tangible outcomes as they are asserted. Thinking can be examined as the overt verbal behavior, and no further prior entities need be postulated as having produced that thinking. In the Wilson cloud chamber the molecules *are* the streaks that appear in the context of observable conditions.

Whether this is a tolerable alternative will, of course, depend upon what you insist are ultimate things, or powers, or dispositions (if you insist on the premise of ultimates) in the world. But we shall save this for the moment, until we reach the additional consideration of the types of explanations that science offers. It does, however, have the virtue of being rid of mysterious metaphysical existences.

WHAT DOES A SCIENTIFIC ASSERTION ASSERT?

Several things can be noted readily about a scientific assertion:

1. It asserts that the description offered is faithful (in a sufficient degree) to the event being examined. That is, features of some event are accurately symbolized in the statement made.

2. It asserts, implicitly or explicitly, the class of events of which this event is a member.

3. It asserts that a given event is related to other events, ostensively and nonostensively, in the way described. This is in part descriptive, and in part predictive. But the prediction is generated out of the descriptive part of the assertion.

4. It asserts that the behavior of the event is a manifestation of a law that enables us to describe and predict the behavior of all events

that fall within this class. In this case it asserts, or reasserts, a generalization that is not simply accidental but falls within a law stated or implied.

5. Finally, in light of this last, a scientific statement asserts, implicitly more often than explicitly, that what we know is a set of conclusions derived from and dependent upon a model of organization, a set of procedural activities and explanations within which the factual and the hypothetical elements are integrated. Every such assertion, thus, is a heuristic statement of both the behavior of actual events and the dispositions of these events that would or could occur in later, not yet known, situations.

In this context there are also implied the metaphysical and the epistemological assumptions on which the model is, from the outset, constructed. For it entails within itself implications about the structure of nature, the conditions of what can be known, the ways in which the knowing occurs, and what knowledge entails. It bespeaks a concept of the order or lawfulness of nature, the human capacities by means of which these orders or laws are known and put to use, and what the structure of knowledge is.

TYPES OF SCIENTIFIC EXPLANATION

In principle, it seems fair to say, an explanation is an effort to promote an understanding by developing a more complete context for some thing or some idea ordinarily seen in isolation. Different *types* of explanation, then, involve different kinds of contexts. Thus, what one context includes is likely not to appear in another; and it is this that is at the heart of the disputes among explanations.

Causal explanations.   The most familiar types of explanations offered are *causal* explanations. That is, to put it as simply as possible, that on the occasion of A happening, B takes place. In some way, when a given event, A, takes place, it is followed by B, which is a product or an outcome of the event we call A. Water boils because heat has been applied to it. Mercury congeals because cold has been applied to it to a given degree. The sequence is considered complete because something in the activities of A has produced something we have identified as the product, or consequence, B.

For the longest part of the history of science, this has been not only the primary but also the exclusive explanation for the appearance of any B. Out of long tradition of acceptance, when any event occurs, we are driven to looking for those specific and particular events that, behaving in a determinate way, produce from within themselves the events identified as *B*. So, in medical science, when we are able to observe an event, say, a cold in the head, we look for those events outside and within the body whose behaviors produce that cold. When we sneeze, cough, show fever, we look for causes. Only relatively recently have we identified specific germs, or viruses, that, in their behaviors, affect the organism in such a way that this same behavior appears in other parts of the organism, in the form of fever, phlegm, and perspiration. The simple absurdity of this last, however, obliges us to further considerations, although the persuasive character of this anthropomorphic view is obvious. (Cold germs do not have the colds that they pass on to us.)

What happens when, by means of a model, we are able to distinguish between the observables and the unobservables in nature? What happens when we come at last to recognize the difference between the measurable fever and the unobservable event we call a virus? This is admittedly an oversimplified illustration, but I think it is not altogether a violation of the issue. For a virus is a nonobservable event, as atoms or molecules are, strictly speaking, unobservable events. If so, then clearly anything we say about the virus is hypothetical. It is either known to be false, or there is no possible way to verify the claims made. But such a hypothesis, contained within a larger theory of the orderly connectedness of things, directs us to look for some particular event or action that would fill in the required continuity. If it is not a virus, then it will be something else. The theory demands it.

Covering laws.   Nevertheless, this mode of explaining the world has been, since Hume and Kant, all but shattered, though it has lingered, impervious, in the realms of common sense. Since Hume, especially, we have either had to demonstrate objective causal sequences, or we have had to acknowledge that the principle of causality is a mental projection on some aspects of ostensive reality, and an admission that we cannot observe the actual operation of objective event *A*, which, it is claimed, has produced objective event *B*. Now, if causality is a hypothesis (a mental construct for which no actual evidence can be shown), then we can ask, Are there no other mental constructs that might supply a better hypothesis for explanation and prediction than this? Are we, perhaps, looking at the world in the wrong way?

Modern scientists, and especially modern philosophers, have reasoned, as a more defensible alternative, to what is called the "covering law" method of explanation, which was considered in chapter 6. This concept presupposes a number of conditions in the world, most of which are quite readily acceptable on logical, familiar grounds. The

first is the assumption of a uniformity in nature such that things belonging to a common class belong to that class not only because they
share features with other members of that class, but because they behave, under similar conditions, in the same or similar ways as do all
other members of that class. This is similar to the causal assumption,
but viewed more coherently. Within a covering law, having a cold is
explained by pointing to the ostensive facts in a hypothetical form: *If*
you are running a fever of X degrees, and *if* you are throwing off
phlegm, and *if* you have the following aches and pains in your body,
then you are suffering from a virus infection that we call the Cold
Virus. More than anything, this is a manifestation of the fact that as
modern science has advanced, the separateness in the model between
what is observable and what is hypothetical has been so completely
integrated that the one cannot be attended to except in the presence
of the other. For modern science is as committed to the unobservables
as it is to the observables. That is, to the logical as to the empirical;
to what we *say* as to what we *see*. As it develops, therefore, the hypothetico-deductive approach to explaining the things of the world is
more than ever primary, and since it remains a powerful element in
its processes, science has become less and less inductive. In this
growth the sense of the absoluteness of the behavior of singular things
as the basic determinant of the findings of science has dissolved.
Science reappears as the writing of the laws of the possibilities of the
behavior of things, and it is less and less the simple, direct, and accurate description of the way particular, isolated things appear.
Lawfulness is now a much more defensible idea than are individual
perceptions of individual things. Laws provide a better *context* for
perception.

Stochastic explanations (good guesses).   The third mode of explanation that is current and important to us is the *stochastic* explanation.
The basis for the development of stochastic explanations is to be found
in the fact that causal explanations applied to the growing complexities in the modern world have been found much too limited, for they
are concerned with isolated events and do not provide sufficiently defensible explanations of masses of data.

   Every causal explanation depends upon a complete, exhaustive,
and accurate description of empirical events in their particularity. To
that end it must be limited to those particulars only which are being
examined. The general principle we call Causality imposes the obligation to seek out the specifics of what, *in fact,* is really present when
this or that specific fact appears. Unless we propound, as Aristotle and
St. Thomas did, a prime, continuing cause, every causal explanation is

isolated and disconnected from every other explanation. And thus, in order to recommend and explain the integrities in nature and in human experience, continuities in things, in time and place, in phases of events, in generation and degeneration of people and things, the concept of causality has to be placed within a noncausal conception. Aristotle calls it the uncaused cause. Modern thinkers call it Covering Laws. From within either of these we are able to account for singular specific cause-effect relationships. Moreover, even when we speak of multiple causes, the same type of descriptive, empirical assertions are made, and thus the truth of these claims must then be open to verification. So, for example, a causal explanation of molecular movement demands a whole series of verifiable statements that claim to be the conditions and circumstances for the event itself. But such a mode of explanation, predicated on the wider hypotheses of harmonies or lawfulness, is just as likely to be false as true; for the evidence becomes increasingly difficult to obtain as events to be explained become increasingly numerous and complex in character and in traits. The event becomes so multiplied in its parts that wholeness, law itself, becomes strained. Nevertheless, that it remains the most widely employed mode of explanation is not to be denied, and whatever limitations it presents to a fuller understanding of the world does not diminish its power where it remains applicable. (That is, where descriptions and verifications of singular events remain possible. The trouble is, events have ceased to be singular and have come to be seen as multiple behaviors.)

The curious thing about causal explanation is that it rests, not only on the concepts of "monadic" singularities (that view that sees all events as little, self-enclosed, eyeless worlds in themselves), but also on the metaphysics of orderliness in nature. Both conditions modern science has resolutely challenged. The world is apparently not at all comprised either of substantive singularities or of "natural" laws, as earlier metaphysics held it to be. With the development of theories of infinite numbers of particles of *energy*, all of which show identical or similar behaviors in motion and change in the universe, the efforts to find evidence for and describe in any discreet way the causal effects of any particular, substantive particle on any other particular substantive particle have simply disappeared. And any attempt to describe the totality of an event in terms of its causes is inadequate, in light of what has come to be accepted as the internal behaviors of such events. What must take its place, then, is an explanatory system that will take into account the *behaviors* of the postulated atomic structure of the things of the world. And for the moment these behaviors are described as random, for the lack of an organizing theory. With the (tentative)

agreement about that randomness, statements of *probability* will replace the deterministic statements of the causal explanation of substances. (The term *stochastic* means a well-placed guess about random behaviors observed.) What it comes to mean, in its simplest
terms, is this: We cannot possibly account for, or predict, the behavior
of single particles in nature any more than we can of single human
beings in their variety of potentials, under an infinite variety of pres-
sures, forces, or influences. All we can do, then, is observe *ranges* and
frequencies of behavior after they have become evident, and establish tables of this behavior over given periods of time in given, described conditions. From such tables we guess what will *probably* happen at some later time in similar conditions.

It is not hard to anticipate the shock that such a hypothesis produces. So completely committed are so many of us to the model of
causal explanations, to the deduction of conclusions from some obviously true and ultimately testable premise about some substantial
event in nature, that the suggestion that more and more events are
discovered to behave in a completely "uncaused" way is too hard to
swallow. At the psychological level, even well-educated people, who
have, however, not been exposed to scientific advances other than in
their technological achievements (electric lights, television, inter-
planetary rockets and satellites), continue to think causally. The abandonment of exactness in explanations renders the world too random
and chaotic to cope with. And thus the consequences of the abandonment of the causal explanatory model cut very deeply into the visions
most of us have about nature, about our societies, our histories, and
ourselves. If there can be claims of uncaused events, does not this
mean that we will be making the most astounding further claims, not
only of the characteristics and origins of things, but also of the influence of otherwise unobservable powers? Why, the whole problem of
spontaneous combustion, so neatly dissolved in the nineteenth century, now returns to plague us as being increasingly probable. Do we
not have to reconsider again this possibility, if substantive events can
no longer be invoked as the causes of other substantive events in their
singularity? Might not this even mean that some things can appear
noncaused? Doesn't this mean that human beings can perform acts
that no causal law will make predictable? Do they, after all, possess
powers that no catalogue of their traits can account for? What we
once thought laws of nature may not be laws at all, but only limited,
particular descriptions of limited, particular events. The shock waves
are deep. For the world does seem to be reduced, as Russell once said,
to a state of just one damned thing after another.

Of course, not all these dire consequences came so late, and not just from the probability approach. This began much longer ago, when sixteenth- and seventeenth-century scientists altered the basic model of inquiry on the altered analogy of human unpredictability. From this model, what we can know is what we can, in some way or other, see or hear, and measure; and however much we could see, we could never draw up a law that a later observation could not overthrow. The probability approach was only consistent with this earlier development, but by means of it there was brought about the abandonment of any kind of absolutism, or determinism. In place of this latter, there is little difficulty in employing the concept of *probability*. Nevertheless, from this there is the added, perhaps the uncomfortable but undeniably exciting, concommitant of making direct, continued, inductive inquiry into clusterings of events the basis of every standard of procedure. It lessens the number of times that we will find ourselves completely surprised by nature, when what falls outside the limits of lawful activities cannot be accounted for. But this only points to the need of writing a more flexible and discriminating law. Not to be dominated by the determinism of the law of causality is to become increasingly alert to the number of times that the "unexpected" happens. What we would tend to dismiss within a causal model, the new model directs us to give increasingly careful attention to.

The fundamental role of thinking as model making is never so clearly seen as when, in a revolutionary shift, we come to recognize that what we had assumed was inviolable was not inviolable; that it was all the time only an analogy transformed into a dogma or a myth; and that a better model would enable us to see more and perhaps to give a better account of the world. If we do not reduce science to a quest for a causal accounting of the features and behaviors of things, we may even see more features and more behaviors, oppression and inquisition notwithstanding. (Brahe, Bruno, and Galileo all suffered persecution for altering models-turned-dogmas.) What we have available are new means of seeing things in widening contexts of inquiry, in widening contexts of relationships of things with other things. This is, after all, most remarkably demonstrated in Heisenberg's principle of Indeterminacy: events behave in such ways that the very instruments employed in observation continue to alter that behavior. The more one knows about any one aspect of behavior, the more one knows about the instrument (in our terms, the model) affecting that behavior; but the most that we can know is its probable behavior. This is what "knowing" means in any realm.

A scientific model, we know, is deliberately established in order to make possible descriptions of the data being examined. Thus, it will include some type of representation of the data in it. But as it is concerned with process, it also includes certain presuppositions, both general and particular, about the possibilities of the behaviors of those things for which we seek understanding. And it must also include symbols for the conceptual instruments that guide the inquiry and make certain observations possible and understandable.

Thus, to know what a scientific *model* does is to know what science does at any time. What models of inquiry make possible is a knowledge of the symbolic context of operations of systems of things, an increasingly accurate description of the states and the behaviors of things, individually, in their internal systemic relationships, and externally in their relationships to other elements of the system. It makes possible, too, a many-faceted explanation, sometimes including predictability, but always advancing the clarity of understanding of the ways things behave in specific situations. What models make possible, especially, is the writing of laws of the *probability* of the behaviors of things examined.

SCIENTIFIC ANALOGIES

So we come to those other elements of any model for thinking, the analogies and metaphors that play so important, productive and irreducible a role. Will any analogies whatever be appropriate in scientific thinking? If not, are there determinations we can make about what kinds of analogies can be used? Or is it perhaps that any analogy whatever can stand in the position of being eligible for scientific thinking, but that it must first be transformed in some specific way so that it can serve the purposes of science?

If we remember that the primary concern of science is the increasingly critical exploration of the things of nature in order more adequately to describe and explain them in their multifold states and behaviors, then it must be clear that whatever analogies we employ must, in some way, make that function more effective. This would suggest, and quite properly, that in any scientific analogy, whatever it is we are seeking to explain, whether some observable event in nature (such as the behavior of sun, stars, and various moons), or unobservable (such as genes, atoms, or quarks), the analogy itself needs to be derived from some observable realm, even if it is not a replication of the event under inquiry. Yet, as proper as it seems, this is not altogether true. For, it is entirely possible to use, as the source of some analogy, some theory, given the form of a *theoretical model* that has already some currency. The theoretical model has been formed in such a way that it makes observable what would otherwise be left completely conceptual, or theoretical. For the explanatory effectiveness of science does, finally, rest on the descriptions of things.

Typical analogies used in science are certainly not hard to come upon. The behavior of water is used to analogize the behavior of sound and of light. The behavior of billiard balls is used as analogue for the behavior of molecules of gas. The way in which a drop of water breaks up into smaller drops has been suggested as an analogy for nuclear fission. In each case, a specific or central feature, or phase of the behavior, or the configuration of the matter within that analogous event, brought centrally into the model directs the focus of attention to a similar aspect in the thing being modeled. In whatever case, a description of the event, or an aspect, or a function of it built into the model is expected to be a description of the thing being explored.

We must, however, remember the fundamental traits of an analogy. It is not a true copy, a replication, of the original event. It may, indeed, have some aspects that are replications, but as a whole, it is analogical because in the face of all the differences in features, certain similarities of relationships have been recommended, for heuristic purposes, as "holding" between both events.

On the basis of a beginning, purely verbal expectation in a primary exploration, we sometimes discover an event that can be employed, or transformed, so that it can be used as a model for our inquiry. Sometimes, however, we are required to construct an analogy from imaginative projection, and by so doing we add the function of comparison to the other functions that analogies make possible. However developed, from the clarity of the analogy we are able to extend those principles that are involved in the behavior of the analogical model to the matters in the primary domain about which greater understanding is sought.

When the model is representative of the event being explored, in the sense that the model is to a large degree a copy of that event reconstructed to scale, the copied event has the security of immediately observable faithfulness. But where such representation is not possible, the quest for sources is greatly expanded. Anything at all about which we can establish or suggest similarities to features or relationships or behaviors of the original is eligible to become a source for the analogical model we construct. There is a freedom here that turns out to be an additional burden in inquiry, for we are first put to the task of showing the warrant for claiming an analogical relationship that is sufficiently similar to the thing investigated. But when we catch on to the clue that *similarity* provides for us, the range of inventiveness made possible is the most promising phase of scientific thinking (see chapter 2). The whole world becomes a reservoir of resources for the quest for more illuminating descriptions, more perceptive explanations of even the most ordinary events. For, where a copy of a given event serves as the source for a model of scientific analysis, the copy itself is sternly restrictive. In analogy, where anything at all may be pressed into service to be built up as a model, possibility, not actuality, is the only restraint. The only proviso is that whatever source we employ, the elements of the analogy selected be transformed so that a similarity of relationships can be shown between it and the event examined. Without this, the inquiry into the model would drift away from the world we seek to explore and into a domain of its own, disconnected from our original quest into pure fancy, for the description is a description of nothing germane.

What I have said in the last paragraph holds equally true when we consider scientific thinking pursued in strictly theoretical models, for the contemplation of imaginary worlds. For, in theoretical models and analogies we are concerned, not with things observed, or with evidence of their internal, observable, or momentarily unobservable structures or behaviors, but with *theories* from which assertions are made about those one-way-or-another observables. This difference is crucial. If we forget that a given model is theoretical, we forget, too, that what we are exploring is a theory, a set of assumptions built into a total "picture" that actual events do not reveal. But this is essential to scientific procedure, for it is by means of a theoretical model, and the explanatory system it provides, that we are led to a better, fuller understanding of some actual event. In an earlier discussion we were concerned with an ostensively descriptive model, from which descriptive explanations might flow. But when a theory is our primary domain, we are involved with that from which little or no descriptions of actual things can be derived, except by analogy. That is, by analogy we recommend a description of some thing in order to theorize further about its inner structures, or its inner functions, conditions, or relationships. So, for example, a wave theory of light will impute to light the kind of structure that would make a wave movement in water possible. This model *imputes* structures and behaviors to light. It is not an actual description of its existential features and powers. It is, rather, intended to explain what is meant by a wave, what is being assumed as to the mode of its behavior, what is theorized about the laws, causes, probabilities, or conditions of its behavior.

Now, it must be clear that analogies enter into the creation of theoretical models far more frequently and certainly more obviously than they do in representative models of the things of the world. Where we are considering only theoretical entities, it would appear that the only way we can develop a model is to employ some analogy. But in this case, curiously yet clearly enough, what we have is theoretical analogy of a theoretical set of assumptions, presuppositions, or postulates. Of course, it is possible to create a model by using idealized aspects of a physical event's behavior to set forth what is being recommented as the internal, theoretical state of something. In order to explain how gases behave, the analogy that has been used is the theorized internal force of a perfectly elastic billiard ball (which, of course, does not exist and is thus quite imaginary). The "picture" we create to show this is not the theoretical model, but simply a way of making that model available for visual, descriptive purposes. But from such an ideal representation, that is, from such a "picture," we could not derive what we could from a theory and from the theoretical model created for its analysis, unless it also had built into it such formulas for the measurement of transactions that make derivations possible.

The explanations, systematizations, and law constructions that theories are said to make possible are, in fact, made possible from the theoretical analogical models that present clear, focused, organized forms of those theories. They make it possible to produce whole ranges of assertions about the traits and behaviors of the things of the world that the theories are theories about. And thus, imaginative choosing and continual mental testing of these analogies, drawn as they are from whatever source, become a primary phase of the methodology of scientific thinking.

Some Conclusions and Recommendations

Let us summarize some of the conclusions drawn by our analysis of the processes of scientific thinking. For, as complicated and as numerous as they may appear, a familiarity with them and an understanding and habituation in their use is required if scientific thinking is to be recognized, analyzed, and improved.

It has not been the intention here to argue against the assumptions of consistency and predictability in the things of the world. This would indeed be disingenuous, for without those traits, science would be neither a possible nor a worthwhile undertaking. What has been attempted is a demonstration of the view that what appears to be simple and immediate, requiring only that we pay direct and close attention to the data of the world, is not simple, and almost never immediate. The more closely we look at things, the more we disturb those things. What appear at first blush so simply reportable, come to be recognized as matters in different stages of momentary arrest, as matters that move from one complex state to another. If things were really as simple and as immediate as the common-sensists urge upon us, then thought could truly be construed as an obstruction, an obscuring of that simplicity. And indeed, it seems always to have been the case that the intense appeal for simplicity, for immediacy, for "simple common-sense responses" to the world, has been the primary appeal of the antiintellectual: in art, the philistine; in history, the chronologists; in the social sciences, the mechanical recorders; in the sciences, a whole range of intellectual Luddites, who believe that every machine is artificial and, therefore, a threat to the simple honesty of individual observers and workers.

Essentially, what is being said here is that in respect to the problems identified with scientific thinking it is not enough to say that one thinks about the world only to the degree that one has directly experienced it. It is not enough to say that science, primarily concerned with a description of what there is in ever increasing precision, need only direct itself to inventing better and better instruments for seeing things, and to improve one's command of language to the point that what can be seen can be described so accurately that in the communication the description is received as exactly as it was stated and intended.

The inadequacy of this has at least two sides. First, the view that what there is in the world can, sooner or later, be seen in its own forms or structures, if we have but patience enough and tools powerful enough. The inadequacy here lies in the fact that it contains a presupposition about nature that cannot withstand close scrutiny. And second, following directly from this, the view that if we could describe all that there is, we would then come to understand it, to know all that there is to be known about it. The inadequacy here, obviously, is to assume that in describing something we have also explained it. But an explanation, the presentation of an event in the context of its career, and its changes and its affects, which make for scientific understanding, derives from imaginative conjecture on the part of some inquirer, not simply from direct observation.[7]

On both accounts science must be more than just a matter of looking, having a language, and then describing what one has seen. What is required is the recognition that every description already presupposes a great deal more than the event gives direct and immediate evidence for. What Niels Bohr has called the awareness of the "concep-

7. N. Rescher, *Scientific Explanation* (New York: Free Press, 1970), parts 1 and 3, esp. pp. 8–10.

tual framework," which we have called the model, is "adapted to account for previous experience," a framework, or a model, which we recognize may at any time "prove too narrow to comprehend new experience."[8]

I have shown how often it is that in such continuing quests for clearer and more faithful descriptions and more valid and more clearly heuristic explanations, the very models that make inquiry possible are being tested, and will require to be reconstructed or even abandoned in favor of better models. I quote Bohr again:

> Scientific research in many domains of knowledge has indeed time and again proved the necessity of abandoning or remold-ing points of view which, because of their fruitfulness and ap-parently unrestricted applicability, were regarded as indispens-ible for rational explanation.[9]

The need, at times, to "abandon a point of view" only underscores the need for some point of view made manifest in some model.

Scientific thinking thus gives us the clearest paradigm for continu-ity and discontinuity in science. Sometimes models already successfully employed at one phase of experience become the beginning point for later experience and inquiry, and alter in that later inquiry. Some-times prevailing models must be abandoned, and new ones created. But in every case the model must contain, in theoretical or hypothet-ical forms, all that is pertinently available to us at the point of entry into an inquiry. Moreover, it has had to have built into it an ordered, integrated unity, providing for us either the observed or the antici-pated (hypothetized) wholeness of that event from which explana-tions will flow. In this sense, at least, it is possible to argue that a complete description *of the model* entails within it implicitly an ex-planation of the events being modeled.

Now, an explanation will be either empirical, when the model addresses itself sufficiently to what ostensibly exists, or to what can in principle exist in observable form; or it will be theoretical, when the model is constructed to contain purely theoretical or imaginary en-tities, such entities as could never, even in principle, be observed in actuality.

How, then, do we learn to think scientifically? By learning how to construct or to follow such models as permit an inquiry into the em-pirical events in the world. We learn as we learn to construct com-

8. N. Bohr, *Atomic Physics and Human Knowledge* (New York: Wiley, 1958), pp. 67–101.
9. Ibid.

pleted pictures of otherwise incomplete physical worlds that are of concern to us. (Not the world as a whole, of course, for science deals only with parts of it at a time.) Whatever we permit to enter into the model must have logical as well as empirical justification for being included in the making of a unity of the events explored. And whatever we allow to enter into that model takes on the significance that the whole of the model gives to it. Whatever meaning a given element has, it has because it is part of the totality, the integrity, of the model itself.

When elements within a model are tested, they are primarily tested for the way they "fit" into and contribute to making up the whole. When the model as a whole is tested, it is tested for the meanings that the unity, which is the model, makes understandable about the empirical events under our scrutiny.

So, for example, when we consider again the recommendation that Moore offers (in chapter 2) for learning to think scientifically, or when we commit ourselves to developing the skills that Dewey sets forth seriatim in his *How We Think*, we may recognize that we have only an initiating stage of a larger set of activities. Of course it is advisable to discern the problem we are confronted with; to set forth the actual conditions that seem to be present; to proffer a hypothesis for the resolution; to put the hypothesis to the test, in some experimental way; and then to rewrite the hypothesis in light of the evidence that the experiment has made available to us. But only when we recognize that that process is better understood as the process of constructing a complete model of the event, including those aspects of the event that we cannot observe but that we hypothesize, so that the whole of the event is brought into a working continuity of completeness, can we more fully appreciate what has been for so long called "the scientific method." In short, we must learn to develop what is called "a working model," a model in which all the elements we can get to are filled out with elements we either have not yet gotten to or are elements we can never get to. When all these are transformed into a "picture" of the thing in its completion, behaving the way we have theorized or hypothesized it works, or ought to work, we are thinking scientifically.

In this process of constructing completions in order to see what is absent to us, the development of analogies and metaphors relevant to the matters on hand becomes the fundamental requirement of the mental act, in science as in any other inquiry by human beings concerned with the many domains of their manifold world. Even in reading or performing *Hamlet*, we need to develop those further wholes, those completions, lest Hamlet be reduced to "words, words, words."

BIBLIOGRAPHY

Achinstein, P.   *The Concept of Science.* Baltimore: Johns Hopkins University Press, 1968.

Allport, G.   *Personality: A Psychological Interpretation.* New York: Henry Holt, 1937.

Arbib, N. A.   *The Metaphorical Brain.* New York: John Wiley, 1972.

Arieti, S.   *Creativity, the Magic Synthesis.* New York: Basic Books, 1976.

Austin, J. L.   *How to Do Things with Words.* London: Oxford University Press, 1962.

Belth, M.   *Education as a Discipline.* Boston: Allyn & Bacon, 1965.

———.   *New World of Education.* Boston: Allyn & Bacon, 1970.

Berger, P. L., and Luckmann, T.   *Social Construction of Reality.* New York: Doubleday Anchor, 1967.

Bettelheim, B.   *The Uses of Enchantment.* New York: Alfred A. Knopf, 1976.

Black, M.   *Models and Metaphors.* Ithaca: Cornell University Press, 1962.

Bloomfield, L.   *Linguistic Aspects of Science.* In *International Encyclopedia of Science,* vol. 1, part 1. Chicago: University of Chicago Press, 1955.

Bohr, N.   *Atomic Physics and Human Knowledge.* New York: John Wiley, 1958.

Borst, C. V., ed.   *The Mind/Brain Identity Theory.* London: Macmillan, 1970.

Boulding, K.   *A Primer on Social Dynamics.* New York: Free Press, 1970.

Bruner, J., et al.   *A Study of Thinking.* New York: John Wiley, 1956.

Burns, T.   *Sociological Explanation.* In *Social Theory and Philosophical Analysis,* edited by Emmet and MacIntyre. London: Macmillan, 1970.

Campbell, N.   *Foundations of Science* [also titled *Physics, the Elements*]. New York: Dover, 1957.

Cantril, H.   *The Why's of Man's Experience.* New York: Macmillan, 1950.

Cassirer, E.   *An Essay on Man.* New Haven: Yale University
                      Press, 1944.
————.   *Language and Myth.* New York: Harper & Bros.,
                      1946.
————.   *Philosophy of Symbolic Forms,* vol. 2. New
                      Haven: Yale University Press, 1953.
Chomsky, N.   *Reflections on Language.* New York: Pantheon,
                      1975.
Collingwood, R. G.   *The Idea of History.* New York: Oxford Univer-
                      sity Press, 1956.
————.   *The Principles of Art.* London: Oxford University
                      Press, 1963.
Copi, I. M.   *Introduction to Logic.* New York: Macmillan,
                      1953.
Craik, K.   *The Nature of Explanation.* London: Cambridge
                      University Press, 1967.

D'Angelo, E.   *The Teaching of Critical Thinking.* Amsterdam:
                      B. R. Gruner, N.V., 1971.
de Bono, E.   *Mechanism of The Mind.* London: Jonathon
                      Cape, 1969.
De Latil, P.   *Thinking by Machine.* New York: Houghton Mif-
                      flin, 1957.
Deutsch, K.   *The Nerves of Government.* New York: Free
                      Press, 1966.
Dewey, J.   *How We Think.* Boston: D. C. Heath, 1910.
Dray, W. H.   *Laws and Explanations in History.* London: Ox-
                      ford University Press, 1957.
————.   *Philosophical Analysis in History.* New York:
                      Harper & Row, 1966.
Du Bos, R.   *So Human an Animal.* New York: Charles Scrib-
                      ner's, 1968.
Duncan, H. D.   *Symbols in Society.* London: Oxford University
                      Press, 1968.

Eiseley, L.   *The Mind as Nature.* The Fifth John Dewey Lec-
                      tures. New York: Harper & Row, 1962.
Empson, W.   *Seven Types of Ambiguity.* New York: New Di-
                      rections, 1966.
Ennis, R. H.   *Logic in Teaching.* Englewood Cliffs, N.J.: Pren-
                      tice-Hall, 1969.

Feuer, L.S.   *Einstein and the Generations of Science.* New
                      York: Basic, 1974.

Foucault, M.   *The Archeology of Knowledge.* New York: Pantheon, 1972.

Gallie, W. B.   "Explanation in History and in the Genetic Sciences." In *Theories of History,* edited by P. Gardiner. Glencoe, Ill.: Free Press, 1959.
————.   *Philosophy and the Historical Understanding.* London: Chatto & Windus, 1964.

Gardiner, P.   *The Nature of Historical Explanation.* London: Oxford University Press, 1952.

Geach, P.   *Mental Acts.* London: Routledge & Kegan Paul, 1971.

Gombrich, E. H.   *Art as Illusion.* New York: Pantheon, 1965.

Harré, R.   *Introduction to the Principles of Scientific Thinking.* London: Macmillan, 1970.
————.   *Principles of Scientific Thinking.* London: Macmillan, 1970.
————, and   *The Explanation of Social Behavior.* Oxford:
Secord, P. F.   B. Blackwell, 1972.

Heisenberg, W.   *Physics and Beyond.* New York: Harper & Row, 1971.

Hempel, C.   *Aspects of Scientific Explanation.* New York: Free Press, 1965.
————.   "Explanation in Science and History." In *Philosophical Analysis in History,* edited by W. H. Dray. New York: Harper & Row, 1966.
————.   "Function of General Laws in History." In his *Aspects of Scientific Explanation,* New York: Free Press, 1965.

Henle, P.   *Language, Thought and Culture.* Ann Arbor: University of Michigan Press, 1965.

Hesse, M.   *Models and Analogies in Science.* South Bend, Ind.: University of Notre Dame Press, 1966.

Hexter, J.   *The History Primer.* New York: Basic, 1971.

Hughes, H. S.   *History as Art and as Science,* New York: Harper Torchbook, 1964.

Hospers, J.   *Meaning and Truth in the Arts.* Chapel Hill: University of North Carolina Press, 1946.

James, W.   *Principles of Psychology.* New York: Dover, 1950.

Kayser, C. J.   *Pastures of Wonder.* New York: Columbia University Press, 1929.

Kuhn, T.S.   *The Structure of Scientific Revolution.* Chicago:
                      University of Chicago Press, 1962.

Lakatos, I., and   *Criticism and the Growth of Knowledge.* Lon-
Musgrave, A., eds.   don: Cambridge University Press, 1970. See es-
                      says by Kuhn, Popper, Masterman, and Feyera-
                      bend.
Langer, S.   *Philosophy in a New Key.* New York: Mentor,
                      1951.
————.   *Problems of Art.* New York: Charles Scribner's,
                      1957.
Lewis, C. I., and   *Symbolic Logic.* New York: Dover, 1959.
Langford, C. H.
Lorenz, K.   *On Aggression.* New York: Harcourt, Brace &
                      World, 1963.

Mandelbaum, M.   "Social Laws." In *Philosophical Analysis in His-
                      tory,* edited by W. H. Dray. New York: Harper &
                      Row, 1966.
————.   "Societal Facts." In *Philosophy of Social Explana-
                      tion,* edited by A. Ryan. London: Oxford Univer-
                      sity Press, 1973.
Martin, J. R.   *Explanation, Understanding and Teaching.* New
                      York: McGraw-Hill, 1970.
Marx, L.   *The Machine in the Garden.* New York: Oxford
                      University Press, 1964.
Mead, G. H.   *Mind, Self and Society.* Chicago: University of
                      Chicago Press, 1934.
Moore, W. E.   *Creative and Critical Thinking.* New York:
                      Houghton Mifflin, 1967.
Morison, S. E.   *Oxford History of the American People.* New
                      York: University Press, 1965.
Morse, J. M.   *Prejudice and Literature.* Philadelphia: Temple
                      University Press, 1976.

Nagel, E.   *Structure of Science.* New York: Harcourt, Brace,
                      1961.
Nash, L. K.   *The Nature of the Natural Sciences.* Boston:
                      Little Brown, 1963.
Nelson, G.   *The Language of Art.* Indianapolis: Bobbs-Mer-
                      rill, 1968.
Nisbet, R. A.   *Social Change and History.* London: Oxford Uni-
                      versity Press, 1969.

Oakeshott, M.   *Experience and Its Modes.* London: Cambridge
                     University Press, 1933.
Parsons, T.   *The Social System.* Glencoe, Ill.: Free Press,
                     1951.
————, et al., eds.   *Theories of Society,* vol. 1. Glencoe, Ill.: Free
                     Press, 1961.
Polanyi, M.   *The Tacit Dimension.* London: Routledge & Ke-
                     gan Paul, 1967.
Popper, K.   *The Logic of Scientific Discovery.* New York:
                     Basic, 1959.

Reeves, J.   *Thinking About Thinking.* London: Secker &
                     Warburg, 1965.
Rescher, N.   *Hypothetical Reasoning.* Amsterdam: North Hol-
                     land, 1964.
————.   *Scientific Explanation.* New York: Free Press,
                     1970.
Ryle, G.   *Concept of Mind.* London: Hutchinson's Univer-
                     sity Library, 1955.

Santayana, G.   *The Life of Reason, Reason in Art.* New York:
                     Charles Scribner's, 1953.
Singer, C.   *A Short History of Scientific Ideas.* London: Ox-
                     ford University Press, 1960.
Skinner, B. F.   *Technology of Teaching.* New York: Appleton-
                     Century-Crofts, 1968.

Thomas, L.   *Lives of a Cell.* New York: Doubleday, 1974.
Thouless, R. H.   *Straight and Crooked Thinking.* New York: Si-
                     mon & Schuster, 1932.
Turbayne, C. M.   *The Myth of Metaphor.* New Haven: Yale Uni-
                     versity Press, 1962.

Waismann, F.   *Principles of Linguistic Philosophy.* London:
                     Macmillan, 1965.
Walter, W. G.   *The Living Brain.* New York: W. W. Norton,
                     1953.
Wheelwright, P.   *Metaphor and Reality.* Bloomington: Indiana
                     University Press, 1960.
————.   *The Burning Fountain.* Bloomington: Indiana
                     University Press, 1968.
Wilson, E.   *Axel's Castle.* New York: Charles Scribner's,
                     1969.

Winch, P.   *The Idea of a Social Science.* London: Routledge
                   & Kegan Paul, 1960.
Wish, H.   *Society and Thought in Early America.* New
                   York: Longmans, Green, 1950.
Wittgenstein, L.   *Philosophical Investigations.* New York: Macmil-
                   lan, 1953.
————.   *Tractatus Logico Philosophicus.* London: Rout-
                   ledge & Kegan Paul, 1961.

INDEX

Abelard, P., 136–37
Absurdity, 98–99
Action as analogy for thinking, 11
Adams, H., 137
Adler, M., 172
Alexander I (tsar of Russia), 130
Allport, G., 172
Ambiguity
    deliberate, 115
    in history, 129 f.
Analogical models, development and use of, 45 ff.
Analogies, 51 f.
    civilization and, 44
    as organizing concepts, 52 f.
    root, 51
    substantive content of, 51 f.
    in history, 126–54
    in natural science, 182–94, 214–17
    in the social sciences, 167–69
Analogy, 7 f.
    categorizing by means of, 51 f.
    description and, 32 ff.
    as distinct from model and metaphor, 75
    persuasiveness in, 42
    relevance in, 50–51
    resistance to, 19
    rules for acceptable, 35 f.
    rules for explanatory, 39 f.
    truth and falsity in, 6
    uses of in poetry, 97
Anthropomorphic fallacy, 58–59, 91
Aristotle, 9, 12, 78, 92, 100, 210, 211
Arnold, M., 113, 115–16
Art as forming, 100–101, 108–13, 122–25
Athens, 150
Augustine, St., 183–84

Barth, J., 48
Beliefs, social sciences treatment of, 156–58, 163–65

Bergson, H., 196
Berlin, I., 152–53
Bernstein, L., 95n.
Bettelheim, B., 69n., 84
Black, M., 47, 69–70, 72, 73n., 77, 84
Blake, W., 124
Bohr, N., 218–19
Brahe, T., 213
Brain as metaphor for mind, 8, 16–17
Browning, E. B., 116, 120
Bruner, J., 12
Bruno, G., 213
Burns, T., 161–62

Caesar, J., 34, 141
"Camelot," 148–50
Cantril, H., 172
Carême, M., 114
Cassirer, E., xviii, 81–82, 95, 99, 101, 200
Catechresis, 79
Categorizing, 51 f.
Causal explanation
    in history, 99 f.
    in natural science, 210–14
    in social science, 128 f., 143–47, 176–80
Charles I, 141
Chomsky, N., 12
Christ, 88, 121
City of God, 184
City of Man, 183
Clemenceau, G., 107
Cocteau, J., 122
Coleridge, S. T., 109
Collingwood, R. G., 135
Computers, 8
    as models of thinking, 43
Connotation, 103–4
Covering Law
    in history, 143–44
    in science, 209–10
Creativity, 52, 88

Darwin, C., 51, 124, 130, 151, 182, 183*n*.
De Bono, E., 16, 19–20
Declaration of Independence, 134
De Gaulle, C., 136
Denotation, 86–87
  in poetry, 103–106
Descartes, R., 81
Description, 29ff., 44, 76–77
  in history, 128ff., 141–43
  in natural science, 196–99, 213–14
  rules for, 35–36
  in social science, 162f., 176–80
Dewey, J., xvii, 12, 60, 172, 183, 220
Dickens, C., 175
Dictionaries, 199–201
Discipleship, 26
Disciplines
  evidence and, 64–65
  as model-making activities, 61–62, 84, 93–94
  subject matter and, 189–90
Duncan, H. D., 178*n*., 179–80
Durkheim, E., 165
Durrell, L., 30

Einstein, A., 71, 124
Eisenhower, D. D., 19
Eliot, T. S., 121–22
Euclid, 81
Experience, 65–66
  ways of, 217–20
Explanandum, 46, 61, 91
  construction of, 63f.
Explanans, 46, 91
Explanation, 36ff., 43–45, 85–86
  absense of, in poetry, 95–100
  in history, 99f.
  in natural science, 208–14, 219–20
  necessity for, 38f., 72
  in social science, 128f., 143–47, 165–67, 176–80
Expression, 97–101, 113–14

Form
  in art, 99–101, 109–13
  as metaphoric concern, 106–8
Foucault, M., 82*n*.

France, A., 154
Freud, S., 85, 172, 195–96
Fromm, E., 150, 156
Frost, R., 103

Galbraith, J. K., 156
Galileo, G., 146, 213
Gallie, W. B., 129, 135, 144
Gardiner, P., 130–31
Geach, P., 31, 34
Generalization, 197f.
Goethe, J. W., 115
Gombrich, E. H., 104*n*.
Goodman, N., 103, 106
Grant, U., 149

Hamlet, 85–86, 89–90, 100, 220
Harré, R., 156, 161, 170, 175, 186, 187*n*., 189–90
Heisenberg, W., 213
Heloise, 136–37
Hempel, C., 143–45
Hesse, M., 41*n*., 86, 189
Hexter, J., 147*n*., 150
Historian, task of the, 139–41
Historical analogies, 133–34
Historical description, 128ff., 141–43
Historical evidence, 128–29, 133–34, 136ff., 139–40, 145
Historical explanation, 128f., 143–47
  covering law as, 143–44
  genetic continuity as, 151–54
  motivating reasons as, 144
Historical facts, 133f.
Historical models
  components, 132–33
  metaphors and, 147–54
History
  as distinct from other disciplines, 129–31
  function of law in, 131–33
  logic of, 133, 135ff., 145
  as reservoir of ideals and beliefs, 126–28
  soft models in, 128
  story-telling and, 134–39, 145f.
  truth in, 137–41
Hughes, S., 137
Hume, D., 209